CUBA AND THE "LAST" BASEBALL SEASON

The 1960–62 story of Cuban baseball players' sacrifice in their pursuit of a professional baseball career

José Ignacio Ramírez
Foreword by Luis Tiant Jr.

Cuba and the "Last" Baseball Season: The 1960-62 story of Cuban baseball players' sacrifice in their pursuit of a professional baseball career

Cover concept by José I. and Judy Ramírez. The 1954-55 baseball signed by 24 players and coaches of the Leones de La Habana (Havana Lions) courtesy of and donated by Manuel R. Serrano. Cover layout provided by Covermint Design.

This is a work of nonfiction. However, some names have been changed or not used due to privacy or safety concerns expressed by individuals and or their families.

Book Interior and E-book design by Soumi Goswami

To Paulino Casanova who inspired the true direction of this effort and to the players, their families, staff and the fans of this great game who sacrificed much over the years.

FOREWORD

Reflecting upon the period of time covered primarily by *Cuba and the "Last" Baseball Season*, it brings back a set of memories of long ago about the difficult and challenging decisions made when we did not have the experience to make such decisions, and yet of the decisions that were made.

At a very young age and with the blessing and encouragement of my mother and father I found myself having to change the plans that my wife and I had made to spend our honeymoon in Cuba after been told through a letter from my father that professional baseball was no longer an option in my own country.

A decision to leave behind your family and friends, not knowing what the future holds or whether you will see your loved ones again, can't be underestimated. The decision was made in privacy and silence as one could not always trust how others around you truly thought given the ebb and flow of the political reality during that time. The confusion, and uncertainty that characterizes the state of mind and the sacrifice that many have made are not always fully understood by those who have not had to endure the same experience. And yet, the experience felt as you pursue your dream of reaching the major leagues is not unlike that of others before us, like my father Luis Tiant Sr., who encountered discrimination and racism in the days when he was travelling between Cuba and the United States to play professional baseball. Sadly he was never able to fulfill his dream to play in the majors as I did.

The story for many of us has had a good ending. We were able to continue our professional career, for many that included playing in the majors, a few were reunited with our parents as it happened in my case. My father even saw me play in the World Series and threw the first pitch from the mound in Fenway Park in Boston in front of a huge and cheering crowd with me at his side and my mother, my wife María and his grandchildren sitting in the stands. Some like myself have returned to Cuba, something I had prayed to God to let me do before I die, and were able to be reunited with family and friends of long ago who professed their love and support for what we had done, despite the sacrifices made by everyone.

Looking back, I would make the same decision all over the same.

It is a story of not so long ago that should never be forgotten.

Luis Tiant Jr.

PREFACE

The island of Cuba and the game of baseball, is a union that is impossible to pull apart. According to the film Major League Cuban, it is a "state of mind" which transcends culture and is part of being a Cuban.[1]

The game in Cuba as one considers its full history is inclusive of a more in-depth experience that reflects the rich amateur history of the sport from the very start. But to write such a history in full detail is beyond the scope and intent of this book.

The writing of this book came about as a result of my observations, learnings and at times frustration over what I had read about the history of Cuban baseball players who came to play in the United States over the years. It was not a frustration due necessarily from erroneous information, although I found some. Nor is it an *intentional* approach to rewrite history, which I could not confirm one way or another through my research (although questioned by some). One can simply read the works by authors such as Roberto González Echevarría, Jorge S. Figueredo and Andrés Pascual to learn much about the rich history of Cuban baseball.

My story is more basic than that. Mine is a story that has been previously treated (in my opinion) with limited emphasis and much more casually than it deserves. This became clear as I spent time talking to many former Cuban professional baseball players and or their families who felt forgotten. Paulino Casanova (who sadly passed away in 2017) welcomed me on many occasions at his baseball academy and made it possible for me to connect with players during my research for this project. He was motivated in doing so by what he referred to as the story of the *"olvidados"* (the forgotten ones) and he encouraged me to pursue my efforts. The need to write a book emphasizing the period of time when professional baseball ceased in Cuba became obvious and necessary. And so the research evolved including a number of discussions with former players.

This book initially emphasized the sport and also included personal information about the players. But as time went on, shifted to one that emphasized the personal stories and the historical elements of that period with baseball being used as the context in which it all happened.

INTRODUCTION

It all begins with the story of a teenager who loves the game of baseball, is good at it and dreams of someday becoming a professional baseball player like many of his sport's heroes. Yet for reasons beyond his control, he finds himself unable to do so, prohibited by the powers that be from pursuing his dreams like others did before him. Now, he must seek guidance from his parents about what to do with his life.

But the story is also about another young man who although able to pursue his dream, found himself in a foreign country without knowing its language or culture. To make matters worse, he encountered hatred and prejudice by the very people he was performing for while he made their lives as enjoyable as possible. This experience prompted him to consider abandoning all that he loved in order to escape the environment he found himself in.

This is also the story of another young man who would not, thankfully, have any of the previous experiences but who would observe how his friends struggled and so considered himself lucky. Yet, with a feeling of great regret, he did not see how he was able to help and reduce or eliminate the pain his friends endured.

Much has been published in recent times about Cuban born baseball players and managers both in the U.S. and in Cuba. This increase in amount of information has been driven in part by the *defections* that have taken place over the last twenty-five (25) plus years, from the 1990s up to and including 2017 (as of this writing). Because of the popular appeal of the topic to the general public and the apparent but not so clear shift taking place in the relationship between Cuba and the United States, one can expect more could be written on the subject.

However, *defections* (a much conflicting use of the word and written in italics for that reason) brings about images of being a traitor, of turning one's coat, and of abandonment, to name but three. It is a highly politicized term and not always agreed to by many, and is in conflict or with a different viewpoint about what may have transpired or why. It is a topic not always explored in full. I hope this will become particularly obvious as we consider the story of the *defectors* in a more appropriate context later on.

To that end, I have chosen to reflect on what I consider to be a more balanced and accurate depiction of the Cuban baseball players' experience through the years as they pursued their dream to play professional baseball.

Before these recent arrivals came to light and millions of dollars went their way, in the early 1900s through 1960, many Cuban players came to the U.S. to play in the Negro leagues, in the minors and in the majors. And coincidentally, many "American" players (those born in the U.S.) went to Cuba to play baseball for a variety of reasons.

With those early journeys as a backdrop and in between the *defectors* account lies a more poignant and critical story. It is about the Cuban players and those affiliated with the game that found themselves facing a most unusual situation never experienced before.

This is the story of those who–some at a very young age–learned of their inability to pursue their dreams to play professional baseball in their home country. The choice they were faced with was to either leave behind their family, home, friends and their beloved homeland, knowing they may never see them again in order to play baseball professionally or stay at home and pursue a different way of life.

And so, while this appears to be a story about baseball, it is in fact about the personal struggle these men and their families endured in the hopes of experiencing baseball played at the highest level possible. This particular aspect of the Cuban baseball players' history is confined to a relative short period of time, a time that both preceded and followed the last professional baseball season in Cuba, which came to an end in February of 1961.

Part of this story is a brief recount of the journey taken through the years by Cuban players wishing to play in the Major Leagues broken down into a series of phases. The initial phase (Part I) reflects on the true pioneers who had a hand in bringing baseball to the island and those that through their performance in the Negro, minors and major leagues, created the well-deserved reputation of Cuban players in the field of play.

The second phase (Part II), the primary focus of this book, is about those faced with the heart-wrenching decision to either leave Cuba or stay during the 1960-62 period. It is in some ways as much about baseball as it is a socio-political treatment of a very difficult and controversial but little appreciated period of time by some.

A third phase (Part III) reflects a transition period leading to some confusion. Future players born on the island reached the U.S. as young boys and ultimately were able to play professional baseball. Information about these Cuban players is at times reflected in the *defectors* period, or other times before then. Unfortunately, though, nothing is cut and dried, especially when addressing baseball, Cuba and the United States. So you will find those that "came and went" during the intervening years as personal decisions changed given personal circumstances and the Cuban political realities. I will try to bring as much clarity to this period as possible.

The fourth phase (Part IV) is about the *defectors* who are generally viewed as a movement starting in 1990 and are the subject of much writing and conjecture in recent times.

"Uncertainty and change" (Part V) brings us to the present and the continuing opinions of what the future holds. Change appears to be facing the relationship between Cuba and the U.S. given the changes in recent U.S. presidential elections. It also touches on the move by present and former players to return to Cuba, albeit temporarily. This is a difficult and controversial decision, at times supported and at other times maligned by others.

I will make an effort to bring light to each of these periods or phases, but it will be always with the intent of serving as a context for Part II, that of the 1960-1961-62 period. With that in mind, I will limit or avoid replicating much of what has been written in a variety of sources on the same topic. But I will reference all information to ensure the proper context is established.

The baseball writings by González Echevarría and Figueredo acknowledged here served as rich and proper sources of information, in particular prior to and including the 1960-1961 period.

As a point of clarification, I will use in this book the term "Cuban players" for simplicity purposes when referring to those baseball players born in Cuba. Another "license" I will bestow upon myself is to spell "Habana" or "La Habana" (the original and proper Spanish spelling) rather than its English version "Havana" unless it is formally used in a title, or found written as such in reference material.

I do hope you find the book enjoyable and sufficiently informative on the history and the stories about those who sacrificed much to pursue their chosen careers.

TABLE OF CONTENTS

PART I

"The Pioneers" 1871–1960

Chapter 1

THE EARLY YEARS

The term "pioneer", defined generally as "to build or be the first" is used here to encompass a significant period of time in Cuban baseball history. It is my personal way of paying tribute and recognizing the historical presence and contribution of Cuban players who opened the doors in major league baseball for so many others over the years, including to those in the present time.

The origin of baseball on the island has been and continues to be a topic not always agreed upon or seen the same way by everyone. While sharing and reflecting on the different thoughts, theories and writings on the subject, I take the basic position that it is likely there were many influential forces at work and the game in Cuba experienced an evolution over the years in part due to these influences.

In some accounts, the origins are said to start with the Tainos natives living in Cuba before the Spaniards arrived in 1492, and who were a powerful native community in the eastern part of the island. Some of their entertainment came from a game called "Batos", similar to the word "bate" or "bat" in Spanish, as described by Emérito Santovenia and Raul M. Shelton in their book *Cuba y Su Historia* Tomo Primero, 1966 Rema Press, page 98. The game was played on a large ground or plaza using a ball that was round and elastic, between two teams comprised by as many as twenty participants on each side. Whenever an argument ensued, the Chief, as a person of great authority, would rule on a controversial or a difference of opinion between the teams involved.

How the game was brought to Cuba from the United States following that earlier influence is met with equal differences of opinion. Nemesio Guilló a young man from Cuba, who studied at Spring Hill College in Mobile Alabama, was said to have returned to his native country in 1864 and shared the game with fellow Cubans as he brought in his luggage bats and baseballs.

Around the same period, Esteban Bellán who was born in the city of La Habana was sent to the U.S. to study as his parents were concerned he might be conscripted to fight in the War of Independence between Cuba and Spain (aka the Spanish-American War). At this early stage the sacrifice made by his parents to send him away from their home would become in essence, the start of the migration and sacrifices that continue to this day. In 1860, the *Victorys* of Troy New York founded a baseball social club (one of 62 enrolled in the National Association). However, by 1864, there were only 28 teams due to the U.S. Civil War hostilities. An earlier version of Belláns history had Bellán enrolled from 1869 through 1873, but his enrollment date at Fordham University in 1863-68 was corrected by the University's library Archivist Maurice L. Ahern in a letter to a Warren F. Broderick. He would play in the first college game with nine men on each side against St. Francis Xavier College in 1859, and much later in 1868 played 20 games scoring 78 runs with the Union Morrisania team. His baseball "career" continued as he became a member of the Troy Haymakers, a team from the National Association and thus became a professional baseball player as their third baseman, thus becoming the first Latino to play professional baseball in the United States in 1871.

During that time, in 1866, U.S. ship sailors played a team of Cuban stevedores or dock workers, which provided another influential element during those early years providing exposure to the game of baseball.[2]

In 1868, Emilio Sabourín (born September 5, 1853/4) founded the Habana club. He was later arrested by the Spanish authorities for conspiring against the colonial regime and sent to prison in Ceuta in the country of Morocco located in Northern Africa where he died.[3]

Even though he died while suffering from tuberculosis on the 5th of July of 1897, he clearly was a victim of the Spanish authorities since the game was prohibited by the Spaniards during the early part of Cuba's War of Independence. Sabourín would in effect pay with his life for his love for the game and his country, a sad consequence that is reflected in similar ways during the current times as a result of the present political environment in Cuba.

Bellán played for the Habana team against Matanzas (founded in 1874) on December 27 1874 as a catcher with his team winning by a score of 51 to 9 in a game said to be the first organized game played in the field named Palmar del Junco built that same year.[4]

The Zaldo brothers (Charles, Henry aka Teodoro and Frederick) attended Fordham University between 1875 and 1878 and returned to Cuba in 1878, Teodoro founded the Almendares team.[5]

Against this backdrop, the Cuban professional Baseball League was founded in 1878 and the first game was played on December 29 with Habana winning. Bellán was its manager with Almendares for the opposing team. That first season (1878-79), the Habana club registered a 4-0 record and repeated as champions in the 1879-80 season with a 5-2 record. During the 1880-81 and 1881-82 seasons no champions were declared but Habana with Bellán as its manager came back as champions during the 1882-83 season with a 5-1 record.[6]

Early baseball in Cuba, just as in the United States, was an amateur sport, first organized by gentlemen's athletic clubs. Games were played on Sundays and were typically preceded by a picnic and followed by a dance.

As early as 1878 a game between the Almendares and Hops Bitter Team from Worcester Massachusetts was held.[7] Foreign baseball tours began in 1879 by Frank Bancroft and in 1886 when the A's and the Phillies arrived in Cuba. One may argue that the migration in reverse (U.S. to Cuba) started during this time before the end of the 19th Century.

As the sport grew in Cuba, by 1890 there were five teams in the Cuban Baseball League namely Fe, Progreso, Almendares, Habana and Matancista.

In 1891, Alfred Lawson led two American teams on tours of Cuba. The first team to tour, in January and February, featured a mix of major and minor leaguers. The second team, the "All Americans", came in December and comprised major-league players that included young stars like Bill Dahlen and John McGraw.

From 1895 through 1897, baseball was not played on the island due to the Cuban War of Independence. But in 1897–98 the Spanish government allowed baseball to be played even though the revolution against the Spaniards continued in the countryside. The season was ended early, however, when the Spanish–American War as it is known in the United States broke out. Under American occupation, in February 1899, the Cuban Baseball League returned.

It is no wonder that, as we can see in this limited perspective, the history of the early days of Cuban baseball is filled with opportunities for discourse and opinions. Any attempt to establish the one element or identify the one person that was instrumental in influencing baseball in Cuba does not acknowledge the contribution made by so many others to establish the game in Cuba as its "national sport." It was an evolution that took place over a short period of time due to many equally important and significant factors deserving recognition.

Author's note: Some of the above information does not come from one specific source but was obtained from a number of writings found in the "Resources Consulted" section.

The turn of the twentieth century brought about the well-established movement (some would use the term migration) of players between Cuba and the U.S. This is a movement that continues to this day under different and significant conditions and circumstances. It is important to note and establish at this juncture a few points for consideration as to why this movement could take place.

One is that the Cuban baseball season, in some respects similar to the U.S. was not a twelve-month endeavor by those that participated in it. Those that wished to pursue playing baseball as a career needed to find opportunities wherever they were available. This is much like in today's society where professionals in many areas will travel sometimes a great distance, even to other countries in order to pursue their professional interests by either moving away from their home countries, permanently or temporarily. Engineers, teachers and even writers are but a few examples. They are not considered mercenaries or other derogatory terms being used by some, but simply people who wish to follow their chosen profession wherever it takes them, so they can learn, provide financial support for themselves and their families, as well as experience a different way of life and contribute in their own way.

A second consideration is the opportunity one is provided to demonstrate or challenge oneself against the best in his or her field, allowing them to play with and against the best, wherever they are. This leads many to migrate and or move elsewhere. We see that today as players in different sports such as basketball, and soccer, will move from team to team and in between different countries, sometimes inside the same year.

A third point takes into account governmental policies and political considerations that may have prevented or made it difficult for people to do what they do best at their own home and have therefore found it necessary to go elsewhere. This will become more obvious as you read further.

There may be other factors at play, but for now suffices to say that much of what you will read going forward was driven by some or all of these considerations.

Parenthetically, I submit that there is always more than one reason existing for the movement of players from one country to another to take place. Reality is not always best addressed through a simplicity approach.

As the history continued, baseball tours represented a significant aspect during the early years of the twentieth century. During that time, the Cuban baseball league was integrated along racial lines due in part to the "integration" and diversity of those that fought and died during the Cuba's War of Independence. There are two important examples: the first, Antonio Maceo a black man called the Bronze Titan for his color and stature was a much respected and hero of the war in Cuba against Spain. Secondly, the Cuban "Father of the Nation", Carlos

Manuel de Céspedes began the 10 Year War against Spain by freeing the slaves and asking them to join him in his quest to seek Cuba's independence.[8]

The first Cuban all-white tour around New York took place in 1900, and soon thereafter in 1905 became the Cuban Stars. In 1907 and 1908, the Brooklyn Royals Giants (from the Negro league such as Rube Foster and Bill Monroe, among others) played in Cuba. Also, in 1908, the major league team Cincinnati Reds played in Cuba against a team that featured Rafael Almeida, Armando Marsans and José Méndez. Marsans scored the game's only run and Méndez pitched a one-hit shutout.

Major league teams would visit the island up through 1953.

In 1910 the Cuban teams beat the World Series champion, the Philadelphia Athletics 6 games to 4, leading the embarrassed Commissioner of baseball to issue a ban on post-season exhibition games by the reigning World Series champion.

Soon other teams were also bringing in Negro League stars, culminating in the 1912 Habana club, which easily took the title with a team featuring Hall-of-Famers Joe Williams, John Henry Lloyd, and Pete Hill, as well as Home Run Johnson and Cuban stars Julián Castillo (January 23, 1880-December 1948), Carlos Morán, and Luis Padrón.

By this time, the movement of Cuban players to the U.S. had begun in earnest. Armando Marsans, whose family had moved to New York in 1898 to get away from the Cuban War of Independence, liked to play baseball in Central Park even though they returned to Cuba a year later. Marsans joined the New Britain Connecticut league in 1908 and by 1910 was in the Cincinnati Reds roster where he would have a batting average of .297 with 37 stolen bases. Marsans, who was born on October 3rd, 1887, passed away on September 3rd, 1960 in La Habana and is buried in the city's Christopher Columbus Cemetery. Another player not as well known as Marsans, who had moved to the U.S. at the end of the century was Charles Chick Pedroes. He was born in Cuba and played in two games in 1902 for the Orphans, the team that is known today as the Chicago Cubs. His "career" lasted six times at bat, striking out twice with no hits to his name.

During the 1910s a number of white Cuban players began to break into major league ranks. These included the outstanding Cincinnati Reds pitcher Adolfo (Dolf) Luque, catcher Miguel Angel (Mike) González, and outfielder Armando Marsans. Black Cuban players competed regularly in the Negro Leagues, where Cristóbal Torriente and José Méndez became stars. Between 1911 and 1914, Rafael Almeida (who passed away on March 18, 1969 in La Habana), Miguel Angel González, Merito Acosta, and Angel Aragon would reach the majors among others. One of the greatest Cuban players of all-time, Adolfo Luque, got a contract in late 1914 by the Boston Braves under manager George Stallings and reached the majors with the Reds in 1918.[9] Adolfo Domingo de Guzman Luque born on August 14, 1890, passed away on July 3rd in 1957 and is buried in the Christopher Columbus Cemetery in La Habana.

Outside of the majors, Cubans were reaching other leagues as well. As an example, in the Northwest league of the U.S., Jacinto (Jack) Calvo would arrive to the Victoria team in 1914.[10]

Meanwhile, talented Cuban players who were black would travel to the U.S. as part of a baseball tour and had the opportunity to showcase their abilities and to earn a salary. They were free to pursue their chosen profession like all other players and travel from their home country. In 1909 José Méndez went on a tour with the Cuban Stars to New York and Chicago where he beat the Roger Park team and allowed no hits, no runs, or walks in 10 innings. Games were played in Chicago, Cincinnati, Kansas City, and Philadelphia.[11] Méndez was the first to play in the Negro leagues, with the Monarchs 1920-26. He also became a manager in 1924.[12] Although he had played in the Cuban league since 1908, Article 98 banned blacks in Cuba, but it was abrogated in 1900 and black players rose to prominence. However, "El Diamante Negro" was barred from playing in the majors in the U.S. because of his color. Frank Bancroft was quoted as saying when he managed Cincinnati against Almendares in 1908 that "If that pitcher Méndez was white, I'm sure it would not take him many months to be one of the stars of the National League".[13] José de la Caridad Méndez March 19, 1887- October 31, 1928 is buried in the Christopher Columbus Cemetery in La Habana along other baseball greats.

Cristobal Torriente another great Cuban player in the Negro leagues, from 1918-25, played for the Chicago American Giants. Much has been written about how he "outclassed" Babe Ruth at a game in Cuba on November 20, 1920 hitting three home runs and a double. Ruth was 0-3. During the 1920s, top Negro League stars such as Oscar Charleston, Cool Papa Bell and Satchel Paige were teammates of Cuban stars such as Martín Dihigo and Cristóbal Torriente. Torriente who was born on November 16, 1893, passed away on the 11th of April in 1938 of tuberculosis and is buried in the Christopher Columbus Cemetery in La Habana.

Martín Dihigo, in order to show his baseball ability and make some extra money went to the U.S. to play in the Negro leagues, touring with the Cuban Stars Homestead Grays.[14] A humorous anecdote relates how Johnny Mize, who played with Dihigo in the Dominican Republic, said, "I thought I was having a pretty good year myself down there and they were walking him to pitch to me".[15] Unlike other greats, Dihigo is buried in the Municipal Cemetery of Cruces in Cienfuegos, Cuba having passed away on May 20, 1971.

Interestingly and sadly at the same time Cuban blacks would speak Spanish and were able to be served in restaurants in the U.S. because they were considered foreigners, unlike black Americans who were not treated as well. American black players, in some cases, tried to follow the same practice by speaking a few words in Spanish.[16]

Cuban blacks went North during the summer months to play in the Negro Leagues and American blacks went to Cuba during the winter. Like many others, players would migrate to where they could work at their craft and enjoy their chosen profession without government interference.

Baseball in Cuba continued to grow in the midst of all this intercountry travel as players learned that by going to each other's countries they were able to display their skills, earn a salary playing ball throughout the entire year, challenge their own abilities and be able to cope with racial policies like those found in the U.S.

In Cuba, the Gran Estadio de La Habana was built in 1920 with a capacity of approximately thirty-one thousand fans, and *La Tropical* baseball field was built in 1930.[17] La Tropical was a popular beer in Cuba and the site not only provided a venue to play baseball but other attractions and events were also held there. The Gran Estadio was replaced in 1946 by the Estadio del Cerro and, by that time, La Tropical was no longer used regularly by the Cuban Baseball league.[18]

The economic depression of the early 1930s and the Cuban political scene both prevented *imports* during the 1934-35 season as the Gerardo Machado government in Cuba was toppled from power following the cancellation of the 1933-34 season. On August 8, 1932, Cuba would lose one of its great baseball pioneers as Esteban Bellán passed away in the capital city of La Habana.

Chapter 2

THE MIGRATION MOVEMENT GROWS

In 1937 and 1938 the New York Giants and the Homestead Grays winners of the National League respectively played in Cuba. In fact the New York Giants held their spring training camp in Habana during that time.

Starting in 1936, the owner of the Washington Senators Clark Griffin had in his employ Joe Cambria who in turn began to look for Cuban talent in earnest. During that year he signed Roberto Estalella, Ismael (Mulo) Morales, Manuel Fortes, Rafael Suárez, Regino Otero, Tomás de la Cruz (who passed away on September 6, 1958 in La Habana), Lázaro Salazar, Fermín Guerra, Jorge Comellas and Armando Paituvi. They were asked to report to their team up North in 1937 using the P&O Steamship Company.

This would mark a significant increase of Cubans in the U.S. baseball scene, a rise that continued through 1960.

It is important to note that at this time that travel by teams (not only players) out of Cuba was taking place even as the island's presence as a baseball power house was being established. During the International Baseball Association (IBA) games between 1938 and 1953, Cuba's team won first place fourteen times, came second once and third place twice.

The Amateur World Series was played in Cuba in 1940 with the local team and Venezuela fighting for the coveted first place. Venezuela won that game and, as the game ended, fans took to the field and players feared for their life, only to realize that the fans raised them in their shoulders and congratulated the victors for having played such a good game.[19]

U.S. teams went to Cuba to train. However, during World War II, travel restrictions cut down the supply of U.S. players and by the early 1940s it was stopped temporarily for the duration of the war. The Brooklyn Dodgers held spring training there in 1941, 42 and 47. This last one became better known as Jackie Robinson played in Cuba during his last spring training before breaking the major league color barrier in the U.S. He stayed in the Hotel Boston in La Habana rather than a national segregated room "I can't afford a chance and have a single incident occur"[20]

Baseball in Cuba had many traditions and unique happenings, including the experiences of long games. The earliest among the longest games took place on December 2, 1943 at the Gran Estadio de la Cervecería Tropical. A four-hour and twenty-five minute game played between the *Elefantes* (Elephants) of Cienfuegos and the Marianao *Frailes Grises,* ran over twenty innings. Luis Tiant (the father) pitched 14 innings but was the losing pitcher by a score of 6 to 5.[21]

Following the end of World War II attendance improved and teams began to match their record in the mid-1940s. The Gran Stadium of Habana opened in 1946-47.

During that time, the baseball organization in the U.S. pursued certain actions to combat Mexico's interests in signing baseball players from the major leagues by trying to control the flow of players from the Caribbean. Finally, in 1947, an agreement was realized between the Cuban League and the National Association of Professional Baseball Leagues to bring talented minor league and first year major league players to Cuba during the winter.

In 1946 a team joined the Class C Florida International League known as the Havana Cubans owned by Merito Acosta, Joe Cambria and George Foster, playing their home games in La Tropical Stadium in Habana.

A source of personal and family pride was that Rogelio (Limonar) Martinez my father's first cousin, also born in the town of Cidra in the province of Matanzas, broke into the majors for a very brief time in 1950.[22] Limonar's playing in the U.S. was simply an extension of (like many other players) wishing to continue his career throughout the year in order to practice his chosen profession and support his family. Further information about his baseball career can be found included in the Bio Project at SABR.org by Rory Costello.

Also that same year (1950) Conrado Marrero would break into the majors playing through the 1954 season and a popular player for many years thereafter until his passing in 2014 in Cuba.

It was during the 1956 season that my father took me to my first professional baseball game. Sitting on the Grandstand section between home plate and first base, I watched intently as Forrest (Spook) Jacobs, who would win the 1956 batting title, played 2nd base for my favorite team, the Habana Lions. I wear their baseball cap to this day and have owned season ticket seats with my older son (José Ignacio Jr.) in Fenway Park in Boston from our seats not coincidentally located in the Grandstand section between home plate and first base.

The 1957-58 season was the last full season of professional baseball on the island before the Castro revolution took over the Cuban government. The official score card for the season, which sold for 5 cents, was sponsored by "Coñac 3 Toneles" and featured the four clubs and the roster of players for each. Many of the Cubans were well known in the U.S. and Cuba, and will be featured later on in this writing. Also, one would find playing for Cienfuegos #28 T. Francona, for Habana #2 Forrest Jacobs, for Almendares #16 the very popular Rocky Nelson, and for the eventual champion Marianao #12 Bob Shaw who had a 14 and 5 record in 30 games.

As the 50s era ended on March 21, 1959, less than three months after the Fidel Castro's revolution got into power, the Los Angeles Dodgers and Cincinnati Reds played what would be the last game between major league teams in Cuba for the next four decades.

Throughout the 1950s Cuba performed very well in the annual Caribbean Series. They also fielded a summer team, the Havana Sugar Kings, at first in the Florida International League, and later in the International League.

However not all players were stars or of a caliber to warrant achieving a spot in a major league roster. Many, in order to pursue their dream of being a professional baseball player, played in large U.S. cities and small town not always known by the average fan.

A particular community well known to this writer, is the town of Palatka Florida, located in the north central part of Florida divided by the St. John's River. The longest river in the state became better known recently during the hurricane Irma in 2017 as it flooded passing by the city of Jacksonville to the Atlantic Ocean. It was in that community where I lived and went to school for a brief period of time and enjoyed the experience of living in a friendly and welcoming community in the early 60s. During 1947, Palatka players born in Cuba included Julio Gómez who played but one season in the Cuban league during 1953-54 and for the Havana Cubans in 1946 and 47, and José Manuel Nápoles y de Ylla who came to the U.S. in 1946 for a couple of months to play baseball, according to immigration records. He would return the following year on March 11, 1947 with the stated intent to remain permanently. Armando Valdés born in 1920, who played for the Habana Cubans in 1946 and stayed in the U.S. until 1949, made Palatka their baseball home. Three players would follow them to play for the Palatka Azaleas of the Florida State League Class D in 1949 Angel Catayo González who played two seasons in Cuba (1946-48) and stayed in the U.S. till 1952, Ramón Díaz Salgado who played one season in Cuba during the 1946-47 season but remained in the U.S. until 1957, and Julio Miguel López (Montelongo).

Montelongo a pitcher for the Azaleas, was 25 years old when he won 11 games losing but 6 games, and had a very good ERA of 2.62. Unfortunately his career in the U.S. ended in 1953 at the age of 29 playing for the Class B team of the Lake Charles Lakers in the Gulf Coast League.

Below one can find a copy of "Montelongo's" Vintage card Colecciones Victoria for sale at Cubacollectibles.com as a pitcher for the Marianao club in the Cuban Professional League. He also played as a catcher for the Cubaneleco club as an amateur.

Many of these players would remain in the U.S. playing in the minors beyond the time they played in Cuba because of their ability to "catch on" with a team and therefore able to pursue their career of choice.

The fifties were indeed years where Cuban players were ever present in the majors. The following reflects the number of Cubans who played in Major League Baseball through these years.[23]

1901–09 = 1

1910–19 = 12

1920–29 = 5

1930–39 = 3

1940–49 = 22

1950–59 = 36

Some of these players distinguished themselves by being named to the All Star games in the majors, such as Sandalio (Sandy) Consuegra and Conrado (Connie) Eugenio Marrero, who would live to the old age of 103 (April 25, 1911-April 23, 2014), passing away in La Habana.

As this era of baseball came to an end, it is worthwhile noting the reality that movement between the U.S. and Cuba had a very long rich history and tradition going back to the late 1900s. So whatever we may be experiencing today, it is not the first time nor is it unique in the annals of the movement of players between the two countries. However, even if the circumstances driving the movement has shifted, the motivation by the players has not. This is due (and worth repeating) to the interests by players to continue to play baseball, earn a year round and fair salary, and or challenge themselves to play against the best talent available. It is also noteworthy to consider that political conditions such as the Cuban War of Independence, Spanish Government prohibition and U.S. Racist policies were factors and had an impact on players in their quest to play the game that they loved. The other reality about the previous history is that players traveled as they did because they simply could do so freely without fear or restrictions, an experience sadly not present today in Cuba by players and citizens in general.

PART II

"To Stay or Not to Stay" 1960–62

Chapter 1

A LOOK AT 1959 AND 1960

An effort has been made to identify specific sources for the following information. But the reality is that much of it comes from a variety of written publications, as well as personal interviews given the rich historical data available due to the time period and people's experiences during that time. I have endeavored to acknowledge within the text or within the "Sources Consulted"-section the material that was used as the basis for the information. However, I would recommend further reading of these sources for more information.

To better understand what occurred in Cuba during and after its last professional baseball season (1960-61) it would make sense to look at what took place in the country after January 1959 when the Castro Revolution triumphed.

The end of professional baseball in Cuba is not just a baseball story and history, it is a story of political intrigue, of the suffering experienced by people (not just baseball players), of painful decisions affecting families, and so much more. From our perspective, though, this story is limited to the experience endured by the baseball community and the sport in general.

It all began in 1959. The Castro Revolution triumphed and the government of the dictator Fulgencio Batista had collapsed. The hope by many at the time was that a democratic form of government would return to the island and the country would thrive even further as the Constitution of 1940 was to be implemented. The Constitution had taken effect initially on October 10, 1940 and thought to be one the most inclusive documents written to date.[24] It was, in fact, one of the many promises made by Fidel Castro on July 28, 1957 that never came about.[25]

During that time, the 1959-60 baseball season was in full bloom. Fidel Castro threw out the first ball in the game where the Cienfuegos team, managed by Antonio Castaño, won the championship. Some of the players on that team who either had played or would play in the major league included Camilo Pascual, Pedro Ramos, José Joaquin Azcue, Octavio (Cookie-Cuqui) Rojas and Antonio (Tony) González among others.[26]

On the very first day that the Fidel Castro Revolution controlled the Cuban government, five newspapers said to have been supporters of the Batista regime were confiscated. On the face of it, this did not seem to raise much concern due to the euphoria in place at the time. I remember well, as a young teenager, the celebrations marked in part by many people shooting guns in the air in the middle of the streets in my hometown.

Executions (some public, others inside military institutions) of Batista supporters began. Jails were filled with many who were suspected or accused, causing many people to flee the country.

Early on under Castro's rule a "Youth Pioneer"–like group, composed of children in the primary and early secondary grades, was created, organized under the government's control, in order to educate them in the Marxist ideology and serve in a governmental related role. Much has been written about children sharing with government officials what they had heard people, including family members, say things that were thought to be "counterrevolutionary". This led to much trepidation about what to say in front of anyone. A concern that continues today.

On March 3rd of that first year, the Cuban Government nationalized the Cuban Telephone Company, an affiliate of ITT, and reduced telephone rates. Reducing rates was likely a welcomed action by many, but confiscation of private property without proper indemnity (the act of compensating for damage or loss) had begun.

Two months later, in the month of May, Castro signed the Agrarian Reform Act, which was stated as expropriating land from owners of over 1,000 acres of farmlands (again without indemnity), and forbade foreign land ownership. The Act would continue to change as time went on to include smaller and smaller tracts of land from their rightful owners. During this time, baseball players who had contracts with teams in the U.S. continued their regular life style travelling to and from Cuba playing baseball as so many had done since the start of the century.

In 1959, the Cuban Sugar Kings came back from a last place finish the previous year to win the Little World Series in a game played in Habana against the Minneapolis team managed by Gene Mauch and whose second base was Hall of Fame member Carl Yastrzemski. Owner and President Bobby Maduro brought in Pedro (Preston) Gómez as the manager, and the team used some of their younger players such as Leonardo (Leo) Cárdenas and Antonio (Tony) González, the team's MVP with a .300 season. Yet the team would end in third place during the regular season, behind Buffalo and Columbus. The story of the last game deserves a careful reading well documented in Jorge S. Figueredo's book "Cuban Baseball A Statistical History, 1878-1961" on page 458.

A total of 72 games were played during the 1959-60 season won by Cienfuegos (the Elephants) followed by Marianao (Tigers), Habana (Lions) and Almendares (Scorpions). The managers of that season were respectively Tony Castaño, Napoleón Reyes, and Fermín Guerra with Oscar Rodríguez and Clemente Carreras sharing the managerial season with the Almendares squad.

Early in 1960, and in the midst of the political instability that existed, the International League decided to give owners the power to move their teams which would in effect open the door for the Cuban Sugar Kings to move their franchise. During that time, controls over the Cuban press had begun in earnest and by May of that year only two independent (non-government controlled) newspapers remained. However, *El Diario de la Marina* (which had been in existence for

128 years) and *Prensa Libre* would be taken over during that month on May 13th and the 16th respectively. At that point, all of the newspapers were in control of the Castro government and CMQ would be the lone holdout television station (but would be also confiscated before the end of the year).[27]

Confiscation of private property continued through the month of June, and on June 29, the Cuban government nationalized the Texaco oil refinery. In July the Esso and Shell oil refineries were taken over. On July 3, in response to these seizures, the U.S. Congress passed the *Sugar Act*, eliminating Cuba's remaining sugar quota, and two days later Cuba retaliated by nationalizing all U.S. businesses and commercial property.

Chapter 2

ROBERTO (BOBBY) MADURO AND THE CUBAN SUGAR KINGS

In 1954, the AAA Reds franchise in Springfield, Massachusetts purchased in 1953 by Cuban Roberto (Bobby) Maduro and became the Cuban Sugar Kings. The story of the short but successful franchise is well known because the Cuban Sugar Kings sent no less than 30 players to the "bigs" during the 50s.

During that same month of July 1960, the International League agreed to revoke the Cuban Sugar Kings franchise and owner Bobby Maduro had to scramble to find a suitable location for his team in the middle of their season. The franchise moved from Habana to Jersey City, New Jersey.

Much has been written (rightfully so) about Roberto (Bobby) Maduro but it seems appropriate here to give a glimpse of the man that did so much for baseball in Cuba. He deserves much more recognition than he is given today.

Early in life, Bobby Maduro attended Cornell University. He remained there through his third year, in 1936, when his father's health made it necessary for him to help with the family business in Cuba. This early exposure enabled him to learn to speak fluent English. Among his many contributions, he built the Gran Estadio de La Habana, also known as Stadium del Cerro, with Miguel Suarez for almost $2MI. Also, during his business career he owned the Cienfuegos baseball team in the Cuban League.

In 1946 the Havana Cubans were owned by Merito Acosta, Joe Cambria and George Foster but in 1954 when the team was in Springfield Massachusetts, it was transferred to the International League becoming the Havana Sugar Kings with Maduro as its owner.

According to José "Chamby" Campos, Maduro's priority during that time was to improve baseball in Cuba. He joined and became a sponsor and promoter of an academy of baseball for boys known as *Los Cubanitos* (the little Cubans) founded by Mako Pérez where baseball was taught. Over 4,000 children throughout the island participated as well as received financial assistance to pursue their education.

When Fidel Castro went to the city of New York soon after the revolution was won he asked to meet with Maduro who had expressed his concern over his club's ability to survive financially. Maduro worried it might possibly be transferred out of Cuba to the U.S. Castro promised, and in fact delivered, through the Revolution infrastructure, the funds that were needed at the time.

As it happened, the team, which was affiliated with the Cincinnati Reds of the National League, was nevertheless moved to Jersey City, as indicated earlier, but Maduro stayed in Cuba to attend to his many business ventures while still following the Kings whom he had left in the hands of his General Manager Paul Miller to run the day-to-day club's business.

Maduro's family came to the U.S. according to immigration records in the early 60s. As examples, daughters Beatriz, Rosario and Isabel born in 1950, 1953 and 1957, respectively, became permanent residents in the U.S. on March 27, 1965. It is worthy of note that Regino Otero would serve as a witness to their becoming U.S. citizens according to the naturalization records. Maduro's son Jorge, born in 1947 became a permanent resident on December 17, 1965 and Maduro's wife Isolina, born in 1919, was a permanent resident since 1964. A Resident Status signified that the person had arrived a few years earlier. In Isolina's case, likely in 1960, given the rules at the time requiring a five-year prior arrival. As this author also would experience. Maduro himself made several trips between Cuba and the U.S. during 1960 (August 12, September 17, December 17) that are shown on official travel records as he attempted to deal with the uncertainty of the times. These trips were followed by a trip on January 20, 1961 (the day before this author would be leaving Cuba as part of the Pedro Pan program). Maduro left on April 13 just before the Bay of Pigs invasion, not wishing to return and in fact leaving with $5 in his pocket.[28] Ultimately and sadly, Bobby Maduro would lose everything (as did many before and after him) to the Fidel Castro regime, including his bus company, insurance business, and real estate property.

During his years in exile, Bobby Maduro would continue to advocate and support baseball. He created a version of the *Cubanitos* (the little Cubans) in Miami and later was named to an intermediary role between Major League Baseball and the Winter Leagues. This latter role, in fact, enabled some of the Cuban players in exile to play in the winter leagues and he would continue to help his fellow baseball friends. As a vivid example of this, José Campos relates how Maduro recommended Rafael Avila to become a Baseball Scout for the Los Angeles Dodgers. One of his last projects was the organizing of an Inter-American league, which unfortunately was short-lived, composed of teams in Miami, Venezuela, Panamá, Dominican Republic and Puerto Rico. Given his many contributions to the game, there are many who believe he deserves to be a member of the Hall of Fame in Cooperstown. In fact, he was selected to the Cuban Baseball of Fame in Miami for all that he meant to the sport of baseball in Cuba and elsewhere.

Maduro became a U.S. Citizen in 1967 and two years later, his wife Isolina would do so, according to their Naturalization Application records. Bobby Maduro would return but only once to his home country to place flowers in the Colón cemetery at his son's (Felipe) grave.[29]

The Cuban Sugar Kings 1960 roster included fourteen Cuban-born players. All but one left Cuba after the Cuban League was abolished, despite a suggested assertion by Manager Castaño that some may wish to stay in Cuba (as he did). That story was reported in the Stars and Stripes.[30] As reported, Castaño indicated that five or six players would quit if the move to Jersey City were to take place. The news of the impending move was decided by League President Frank Shaughnessy and was announced to the players prior to a game. Castaño had been previously notified by phone. He said "It's tough. I feel sorry for everybody". He did not share his own decision to leave or not was not shared with the players and sealed it in an envelope to be opened at the end of the following series in Miami. All Americans, except two had previously brought their families out of Cuba, and their general attitude was summarized by Yo Yo Davalillo, who said "I will go with the team. It's my work and I've got a family to support." For the Cubans, Enrique Izquierdo told reporters, "I work for the Cubans and I'll go where they go." This sentiment was echoed by pitcher Orlando Peña. As it turned out, all the Cubans stayed with the team. The story of the 1960 Sugar Kings also the Jersey City Jerseys, is the story of the dream of players who simply wanted to play baseball and make it to the Majors. Following the announced move to Jersey City, the players were given the opportunity to go to Cuba and bring their families to the U.S. with them.

Manager Tony Castaño resigned from the team in protest and stayed in Cuba. Napoleón Reyes was then named manager of the team and was promptly denounced by the Castro government for accepting the job. The team closed the season ending in fifth place with a record of 76 wins and 77 losses.

The Cuban born players on the roster ranged from the age of 20 to 29 years of age and included:

Rogelio Alvarez

Andrés Ayón

José Joaquin Azcue

Leonardo (Leo) Cárdenas

Pedro Carrillo

Miguel (Mike) Cuellar

Enrique (Hank) Izquierdo

Enrique Maroto

Daniel Morejón

Orlando Peña

Octavio (Cuqui/Cookie) Rojas

Raúl Sánchez

Mario Zambrano

Elio Toboso

This last player, Elio Toboso, requires some further attention. He would be the one 1960 Cuban Sugar King Player that did not move to the U.S. after the dissolution of the Cuban League the following year and very little information has been written about him.

Due to my personal connections in the area, I was able to secure personal information about Toboso. Francisco Elio Toboso was born in the San Antonio Sugar Mill in the town of Madruga, situated about an hour southeast of the capital city of La Habana. Madruga is a town divided by the central road, *Carretera Central*, crossing the island of Cuba and is within 15 minutes of my hometown of Aguacate.

Toboso was born on April 4, 1937. His parents Ana and Roberto, were laborers in the area. Elio went to the school located at the San Antonio Sugar Mill and would proceed through the middle school grades. As a youngster, he was interested in baseball, influenced by his parents and uncles who played on the *Picolino* local team. He was said to be so engaged in the sport that he, along with his brothers and other children, formed a team and played against other nearby clubs. After a while, they would be playing against teams composed of older children. Elio was known for his hitting and fielding abilities and for being a smart player who ran the bases well, to the point that others recognized him as showing great promise.

Tony Castaño who was a scout seaching for potential major league talent, signed him up as part of the Cincinnati organization which provided Toboso with the opportunity to travel to the U.S. This was the same Castaño that would be his manager with the 1960 Cuban Sugar Kings.

As Toboso moved up in class he became an outfielder, a position he played during the rest of his career. He broke into professional baseball in the U.S. playing for the Crestview Braves, a Class D team in the Alabama-Florida league, in 1956 at the age of 19. He also played the following year for the Palatka Redlegs. Rosales shared that a newspaper reporter once wrote that Toboso was someone that didn't need to be motivated for he was the "jewel" of Cuban baseball. Rosales suggested that the lack of English language prevented Toboso from being a better player, but he was clearly the best centerfielder that played in a Palatka uniform. He played through 1961 playing the outfield for the Jacksonville Jets at the Class A level in the South Atlantic League, with a .273 batting average during his six seasons in the minors.

During the 1958-59 season and subsequent season he played in the Cuban league for the Habana club, ending up with a batting average of 0.053 in 19 times at the plate. His record with the 1960 Cuban Sugar Kings was limited to playing in only seven games, with three times at bat and no hits which may account in part for why he is not remembered by his former teammates. During 1960 season he travelled to Mexico where he played for the Monterrey Sultanes where he had a more robust batting record of .266.

While it is said by some that he played in the 60-61 Cuban season, the record suggests otherwise. It appears that Toboso, and many others were assigned to a particular team but would not be in the team's playing active roster. Instead, these players were used only during practices. The thinking behind this according to former players I interviewed, is that during that last season, the Cuban talent was of a sufficiently high caliber that they could not accommodate everyone that wanted to play. Octavio Cuqui Rojas was among those who would say that there was simply no room for everybody on a 25 player roster.[31]

When the last professional season ended in Cuba, Toboso was approached by representatives of the town of Madruga to help develop youngsters in the game of baseball. He accepted the offer and, according to those who knew him, contributed as best he could. He did not maintain any known communications or relations with his former teammates which accounts in part for why little was known about him by those interviewed for this book.

As the year passed, Toboso fell victim to alcoholism one of the causes of his death on July 18, 2006. His remains are buried in the Madruga cemetery. Due to the number of years that have passed there are not too many people left in his own hometown who remember him.

Year	Age	Tm	Lg	Lev	Aff
1956	19	Crestview Braves	Alabama-Florida League	D	CHC
1957	20	Palatka Redlegs	Florida State League	D	CIN
1958	21	Wenatchee Chiefs	Northwest League	B	CIN
1959	22	Havana Sugar Kings	International League	AAA	CIN
1959	22	Memphis Chickasaws	Southern Association	AA	
1960	23	Columbia Reds	South Atlantic League	A	CIN
1960	23	Monterrey Sultanes	Mexican League	AA	
1960	23	Havana Sugar Kings/ Jersey City Jerseys	International League	AAA	CIN
1961	24	Jacksonville Jets	South Atlantic League	A	

I want to offer special thanks (also recognized in the Acknowledgement page) to Efraín Rosales who knew and played with Toboso during their youth and also Leonel Morales, a true baseball fan who met Toboso as an older man. Both of these men continue to live in Cuba today and were able to provide information not readily available.

Toboso baseball record in the U.S. is as follows: Courtesy of baseball-reference.com

Chapter 3

1960 CONTINUES

While the activity surrounding the Cuban Sugar Kings was going on, the Castro regime continued to seize and nationalize private industries. In mid-September sixteen cigar companies, fourteen cigarette plants and twenty tobacco warehouses including the H. Upmann factory (home of Montecristo), and Partagás fell victims to the regime policies. To make matters more critical at an international level, all U.S. banks were taken over by the Cuban government, including the First National City Bank of New York, First National Bank of Boston and Chase Manhattan Bank. By mid-October the Urban Reform Law No. 890 went into effect, with 382 locally owned firms, including sugar mills, banks and large industries, being *nationalized* a euphemism for confiscation.

The U.S. government's answer to the seizure of U.S. companies was to impose a partial economic embargo on Cuba that excluded food and medicine. This brought a response by the Cuban government to nationalize additional properties owned by American interests, and, in fact, all foreign oil refineries and American Sugar Mills were confiscated. And, by the end of 1960, all local unions firmly in control of communist elements had ousted their elected officials.[32]

Block committees designed to have neighbors watch each other and report unusual activity were created. Unusual activity could include people taking their furniture out of their own homes since the government concluded that these homes would someday belong to the State if homeowners were to leave Cuba. As this distorted thinking was applied, homeowners were accused of "taking government property" for removing their own belongings out of their homes. The Urban Reform Act which gave the State the exclusive right to lease rental property was also passed.

At this point Cuban owned industries and businesses were taken over by the State as well, and all privately owned Cuban banks were now in the hands of the State.

If one were to look at this situation at the most superficial level, it would be reasonable to conclude that the end of remaining private properties such as baseball clubs was on hand. And yet, the baseball players I interviewed indicated they did not think so at the time. But as we now know, the end of the private baseball clubs was imminent.

Meanwhile the sport of baseball continued. The team from Cuba (Cienfuegos) won the XII Caribbean Series in Panamá followed by Puerto Rico and Venezuela.

Chapter 4

THE "LAST" SEASON BEGINS, TIME TO MAKE A DECISION

What would become the last professional baseball season in Cuba began on October 14, 1960. American players were no longer allowed to participate. All teams were made up of Cuban born players who took this opportunity to "try out" for the teams because competition from players out of the country was no longer in their way. During that last season League President Narciso Camejo and the Cuban players were organized into a trade association headed by baseball great Orestes Miñoso who agreed to reduce their salaries in exchange for being allowed to return to play in the U.S. in the spring of 1961.[33]

At the end of 1960 many parents held concerns and fears about legislation said to be under consideration known as *Patria Potestad.* The legislation, as it was feared would give the State control over the education and raising of children, and so parents scrambled to find ways to send children to a safer environment outside of Cuba. This fear was grounded in part by the previous historical experiences of Spanish children from the Basque region who were taken to Russia during the Spanish Civil War (1936-39). Many Cubans (like myself) had families that went back to that northeast region in Spain and were familiar with the history.

The Program established to allay the parents' fear, known today as "Pedro Pan" welcomed its first unaccompanied children (mostly between the ages of 6 and 17) to the U.S. on December 26 of that year. It would continue through October of 1962 with 14,048 children leaving Cuba for the United States where they were relocated to 190 cities in the continental U.S. and Puerto Rico.[34]. These children were housed, among many other places, in foster homes, refugee camps, and orphanages. Some joined family members who had previously left. On a personal note, I came to the U.S. at the age of fifteen as part of this Program in January of 1961.[35]

By 1961, over 100,000 political émigrés had gathered in the United States. And this number was only a fraction of those who had tried to get out but could not.[36] Between 1959 and 1973, 500 thousand Cubans left their homeland.[37] On January 3rd of 1961, the U.S. broke off official diplomatic relations with Cuba.

Baseball continued its 1960-61 season (the last professional baseball season) ending on February 8 as Cienfuegos managed by Tony Castaño, who had previously managed the Cuban Sugar Kings clinched the championship with a 35-31, record. Cienfuegos was followed by Almendares, behind by only one game, with the Habana Lions in third place, followed by Marianao.

The last season's All Star team consisted of Catcher José Azcue, at First Base Julio Béquer, Second Base Octavio (Cookie-Cuqui) Rojas, Third Base Miguel De la Hoz, Short Stop Leonardo Cárdenas. The Outfielders were Daniel Morejón, Hilario (Sandy) Valdespino, and Román Mejías. The All Star Pitchers were Pedro Ramos, Jiquí Moreno and Rodolfo Arias. Pitcher Luis Tiant Jr. was named the Rookie of the Year with a record of 10 wins and 8 losses.

The announcement of the end of professional baseball in Cuba has been reported through a number of different versions. One version relates to February of 1961 when it was said that Fidel Castro appeared where many of the established players were playing softball and told them that professional ball was being disbanded. "But," he said. "If you want to go and continue your career in the U.S. you are free to go. But if you stay here you are going to stay for good." He also said he would give the players jobs as instructors. It was understood by many at that time that they could go to Mexico and play professional baseball as long as they expressed their intent to return to Cuba such as Andrés Ayón who did just that.[38]

Some of the players I interviewed do not recollect, given the passage of time, or they disputed that it was Fidel Castro who delivered the actual message but that it had been in fact one of his representatives. A related version was provided by Miguel de la Hoz during our interview in 2016. He did not remember that specific encounter. But did remember that a Fidel Castro Representative, a Captain Moro, spoke to the players at the *Ciudad Deportiva* to let them know about the end of professional baseball in Cuba. And did actually relay the message that he, de la Hoz, would have a job with the Castro Government. A third version of the same encounter can be read in the Leopoldo Posada section found later on in this book. He stated that government official Felipe Guerra Matos met with the players and told them professional baseball would be ending that season.

Regardless of which version is accepted, the message was clear that professional baseball was prohibited and these privately owned clubs ceased to exist. Baseball, like industries of all types, suffered in effect the same consequences as all other (industries) did previously. To suggest otherwise shows an inability or unwillingness in my opinion to reflect on the Cuban reality and the aftermath of the Castro Revolution from 1959 through 1961 when the Castro government took over all elements of Cuba's infrastructure. The historical record makes it clear for all to see.

The key basic question players had to answer to make a decision was whether "to stay or not stay" in Cuba. Clearly some players would say "yes" and stayed in Cuba, as we will see later on.

Many said in effect, "no." They did so reflecting on the fact that they were professional baseball players and that their careers were not possible in their own country, as it had been for so many before them. They wished to continue to pursue their dream and play in the major leagues, regardless of the sacrifice that they and their families knew they would experience.

To leave meant in some cases to separate from one's own family and perhaps never seeing them again (as many did). It also meant leaving behind the country where one had been born and raised, of no longer being able to experience the Cuban culture and way of life, and stepping away from the tradition of Cuban baseball and its fans, among many factors.

Those factors were confronted and balanced by the opportunity to play in the "Bigs," with baseball scouts and knowledgeable people telling you as a player that you had the talent to continue to play professional baseball while going to the U.S. and show your ability to play. This was both a challenge and a goal. It is important to note here that many players had by this time received contracts to play with U.S. based teams.

At this point in their lives their future was sufficiently clear, the end of professional baseball and staying in Cuba with their family and friends meant to live and work in an uncertain future and to forfeit the dream that many had envisioned for themselves to play professional baseball, indeed a heart wrenching decision.

What was also clear was that the decision needed to be made while the option to do so was available. Many of the players were very young, in their teens or early twenty's, or were less established and had never made a decision of this magnitude which amounted to be a life-long and painful decision no matter what they finally decided. Some were more established in the majors or were a bit older had already opted to leave Cuba knowing their life would be changed forever while dealing with some of the challenges such as the language barrier with limited or no help available. It is worthwhile noting that the assistance related services available to players today were not part of the normal infrastructure in those days. But those matters paled in comparison to more fundamental issues found in the Cuba's society that many feared would take place.

During the 1960-61 season, while players were wrestling with this life-changing decision, it was told to me during private interviews that some players kept a low profile and travelled to the country side and away from their familiar environment during off days as a way of dealing with the significant political upheaval in those days. Many Cubans thought that things would change for the better at the time, yet they knew and it was obvious that it was communist leaning regime. Players had to be careful where and in front of whom they spoke since they were aware that some of those players were committed to the communist revolution. There were other players whose allegiance seemed to waver back and forth between their support and their rejection of the Castro Cuban revolution. They could not be trusted entirely and so fellow players needed to be discrete about what to say in front of them. Secrecy was the order of the day. Players were told not to say a word about their possible exit from Cuba among other related topics. That fear has continued to the present day as related by so many Cubans wishing to leave their country, including players who have left since 1990 to the present time.

Several names were used during my interviews about those who were viewed to *waver* back and forth between support and rejection of the Castro government. But it is not possible to say with certainty without taking the risk of damaging some players' and their families' reputation within the Cuban community and so I have refrained from including them. Over fifty years later, during my interviews with some of these players, one could still see the anguish and emotional impact in their faces and hear it in their voices when they shared their personal story.

One such story was shared by Leopoldo Posada who wanted the following story to be known, telling me, "It is about time people know what went on in Cuba" during that time, and he requested that it be included in this book.

He recalled how during the 60-61 season he hit a home run against Luis Tiant Jr., who would be named Rookie of the Year. Next time they faced each other, Tiant unleashed a hard throw hitting him in the ribs. The next day, a Sunday, Posada was unable to play due to the injury he had suffered. Monday was a day off and he also did not play on Tuesday or Wednesday, still hurting from the injury to his ribs.

On Thursday, Monchy de Arcos told Posada he had overheard the *barbudos* talking about him, *Barbudos* were what government soldiers were known as, especially those that had fought in the mountains in Cuba because of the long beards they grew during the revolutionary war. They were overheard to say that Posada was actually not playing because he was a counterrevolutionary as his uncle had been. His uncle had been put to death in the Escambray Mountains in December of 1960 during a failed insurrection against Fidel Castro. De Arcos further heard them say that if Posada didn't play that night, he would be put in jail.

Posada, troubled by what he heard, left the clubhouse and asked the trainer to bring the largest bandage he could find and wrap it around his midsection as tight as possible. Then he went to see his Manager, Carrera, and told him he was playing that day. Carrera said, "Are you are crazy?" referring to his injury. Posada responded, "No, put me to play." and he did. Posada was not going to jeopardize his life, or at least his career. This is a true and sad story. It shows how the political environment was in Cuba and what players had to deal with in order to move forward with the life they wanted to experience. Years later, I would share this story with Luis Tiant, who remembered well hitting Posada but had not been aware of the aftermath and the pressure Posada had endured.

In order to make the actual decision many of these young players had to rely on family members to seek advice about what was the "right thing" to do. And it was clear that there was not a lot of time to make such a life changing decision. It is difficult to truly understand, on the emotional level, for those who have not had the experience of having to consider the painful and difficult decision to leave one's home country and family behind to an uncertain future. There are those among us that, because of our age at the time, were spared the need to make that decision. However, for our parents and other adults, including baseball players, it was an experience that to this day has had a significant impact on them and our families. Reflecting on the family separation and its impact, when I left it felt like *me mataron vivo* (they killed me while being alive). Luis Tiant Jr. said, "I lost 17 years of my life with my father. People don't understand. Only Cubans can understand,"[39] the decision to leave was fraught with issues never felt before in their lives. Confusion, facing an uncertain future, "you start thinking and you don't know what you are getting into." It was the type of decision that you are not prepared to make. People who have not had to make this decision cannot fully comprehend the impact that it has for someone at such an early age. Many don't understand that it is not a decision about where you are going but about what you leave behind, your parents, and lifelong friends.[40]

For these players baseball had in effect become politicized and the veil of a fun and happy experience was torn as the family unit, culture and personal relationships were taken away knowing one could never go home again.[41]

One has to wonder what the impact of these uncertain and difficult times had on these players. Many of them were very young, trying to perform their very best on the field of play and possibly make the best impression while contemplating prolonging their professional career outside of their home country.

While this personal crisis was taking place, Narciso Camejo was reelected President of the Cuban Baseball league. However, he requested a Leave of Absence that was granted, and instead left the country just as the club owners had done. This underscored the severity of what was facing these players. Miguel Angel González born September 24, 1890, became President of the League and remained in Cuba, passing away February 19, 1977 at the age of 86, and was buried at the Christopher Columbus Cemetery in La Habana.

As the season ended on February 8, 1961, the process of leaving the country for these players was not a straightforward process. Many left Cuba never to return, while others left and returned at different times, all of it showing on how these times differed from those of the previous era where players would simply travel between Cuba and the U.S. to advance their chosen career.

The process for leaving Cuba had an assist made possible by the fact that the country of Mexico had an agreement with Major

League Baseball to provide visas for players contracted to play with a U.S. team.

Within a short time of making their personal and heart wrenching decision to leave, players were notified that they should go to the Mexican Embassy in Cuba where they could secure a visa to travel safely to the United States via Mexico. In the case of Miguel de la Hoz, Monchy de Arcos was said to be the only person that had such information and would in turn communicate with the players.[42]

Upon arrival to Mexico City many would stay at the Hotel Virreyes, built in 1947, and located in the center of the city. During the 1950's this hotel had hosted many personalities such as the Cuban born boxer, Mantequilla Nápoles, actors Rock Hudson and Barbara Rush which led to an expansion of the rooms available for many more guests including baseball players from Cuba, as it turned out.

Meanwhile in Cuba, in February of 1961, INDER (*Instituto Nacional de Deportes, Educación Física y Recreo*), the National Institute of Physical Education and Recreation was created and decree 936 banned all professional athletics.[43] "The adoption of a Soviet model in 1961 envisioned national sports teams as instruments for propping national propaganda."[44] With a system that had EIDE (*Escuela de Iniciación Deportiva Escolar*), the Early School of Sports brought students up to grade 10, while ESPA *Escuela de Superación y Perfeccionamiento Atlético*, the School of Athletic Improvement, included students from the 10th grade to High School, then followed by municipal teams and the National and Selective Series. This system would lead ultimately in the selection of players to the Cuban National team.[45]

The Bay of Pigs invasion took place in April of that year as the door for players to leave the country began to close. Soon thereafter, on May 1st, Cuba declared itself a Socialist Nation. The private school system was confiscated and closed for eight months while the government endeavored to revamp the country's school system. By June of that year the Education Reform was instituted, which in effect only welcomed teachers who would comply with Marxist ideology.

The regime clamped down on those deemed enemies of the State with executions, jail terms and a minimum of a fair trial system in place. To further reduce any semblance of resistance, clergy were expelled in September of 1961. Public religious services banned, and acts of repudiation began that were designed to intimidate people. These acts were, simply stated, public demonstrations incited by the government to bully people or damage property of those considered to be counter revolutionaries, another way of saying they did not agree with the Castro regime. Family members in Cuba shared with me some years later, how their neighbors who were "accused" of wishing to leave Cuba would have a public demonstration gathered in front of their homes with many throwing eggs at the doors and windows while shouting revolutionary slogans. Many of these acts of repudiation continue today.[46]

It was during this time, in October of 1961, that the Cuban Sugar Kings ultimately moved from Jersey City to Jacksonville Florida, where the team ultimately ceased to exist. It was coincidental that this author was at a Cuban refugee camp for boys outside of that very city but given the conditions of the times never had the opportunity to see the games nor had knowledge of the team being there.[47]

In December of 1961 Fidel Castro declared himself a Marxist-Leninist, and had been from the beginning. At that point, Cubans had to obtain exit permits to leave and enter Cuba and so the door had in effect been shut down.

The final days of professional baseball at the end of the 1960-61 season, did not signified that only those players that were in the teams' rosters would be leaving. The reality was that others had already done so and others would follow in the months to come. While the stories of individual players were somewhat different from one to another, the conditions that they experienced were basically the same.

Against this general backdrop the next few chapters will serve as an introduction to the teams' active rosters in the Cuban Baseball League enabling us to see what each player decision would ultimately leads to.

The basic write up of each player, which is included in no particular order, is not intended to be an exhaustive account of their career. It is to highlight some of their baseball accomplishments during the last season, as well as their baseball history outside of Cuba, and to capture their comings and goings to and from Cuba, which has been a point of interest in this project. To the degree that it was possible, I have traced their exit from Cuba, or whether they remained following the end of the 1960-61 season. Each team roster is written in the order in which the (team) ended that last season.

An Author's note about references and sources: To the degree possible, I have included an image of the corresponding player with the credit to the organization which gave the permission to use these images. The acknowledgement page features these organizations. You will also find included here, as part of each player's story a table showing the teams and the dates they played for outside of Cuba.[48] This table is found at the end of each of their historical summaries in order to provide some context for the story of the players as they left Cuba or chose to stay. I have purposely avoided writing or including the entire set of baseball accomplishments and records for each of these players since that information is readily available in many other and more complete sources. Among those, the primary reference sources I used to show their careers in Cuba were as follows: Figueredo, Jorge S. *Cuban Baseball A Statisitical History 1878-1961.* Jefferson, North Carolina and London: McFarland and Company, 2003, Figueredo, Jorge S. *Who's Who in Cuban Baseball 1878-1961.* Jefferson, North Carolina and London: McFarland and Company, 2003, González, Echevarría, Roberto. *The Pride of Havana A History of Cuban Baseball.* New York Oxford: Oxford University Press, 1999 and baseball-reference.com. Immigration records and other official records such as marriage, U.S. Naturalization Applications, burial and other related information were secured via ancestry.com.

It is worthy of note that I have found inconsistent information related to birthplaces and birthdays to that which has been previously published. I have relied on the information found in the immigration record presuming that players did not wish to jeopardize their travel plans by inserting innacurate information.

Other sources were also used which I have endeavored to either reference throughout the text and or noted as "Additional Sources" at the conclusion of each player's write up.

Chapter 5

CIENFUEGOS

The 1960-61 season was owned by "Cucho" Rodríguez Gali and "Guille" Alonso Bermúdez.

Manager

Antonio (Tony) Castaño

Tony took over the helm of Cienfuegos in mid-season in 1957-1958 and guided them to a 31-41 third-place finish in 1958-1959. In 1959-1960, he led the club to a 48-24 record, winning the championship by 12 games for one of the most successful seasons in league history. His team was a talented one, with players such as Camilo Pascual, Pedro Ramos, Raúl Sánchez, George Altman, Cookie/Cuqui Rojas, Orlando Peña, Leo Cárdenas, Don Eaddy, Dutch Dotterer, Román Mejías, Tony González and Rogelio Alvarez. They went 6-0 on their way to win the 1960 Caribbean Series, the last Caribbean Series to be won by a Cuban team to date. His overall career record in the Cuba League was 135 wins and 122 losses.

Castaño began 1960 as the skipper of the Sugar Kings, an AAA team, but as indicated earlier, he resigned when the club moved to Jersey City, NJ. Tony stayed behind in Cuba while Napoleón Reyes took over the managerial reigns. Castaño's record with the Kings was 38 wins and 39 losses.

During this last season, in 1960-1961, Cienfuegos repeated as champs with a 35-31 record, this time by a much smaller margin, winning by one game over Almendares. Castaño chose to stay in Cuba and became the first skipper of the Azucareros in the new Cuban Series Nacional. He guided them to a 13-14 record, tying for second place with the Orientales.

Immigration records show Castaño leaving Cuba in March of 1961 via Mexico with his destination being the Athletics Training Camp in Pensacola, but that would be a temporary exit. He, in fact, left Cuba permanently in 1966. Castaño became a long-time manager in Mexico, with a record of 862 wins and losing 792 as a skipper in that country's league. He led Puebla to a Mexican League pennant in 1963, the third straight Cuban to manage Mexico's champs, following Amaro in 1961 and Clemente Carrera in 1962. His coaching career in Mexico began in 1962-66, followed by the 1968-71 seasons and again in 1974 through the 1975 season. He also coached for the Colombian National team.

His overall career as a player for fifteen seasons included nine in the U.S. minors where he appeared in 953 games with a .294 batting average, splitting his positions between the infield and the outfield. During his thirteen seasons as a manager he won 938 games and lost 869.

It may seem unusual to some to have seen Castaño leave Cuba in 1961 and then leave again later on in 1966, but the reality is that it is not indeed that unusual. You will read about other players who left Cuba at different times driven in some cases by family obligations that made it difficult for them to deal with at the time they were making these decisions whether to leave or to stay. For others, who left only to return to Cuba it was a hope that somehow things would change, and they would be able to pursue a professional baseball career while continuing to live in Cuba as many had done in prior years. This was not unusual for many Cubans outside of baseball who felt the Castro government would not last. Consequently, immigration records show this *in and out* of Cuba movement, especially during the first year or so after the last season ended, while freedom to travel between the two countries was still relatively possible.

He was recognized by players and the baseball world and inducted into the Cuban Baseball Hall of Fame in 1967 in Miami, alongside Santos Amaro, the player he had beaten for his first batting title during the 1938-39 season in his fourteen seasons in Cuba.

Antonio Castaño was born in Palma Soriano on February 11, 1911 and died on the 13th of October, 1989 in Miami, FL and is buried in the Vista Memorial Gardens in Hialeah Florida.

Additional sources:

Pascual Andrés, eltubeyero22, November 21, 2011.
Bjarkman, Peter C. *A History of Cuban Baseball 1864-2006*. Jefferson, NC, and London: McFarland, 2007.

His managing record is shown here:

Year	Age	Tm	Lg	Lev	Aff	G	W	L
1956	45	Nuevo Laredo	MEX	AA		122	42	78
1960	49	Havana/ Jersey City	IL	AAA	CIN	155	76	77
1962	51	Fresnillo	MXCL	C		119	70	49
1963	52	Puebla	MEX	AA		132	80	52
1964	53	Puebla	MEX	AA		140	79	61
1965	54	Puebla	MEX	AA		139	78	61
1966	55	Poza Rica	MEX	AA		140	61	79
1968	57	Puebla	MEX	AAA		140	72	68
1969	58	Puebla	MEX	AAA		154	72	82
1970	59	Yucatan	MEX	AAA		150	77	73
1971	60	Veracruz	MEX	AAA		145	70	75
1974	63	Puebla	MEX	AAA		137	81	56
1975	64	Puebla	MEX	AAA		138	80	58
13 Seasons						1811	938	869

His playing career is shown below:

Year	Age	Tm	Lg	Lev	Aff
1938	27	Asheville Tourists	Piedmont League	B	STL
1939	28	Sacramento Solons	Pacific Coast League	AA	STL
1940	29	Columbus Red Birds	South Atlantic League	B	STL
1940	29	Asheville Tourists	Piedmont League	B	STL
1941	30	Springfield Cardinals	Middle Atlantic League	C	STL
1941	30	Mobile Shippers	Southeastern League	B	STL
1942	31	Springfield Cardinals	Middle Atlantic League	C	STL
1943	32	Richmond Colts	Piedmont League	B	
1944	33	Toronto Maple Leafs	International League	AA	PIT
1945	34	Toronto Maple Leafs	International League	AA	PHA
1946	35	Veracruz Azules	Mexican League	Ind	
1947	36	Veracruz Azules	Mexican League	Ind	
1948	37	Veracruz Azules	Mexican League	Ind	
1948	37	Puebla Angeles	Mexican League	Ind	
1949	38	Jalisco Charros	Mexican League	Ind	
1950	39	Havana Cubans	Florida International League	B	WSH
1951	40	Veracruz Aguila	Mexican League	Ind	
1952	41	Veracruz Aguila	Mexican League	Ind	
1952	41	Jalisco Charros	Mexican League	Ind	

Pitchers

Dagoberto Concepción Cueto (also known as Bert Cueto)

In his last season in Cuba, Concepción pitched in 15 games but could not muster a win to go along with his one loss and a 3.00 ERA. He pitched in 26 innings, and gave up 25 hits, while striking out 10 and walking 14. He played for Cienfuegos during his four seasons in Cuba.

Born on August 14, 1937 in the town of San Luis in the province of Pinar del Río, Concepción played professional baseball in the U.S. from the 1956 season through 1964. He left his career behind at the age of 26, having played in the U.S., Mexico and Cuba. He made it to the majors playing for the Minnesota Twins in 1961, posting a 1-3 record in seven games. His stats in the minors included a 46-46 win and loss record.

He left Cuba on March 24, 1961 via Mexico, four days after his manager Castaño. He arrived in Fernandina Beach, located outside of Jacksonville, Florida, and stayed at the Kingston Hotel while he joined the Charlotte Hornets. His playing record reflects his decision to stay in the U.S. following the end of the last professional season in Cuba.

Dagoberto Concepción passed away on October 25, 2011 in Charlotte, North Carolina, where he is buried in the Sharon Park Cemetery.

Year	Age	Tm	Lg	Lev
1956	18	Superior Senators	Nebraska State League	D
1957	19	Fort Walton Beach Jets	Alabama-Florida League	D
1958	20	Fox Cities Foxes	Illinois-Indiana-Iowa League	B
1958	20	Missoula Timberjacks	Pioneer League	C
1959	21	Charlotte Hornets	South Atlantic League	A
1960	22	Charleston Senators	American Association	AAA
1960	22	Charlotte Hornets	South Atlantic League	A
1961	23	Syracuse Chiefs	International League	AAA

Year	Age	Tm	Lg	Lev
1961	23	Minnesota Twins	American League	MLB
1962	24	Vancouver Mounties	Pacific Coast League	AAA
1962	24	Spokane Indians	Pacific Coast League	AAA
1963	25	Nashville Volunteers	South Atlantic League	AA
1963	25	Reynosa Broncs	Mexican League	AA
1964	26	Reynosa Broncs	Mexican League	AA
1964	26	Asheville Tourists	Southern League	AA

Roberto León (Pérez) Taño

Born on February 20, 1936, in Vertientes, Camagüey. Taño saw limited action during his two seasons in Cuba (both with Cienfuegos) in a total of eight games, seven of which were during that last season where he had ten strike outs and gave up six walks in seven games with a no win-no loss record in 13 innings. He won six games and had a 2.77 ERA during his professional career in Cuba.

Outside of Cuba, his career spanned from 1956 through 1963 in the U.S. minor leagues, with a pitching record of 6 and 5. He also played in a number of positions but was never able to reach the majors. He arrived in Fernandina Beach, Florida via Mexico on March 24, 1961, just over a month after his 24th birthday, (the same day as Concepción), to join the Charlotte Hornets which were affiliated with the Minnesota Twins. He is among those that stayed after the 60-61 season, as shown by his record in the U.S.

Year	Age	Tm	Lg	Lev
1956	20	Crestview Braves	Alabama-Florida League	D
1956	20	Fort Walton Beach Jets	Alabama-Florida League	D
1957	21	Fort Walton Beach Jets	Alabama-Florida League	D
1958	22	Fox Cities Foxes	Illinois-Indiana-Iowa League	B
1959	23	Charlotte Hornets	South Atlantic League	A

Year	Age	Tm	Lg	Lev
1960	24	Charlotte Hornets	South Atlantic League	A
1961	25	Wilson Tobs	Carolina League	B
1961	25	Charlotte Hornets	South Atlantic League	A
1962	26	Wilson Tobs	Carolina League	B
1963	27	Wilson Tobs	Carolina League	A

Antonio Díaz

Díaz was born on June 13, 1938 in La Habana. He registered a six win-six loss record during the last season in Cuba with five complete games and a 3.54 ERA. During his four seasons in Cuba, all with Cienfuegos, he won 14 games and lost 16 in 86 games. He posted a no hit-no run game during the 57-58 season and was named Rookie of the Year that season. He also played in the 1960 Caribbean series, pitching four innings, and had an ERA of 2.25. His career spanned from 1956 through 1964, posting a minor league record of 60 wins and 51 losses, in addition to his four seasons in Mexico.

He played in the U.S. in 1961, suggesting that he left, at least temporarily, so he could play baseball. Following that season, he played in Mexico through 1964 but ultimately stayed in the U.S.

Additional Source: Iván Davis, telephone interview with author January 31, 2018.

Year	Age	Team	Lg	Class
1956	18	Wellsville Braves	Pennsylvania-Ontario-New York	D
1957	19	Evansville Braves	Illinois-Indiana-Iowa League	B
1958	20	Jacksonville Braves	South Atlantic League	A
1959	21	Austin Senators	Texas League	AA
1960	22	Sacramento Solons	Pacific Coast League	AAA
1961	23	Austin Senators	Texas League	AA

Year	Age	Team	Lg	Class
1961	23	Houston Buffs	American Association	AAA
1961	23	Monterrey Sultanes	Mexican League	AA
1962	24	Monterrey Sultanes	Mexican League	AA
1963	25	Poza Rica Petroleros	Mexican League	AA
1963	25	Puebla Pericos	Mexican League	AA
1963	25	Veracruz Aguilas	Mexican League	AA
1964	26	Puerto Mexico Portenos	Mexican Southeast League	A

Máximo D. (Cárdenas) García

García played but one season in Cuba, (1960-61), appearing in 15 games and had two complete games. There is no record of him having played in the U.S. during his 12-season career, from 1955 through 1966, playing exclusively in Mexico.

He arrived in the U.S. at two different times, Miami on December 1961 from La Habana Cuba and, in April of 1962, when he boarded his flight to Miami from the Dominican Republic. His permanent address was listed in Tampa Florida, according to the travel records.

Year	Age	Tm	Lg	Lev
1955	18	Yucatan Leones	Mexican League	AA
1956	19	Fresnillo Mineros	Central Mexican League	C
1957	20	Nuevo Laredo Tecolotes	Mexican League	AA
1957	20	Saltillo	Central Mexican League	C
1957	20	Durango-Laguna	Central Mexican League	C
1958	21	Nuevo Laredo Tecolotes	Mexican League	AA
1959	22	Nuevo Laredo Tecolotes	Mexican League	AA
1960	23	Puebla Pericos	Mexican League	AA

Year	Age	Tm	Lg	Lev
1961	24	Puebla Pericos	Mexican League	AA
1962	25	Puebla Pericos	Mexican League	AA
1962	25	Veracruz Aguilas	Mexican League	AA
1963	26	Veracruz Aguilas	Mexican League	AA
1964	27	Puebla Pericos	Mexican League	AA
1964	27	Campeche Pirates	Mexican Southeast League	A
1965	28	Campeche Pirates	Mexican Southeast League	A
1966	29	Campeche Pirates	Mexican Southeast League	A

Héctor Anibal Maestri García

Maestri participated in 28 games during this last season and had a record of six wins and eight losses. He played a total of two seasons in Cuba, both with Cienfuegos, winning a total of seven games with eight losses and a 3.78 ERA. He reached the majors on two different occasions with a 0-1 record during his career, from 1956-1966, playing in Cuba, the U.S. and Mexico and with the Toronto Maple Leafs of the International League. He won a total of 71 games, 64 of which were in the U.S. minors. He also played for the Cuban team that won the Caribbean series in 1960 in Panamá.

Héctor Maestri left Cuba on several occasions. He secured a visa from Mexico to travel on November 11, 1961, and also arrived there on February 20, 1962 from Cuba, having secured a visa in Toronto, Canada. Both times he flew to Pompano Beach to join the Washington Senators, according to the travel records. He wanted to return to Cuba to see his newborn son and, even though he was able to leave the country, he did so alone. The Mexican League ultimately provided him with visas for both his wife and two sons leaving Cuba permanently in 1965 via Mexico.

Maestri was the nephew of the well-known and respected Cuban umpire, Amado Maestri. For a period of time, he became the President of the Players Cuban Federation in Exile.

Maestri passed away on February 21, 2014 in Miami Florida.

Additional source: baseballhappenings.net/2014/02

Year	Age	Tm	Lg	Lev
1956	21	Fort Walton Beach Jets	Alabama-Florida League	D
1957	22	Elmira Pioneers	New York-Pennsylvania League	D
1958	23	Elmira Pioneers	New York-Pennsylvania League	D
1959	24	Charlotte Hornets	South Atlantic League	A
1959	24	Fox Cities Foxes	Illinois-Indiana-Iowa League	B
1960	25	Charlotte Hornets	South Atlantic League	A
1960	25	Washington Senators	American League	MLB
1961	26	Columbia Reds	South Atlantic League	A
1961	26	Jersey City Jerseys	International League	AAA
1961	26	Toronto Maple Leafs	International League	AAA
1961	26	Washington Senators	American League	MLB
1962	27	Charlotte Hornets	South Atlantic League	A
1962	27	Toronto Maple Leafs	International League	AAA
1962	27	Syracuse Chiefs	International League	AAA
1965	30	Veracruz Aguilas	Mexican League	AA
1965	30	Charlotte Hornets	Southern League	AA
1966	31	Wilson Tobs	Carolina League	A

Enrique Maroto Mena

Appearing in 17 games during the 1960-61 season, Maroto had a 2-2 record in 56 innings, during the only season he played for Cienfuegos. He played a total of four seasons in Cuba, three of which with the Marianao Tigers. This is the team he played with during the 1957 Caribbean Series where he participated in only one game.

His career included playing for the Kansas City Monarchs in 1954. He was known as a *workhorse* because on more than one occasion, he would pitch in both games of a doubleheader. He pitched in both the 1954 and 1955 Negro League All Star Games. He was signed by the Washington Senators in 1957 and helped integrate the South Atlantic League (Class A Minor League level) over the next two years. His minor league record during these two seasons included seven wins and seven losses, but the Senators never advanced him any further. He returned home to La Habana in 1959 to play for the Havana Sugar Kings of the Class AAA International League. Maroto also played in Mexico and in Nicaragua in 1961-62 and went back to Cuba in 62 but couldn't leave for four years.

Ultimately, having returned to the U.S., Maroto established his permanent Residence Status in 1966 and became a U.S. citizen at a ceremony in Chicago Illinois in April of 1972.

Additional source: The Negro League Revisited by Brent Kelley 324-327

Year	Age	Tm	Lg	Lev
1957	22	Mexico City Diablos Rojos	Mexican League	AA
1957	22	Fresnillo	Central Mexican League	C
1958	23	Charlotte Hornets	South Atlantic League	A
1959	24	Charlotte Hornets	South Atlantic League	A
1960	25	Monterrey Sultanes	Mexican League	AA

Year	Age	Tm	Lg	Lev
1960	25	Havana Sugar Kings/ Jersey City Jerseys	International League	AAA
1961	26	Monterrey Sultanes	Mexican League	AA
1961	26	Mexico City Diablos Rojos	Mexican League	AA

Camilo Alberto Pascual Lus

One of the better known and successful Cuban born pitchers was Camilo Pascual. He went on to an 18-year career in the majors from 1954 through 1971, winning a total of 174 games with teams that had less than stellar records, and made the major league All Star team five times between 1960 and 1964. He arrived in the U.S. in 1951, at the age of 17. He came to Geneva, NY where many Cubans recruited by Joe Cambria were assigned to play. He carried a card on bus rides showing his destination. His record in the minors was 23 wins and 16 losses.

During his eight seasons in Cuba he had a record of 58 wins and 32 losses with 612 strike outs and 253 walks and an ERA of 2.04.

Playing for the Havana Sugar Kings for two seasons he had an 18-12 record, with 165 strike outs, 134 walks and a 2.96 ERA.

Pascual had a 1-1 record during the last season in Cuba pitching for a total of eight innings while appearing in 2 games. One can speculate that he had arm trouble, or that his U.S. team asked him not to play winter ball since he had been a major league pitcher since 1954, having been signed by the Senators in 1952. The actual reason became known during an interview with Miguelito de la Hoz, Pascual shared the fact that he had a bad arm and was unable to take the mound during the season. Arm trouble would not be surprising to understand if Pascual's pitching record for the preceding nine months is considered. During that time, while pitching in the 1959-60 Cuban season, the Caribbean series and then the 1960 Major League season with the Washington Senators, he appeared in 51 games, pitching in 323.2 innings and completing 22 games. His record for that time was 29-13.

With a few games left in the 1960-61 season in Cuba, his arm showed signs of having recovered. Pascual asked for and pitched in two games for a total of eight innings, wishing to test whether recovery had in fact taken place, and also thinking ahead to the upcoming spring training with the Minnesota Twins. He went on to pitch in the majors through the 1971 season. During that last season in Cuba, he was used as a coach with the support of his Manager Antonio Castaño.

His family settled in the U.S. by 1961, and his brother Carlos came to the U.S. in 1962, followed by his parents and sister in 1964-65. Pascual never returned to Cuba after leaving via Mexico on February 28, 1961. As he reflected in a 2017 film, *Major League Cuban*, his job was to play baseball, so he stayed in the U.S. and became a U.S. citizen in 1969 in Miami Florida. However, in the film, Pascual said "I was born there. I made my life there. But I don't have anybody there. If the situation with this government changes, maybe I will visit Cuba."

His baseball career was recognized during his selection to the Cuban Baseball Hall of Fame in Miami, Florida.

Additional sources:

Omelis Hongamen, telephone interview with author, September 28, 2016

Camilo Pascual, telephone interview by Miguel de la Hoz February 1, 2018.

Cardona, Joe and González Ralf "Major League Cuban" a co-production of South Florida PBS and Royal Palms Films 2017.

Tony Oliva by Thom Henninger, University of Minnesota Press Minneapolis London 2015 page 194

Year	Age	Tm	Lg	Lev
1951	17	Geneva Robins	Border League	C
1951	17	Big Spring Broncs	Longhorn League	C
1951	17	Chickasha Chiefs	Sooner State League	D
1952	18	Havana Cubans	Florida International League	B
1952	18	Tampa Smokers	Florida International League	B
1953	19	Havana Cubans	Florida International League	B
1954	20	Washington Senators	American League	MLB
1955	21	Washington Senators	American League	MLB
1956	22	Washington Senators	American League	MLB
1957	23	Washington Senators	American League	MLB
1958	24	Washington Senators	American League	MLB
1959	25	Washington Senators	American League	MLB
1960	26	Washington Senators	American League	MLB
1961	27	Minnesota Twins	American League	MLB
1962	28	Minnesota Twins	American League	MLB
1963	29	Minnesota Twins	American League	MLB

Year	Age	Tm	Lg	Lev
1964	30	Minnesota Twins	American League	MLB
1965	31	Minnesota Twins	American League	MLB
1966	32	Minnesota Twins	American League	MLB
1967	33	Washington Senators	American League	MLB
1968	34	Washington Senators	American League	MLB
1969	35	Washington Senators	American League	MLB
1969	35	Cincinnati Reds	National League	MLB
1970	36	Los Angeles Dodgers	National League	MLB
1971	37	Cleveland Indians	American League	MLB

Pedro Ramos Guerra

Along with Camilo Pascual, Pedro Ramos was an equally well known and effective Cuban pitcher who during the 1960-61 season appeared in 30 games and had an impressive record of 16 wins with only 7 losses, pitching in 216.2 innings with 17 complete games and three shutouts. He struck out 150 batters and walked but 38, with a 2.08

ERA. He was named, deservedly so, the Most Valuable player during that last season.

Ramos played in the Cuban League during seven seasons, all with Cienfuegos, winning 66 games while striking out 547 batters and giving up 258 walks. His ERA during that time was 2.62. He also appeared in three Caribbean Series, had a 5-1 record and was named Rookie of the Year for the 1955-56 season.

Born in the province of Pinar del Río on the western end of Cuba, Ramos, a member of the Cuban Baseball Hall of Fame in Miami, Florida, had a long and distinguished 20-year career, including 15 years in the majors, playing in Cuba, the U.S. and Mexico, where he would manage a team for one season. His major league record included 117 wins with 160 losses and a 4.08 ERA. In the minors he won 37 and lost 14. His managerial record in Mexico was 72 wins and 65 losses.

It did not take long for Ramos to leave Cuba after the season ended on February 8. He, like many other players, made his way to the Mexican Embassy in La Habana and traveled to the U.S. via Mexico City, arriving on February 28. He made a return trip to Cuba in August 2016 after a 55-year absence.

Additional source: oncubamagazine.com

Year	Age	Tm	Lg	Lev
1953	18	Morristown Red Sox	Mountain States League	D
1954	19	Hagerstown Packets	Piedmont League	B
1954	19	Morristown Red Sox	Mountain States League	C
1954	19	Kingsport Cherokees	Mountain States League	C
1955	20	Washington Senators	American League	MLB
1956	21	Washington Senators	American League	MLB
1957	22	Washington Senators	American League	MLB
1958	23	Washington Senators	American League	MLB
1959	24	Washington Senators	American League	MLB
1960	25	Washington Senators	American League	MLB

Year	Age	Tm	Lg	Lev
1961	26	Minnesota Twins	American League	MLB
1962	27	Cleveland Indians	American League	MLB
1963	28	Cleveland Indians	American League	MLB
1964	29	Cleveland Indians	American League	MLB
1964	29	New York Yankees	American League	MLB
1965	30	New York Yankees	American League	MLB
1966	31	New York Yankees	American League	MLB
1967	32	Vancouver Mounties	Pacific Coast League	AAA
1967	32	Philadelphia Phillies	National League	MLB
1968	33	Columbus Jets	International League	AAA
1969	34	Columbus Jets	International League	AAA
1969	34	Indianapolis Indians	American Association	AAA
1969	34	Pittsburgh Pirates	National League	MLB
1969	34	Cincinnati Reds	National League	MLB
1970	35	Jalisco Charros	Mexican League	AAA
1970	35	Washington Senators	American League	MLB
1971	36	Savannah Braves	Dixie Association	AA
1971	36	Richmond Braves	International League	AAA
1972	37	Tidewater Tides	International League	AAA
1972	37	Puebla Pericos	Mexican League	AAA
1973	38	Mexico City Diablos Rojos	Mexican League	AAA
1974	39	Mexico City Diablos Rojos	Mexican League	AAA
1975	40	Mexico City Diablos Rojos	Mexican League	AAA
1975	40	Villahermosa Cardenales	Mexican League	AAA

Raúl Guadalupe Sánchez Rodríguez

Sánchez appeared in seven games during the 1960-61 season, garnering a 3-2 record while pitching a complete game and sporting a 3.94 ERA. During his ten seasons in Cuba, he played for all the professional teams of his time, the Habana, Marianao, Almendares and Cienfuegos for a total of 246 pitching appearances and winning 46 games with a very respectable 3.31 ERA.

He also played in two Caribbean Series winning one game in three appearances, and a 2.12 ERA, and then played two seasons for the Havana Cubans with a record of 16-18 and a 2.09 ERA. Sánchez also played six seasons and 257 games for the Cuban Sugar Kings and had a record of 44 wins, 36 losses and a 3.45 ERA. He was on the team winning the Little World Series in 1959, winning a game with a 2.00 ERA. Born in the Toledo Sugar Mill, on December 20, 1930, Sánchez's career spanned 1951 through 1963, including three years in the majors. He returned to baseball in 1972 to play for the Reynosa Broncos in the Mexican League at the age of 40. He was inducted onto the Cuban Baseball of Fame in Miami, Florida.

The last official record available of his leaving Cuba, showed his exit on June 27, 1960 on his way to (as described) "some hotel in Buffalo NY". But given his continuing career through 1962 in the U.S., this reflects his staying in this country during that time and after the end of the last season. Following the end of his baseball career, he worked in construction. Raúl Sánchez passed away on June 30, 2002 in Pembroke Pines in Florida and is buried in the Flagler Park Cemetery.

Year	Age	Tm	Lg	Lev	Aff
1951	20	Big Spring Broncs	Longhorn League	C	
1951	20	Havana Cubans	Florida International League	B	WSH
1952	21	Havana Cubans	Florida International League	B	WSH
1952	21	Washington Senators	American League	MLB	WSH
1953	22	Chattanooga Lookouts	Southern Association	AA	WSH
1954	23	Havana Sugar Kings	International League	AAA	
1955	24	Havana Sugar Kings	International League	AAA	CIN
1956	25	Havana Sugar Kings	International League	AAA	CIN
1957	26	Cincinnati Redlegs	National League	MLB	CIN
1958	27	Havana Sugar Kings	International League	AAA	CIN
1959	28	Havana Sugar Kings	International League	AAA	CIN
1960	29	Havana Sugar Kings/Jersey City Jerseys	International League	AAA	CIN
1960	29	Cincinnati Reds	National League	MLB	CIN
1961	30	Toronto Maple Leafs	International League	AAA	

Year	Age	Tm	Lg	Lev	Aff
1961	30	Richmond Virginians	International League	AAA	NYY
1962	31	Amarillo Gold Sox	Texas League	AA	NYY
1963	32	Puebla Pericos	Mexican League	AA	
1971	40	Reynosa Broncs	Mexican League	AAA	

Catchers

José Joaquín Azcue López

This resourceful catcher for the Cienfuegos squad had 228 appearances at the plate with a batting average of .289 and 38 runs batted in during the last baseball season. His four seasons in the Cuban League were all with Cienfuegos, batting .267 in 359 plate appearances. He also played in the Caribbean Series with that same team in 1960.

His playing career from 1956, at the age of 16, through 1973 included a season with the Palatka Redlegs in 1957, and 11 seasons in the major leagues, mostly with the Cleveland Indians. And he played for a brief period in Venezuela during 1961-62. He also managed a team in Reno during 1974. Azcue was selected as a member of the 1997 class of the Cuban baseball Hall of Fame in Miami, Florida.

He entered the U.S. in 1962 to join the Kansas City Athletics from the Dominican Republic having played in Vancouver British Columbia for the Vancouver Mounties during the 1961 season. His baseball career clearly reflects a decision to stay in the U.S. after the 1960-61 season in Cuba.

Year	Age	Tm	Lg	Lev
1956	16	Moultrie Reds	Georgia-Florida League	D
1956	16	Douglas Reds	Georgia State League	D
1957	17	Palatka Redlegs	Florida State League	D
1958	18	Savannah Redlegs	South Atlantic League	A
1958	18	Wenatchee Chiefs	Northwest League	B
1959	19	Savannah Reds	South Atlantic League	A
1960	20	Havana Sugar Kings/ Jersey City Jerseys	International League	AAA
1960	20	Cincinnati Reds	National League	MLB
1961	21	Vancouver Mounties	Pacific Coast League	AAA
1962	22	Kansas City Athletics	American League	MLB
1963	23	Portland Beavers	Pacific Coast League	AAA
1963	23	Kansas City Athletics	American League	MLB
1963	23	Cleveland Indians	American League	MLB
1964	24	Cleveland Indians	American League	MLB
1965	25	Cleveland Indians	American League	MLB
1966	26	Cleveland Indians	American League	MLB
1967	27	Cleveland Indians	American League	MLB
1968	28	Cleveland Indians	American League	MLB
1969	29	Cleveland Indians	American League	MLB

Year	Age	Tm	Lg	Lev
1969	29	Boston Red Sox	American League	MLB
1969	29	California Angels	American League	MLB
1970	30	California Angels	American League	MLB
1972	32	Salt Lake City Angels	Pacific Coast League	AAA
1972	32	California Angels	American League	MLB
1972	32	Milwaukee Brewers	American League	MLB
1973	33	San Antonio Brewers	Texas League	AA

Adolfo (Tejerina) Suárez

During his six seasons career in the U.S., Suárez played a number of positions, mostly as a catcher, including two seasons with the Class D Palatka Redlegs, affiliated with Cincinnati during the 1958 and 59 seasons. He was born in Nícaro in the Oriente Province, on the eastern side of Cuba, and later on moved to the Matanzas province. He played two seasons in Cuba as a member of the Cienfuegos squad where he had but 21 appearances at the plate and a batting average of .143. Eighteen of those appearances were during the 1960-61 season.

Although called Arturo in some sources, Adolfo was confirmed as his correct name by fellow player Iván Davis. He arrived in the U.S. in February of 1962 to join, according to the immigration record, the Jacksonville ball club, even though he played that season for the Tri-City Braves of the Northwest league. He lived in Chicago and became a U.S. citizen in 1972 while living in Chicago Illinois.

Additional source: Iván Davis, telephone interview with author, October 24, 2016.

Year	Age	Tm	Lg	Lev
1958	23	Palatka Redlegs	Florida State League	D
1959	24	Palatka Redlegs	Florida State League	D

Year	Age	Tm	Lg	Lev
1959	24	Topeka Hawks	Illinois-Indiana-Iowa League	B
1960	25	Topeka Reds	Illinois-Indiana-Iowa League	B
1960	25	Charleston White Sox	South Atlantic League	A
1961	26	Jersey City Jerseys	International League	AAA
1961	26	Topeka Reds	Illinois-Indiana-Iowa League	B
1962	27	Tri-City Braves	Northwest League	B
1963	28	Tidewater Tides	Carolina League	A

Infielders

Oswaldo (Ossie) Alvarez González

As an infielder, primarily at second base, for Cienfuegos, Alvarez hit .262 in 107 times at bat during the season. He played 238 games for the team during his six seasons in Cuba, with a batting average of .231. He also played two games during the 1960 Caribbean Series, with eight at bats and a .250 batting average.

Born in Bolondrón a town centrally located between the city of Matanzas to the North and the Bay of Pigs area in the South, Alvarez's travel would take him to places far and wide. His career outside of Cuba spanned fifteen seasons, from 1952 and 1966 in the U.S. and Mexico. He also played in the majors for two seasons for the Washington Senators and the Detroit Tigers. During his two seasons in the majors, he appeared in 95 games with 198 times at bat and a .212 batting average. In 10 seasons in the U.S. minors he came to bat 4084 times during 1113 games and had a robust .291 batting average. He also managed in the Mexican League during six seasons between 1966 and 1994, where he had a record of 388 wins and 387 losses. Alvarez became a Latin American scout for the Pittsburgh Pirates and the Arizona Diamondbacks.

He left Cuba on two different occasions following the end of the 1960-61 season. Having secured a visa in Mexico he arrived on his way to Tampa to report to the Cincinnati Reds camp on March 21, 1961. Returning to Cuba, he left again on February 20, 1962 from La Habana on his way to Lakeland Florida where the Detroit Tigers had their training camp. His visa had been secured in Canada.

He died on March 8, 2008 in Guadalajara, Jalisco, Mexico.

Year	Age	Tm	Lg	Lev
1952	18	Big Spring Broncs	Longhorn League	C
1953	19	Roswell Rockets	Longhorn League	C
1954	20	Roswell Rockets	Longhorn League	C
1955	21	Charlotte Hornets	South Atlantic League	A
1955	21	Hobbs Sports	Longhorn League	C
1956	22	Hobbs Sports	Southwestern League	B
1957	23	Midland/Lamesa Indians	Southwestern League	B
1958	24	Washington Senators	American League	MLB
1959	25	Richmond Virginians	International League	AAA

Year	Age	Tm	Lg	Lev
1959	25	Charleston Senators	American Association	AAA
1959	25	Houston Buffs	American Association	AAA
1959	25	Detroit Tigers	American League	MLB
1960	26	Denver Bears	American Association	AAA
1960	26	Tacoma Giants	Pacific Coast League	AAA
1961	27	Austin Senators	Texas League	AA
1961	27	Denver Bears	American Association	AAA
1962	28	Mexico City Diablos Rojos	Mexican League	AA
1963	29	Mexico City Diablos Rojos	Mexican League	AA
1964	30	Rochester Red Wings	International League	AAA
1964	30	Jalisco Charros	Mexican League	AA
1965	31	Jalisco Charros	Mexican League	AA
1966	32	Jalisco Charros	Mexican League	AA

Rogelio Borrego Alvarez Hernández

Born on April 18, 1938 in Pinar del Río, Rogelio Alvarez, as he was best known, played his three seasons in Cuba for Cienfuegos, earning a batting average of .257. During its last season, his average was a healthier .274 with 11 home runs. He, like others mentioned here, also played during the 1960 Caribbean Series in six games, hitting .333 in 24 times at bat and was a member of the Cuban Sugar Kings for three seasons, hitting .239. During the Little World Series, he played all seven games but his hitting was only .217.

His 18-season career outside of Cuba from 1956 when he was signed by Cincinnati to 1973 in the U.S. and Mexico, included two call ups to the majors, in 1960 and 1962 with the Cincinnati Reds. During his two seasons in the majors, Alvarez appeared in 17 games and held a .189 batting average, a lesser performance than in the minors when he appeared in 1463 games during twelve seasons and had a .266 batting average. Alvarez is a member of the Cuban Baseball Hall of Fame in Miami.

The story about Rogelio Alvarez leaving Cuba is a bit more complex and not as well known. He left initially in March of 1961 with a visa from Mexico to Tampa Florida, like many of his fellow players. However, he returned to Cuba only to come back to the U.S. on March 22, 1962 with a visa secured in Toronto, Canada with Tampa as his ultimate designation. An eye-opening account of Alvarez's travels is provided (see source below) that shows the time when he, among other players, decided to travel to Cuba during the 1961 off season to wait for the 1962 spring training. When the time came, the Cuban government would not authorize their travel to Mexico and so the need to seek an intermediary became obvious. The task fell on Tito Fuentes whose father was an old member of the "Party" (the Communist Party) who ultimately made it possible for the players to travel abroad.

During the 1962 season he played for the AAA San Diego Padres and, in September, was called up to play in the majors for the Cincinnati Reds through the end of the month. He then returned to Cuba only to find himself once again unable to leave in the spring of 63. It was reported that the Mexican government had a hand in making it possible for him to ultimately leave Cuba in May of that year when he again played for the Padres.

He passed away in Hialeah, Florida on November 30, 2012 at the age of 74.

Additional source: Crónicas de Andrés Pascual beisbol07

Year	Age	Tm	Lg	Lev
1956	18	Port Arthur Sea Hawks	Big State League	B
1956	18	Yuma Sun Sox	Arizona-Mexico League	C
1957	19	Wenatchee Chiefs	Northwest League	B
1957	19	Clovis Redlegs	Southwestern League	B
1958	20	Havana Sugar Kings	International League	AAA
1959	21	Havana Sugar Kings	International League	AAA
1960	22	Havana Sugar Kings/ Jersey City Jerseys	International League	AAA
1960	22	Cincinnati Reds	National League	MLB
1961	23	Jersey City Jerseys	International League	AAA
1962	24	San Diego Padres	Pacific Coast League	AAA
1962	24	Cincinnati Reds	National League	MLB
1963	25	San Diego Padres	Pacific Coast League	AAA
1964	26	Macon Peaches	Southern League	AA
1965	27	San Diego Padres	Pacific Coast League	AAA
1965	27	Knoxville Smokies	Southern League	AA
1966	28	Knoxville Smokies	Southern League	AA
1966	28	Buffalo Bisons	International League	AAA
1967	29	Knoxville Smokies	Southern League	AA
1967	29	Evansville White Sox	Southern League	AA
1968	30	Veracruz Aguila	Mexican League	AAA

Year	Age	Tm	Lg	Lev
1969	31	Veracruz Aguila	Mexican League	AAA
1970	32	Veracruz Aguila	Mexican League	AAA
1971	33	Veracruz Aguila	Mexican League	AAA
1972	34	Poza Rica Petroleros	Mexican League	AAA
1973	35	Yucatan Leones	Mexican League	AAA

José Angel César

The young man from Mayarí Oriente, born on September 25, 1937, played during the last season in Cuba for both the Habana Lions and Cienfuegos Elephants. He played second base and hit .228 which was consistent with his two-season average in Cuba of .230.

During his six seasons in the U.S., from 1957 through 1962, he was unable to reach the majors but did reach the AAA level on three different occasions. He experienced a total 540 games, coming to bat 1938 times and held a very respectable .297 batting average.

César traveled to Mexico on his way to Tampa and the Cincinnati Reds arriving on March 21, 1961. He returned to Cuba, but then found himself back in the U.S. in March of 1962, having secured a visa in Toronto Canada, and reported to Vero Beach with the Dodgers organization.

Year	Age	Tm	Lg	Lev
1957	19	Tucson Cowboys	Arizona-Mexico League	C
1958	20	Tucson Cowboys	Arizona-Mexico League	C
1959	21	Victoria Rosebuds	Texas League	AA
1959	21	Macon Dodgers	South Atlantic League	A
1960	22	Montreal Royals	International League	AAA
1960	22	Macon Dodgers	South Atlantic League	A
1961	23	Omaha Dodgers	American Association	AAA
1961	23	Greenville Spinners	South Atlantic League	A

Year	Age	Tm	Lg	Lev
1962	24	Greenville Spinners	South Atlantic League	A
1962	24	Omaha Dodgers	American Association	AAA

Leonardo (Leo) Lázaro Cárdenas Alfonso

Primarily a swift fielding short stop, Cárdenas had a batting average of .302 during the 1960-61 season in Cuba with 258 times at bat and 37 runs batted in. During the 1960 Caribbean Series, he played in six games, batting .250. He was a member of the Cuban Sugar Kings for three seasons, including the Little World Series where he played in the seven games, batting .250. He played three seasons in the Cuban League with Habana and Cienfuegos and later played in the U.S., starting with Tucson in 1956, then through 1975 with Texas. He played a total of sixteen seasons in the major leagues, mostly with Cincinnati, as well as Minnesota, Cleveland, California and the Texas Rangers, where he ended his stellar career batting .257 in 1941 games. This slick fielding infielder had a .968 fielding percentage throughout his career in the U.S. He was named to the All Star team in 1965 while a member of the Cincinnati Reds and is a member of the Cuban Baseball Hall of Fame in Miami, Florida.

His playing career makes it clear that he left Cuba following the end of the last season, but the last record found showing him travelling from Havana in June of 1960 to join the Havana Cubans in Buffalo, New York. Born on December 17, 1958 in Matanzas, Cárdenas listed his permanent address in Cuba as the baseball park *Estadio del Cerro.*

Year	Age	Tm	Lg	Lev
1956	17	Tucson Cowboys	Arizona-Mexico League	C
1957	18	Savannah Redlegs	South Atlantic League	A
1958	19	Savannah Redlegs	South Atlantic League	A
1959	20	Havana Sugar Kings	International League	AAA
1960	21	Havana Sugar Kings/ Jersey City Jerseys	International League	AAA
1960	21	Cincinnati Reds	National League	MLB
1961	22	Cincinnati Reds	National League	MLB
1962	23	Cincinnati Reds	National League	MLB
1963	24	Cincinnati Reds	National League	MLB
1964	25	Cincinnati Reds	National League	MLB
1965	26	Cincinnati Reds	National League	MLB
1966	27	Cincinnati Reds	National League	MLB
1967	28	Cincinnati Reds	National League	MLB
1968	29	Cincinnati Reds	National League	MLB
1969	30	Minnesota Twins	American League	MLB
1970	31	Minnesota Twins	American League	MLB
1971	32	Minnesota Twins	American League	MLB
1972	33	California Angels	American League	MLB
1973	34	Cleveland Indians	American League	MLB
1974	35	Texas Rangers	American League	MLB
1975	36	Texas Rangers	American League	MLB

José Martínez Azcuiz

Martínez, not too well known in Cuba, played but one season, its last professional season. He was very young at the time, 18 years old. He batted .231 with 52 times at the plate.

He played in the U.S. for a total of 13 seasons, from 1960 through 1974, including part of two seasons for the Pittsburgh Pirates of the National League in 1969. He batted .268 in 77 games. In 1970 he played in only 19 games hitting .050 in 20 times at bat. He managed the Single A team for the Kansas City Royals of the Florida League.

He was able to secure a visa through Toronto Canada and travelled from Habana to the U.S. to join the Pittsburgh organization on October 30, 1961. José Martínez Azcuiz was born on July 26, 1942 in the city of Cárdenas in the Province of Matanzas and passed away on October 1, 2014 in Orlando Florida.

Year	Age	Tm	Lg	Lev
1960	17	Dubuque Packers	Midwest League	D
1961	18	Grand Forks Chiefs	Northern League	C
1962	19	Asheville Tourists	South Atlantic League	A

Year	Age	Tm	Lg	Lev
1963	20	Batavia Pirates	New York-Pennsylvania League	A
1963	20	Kinston Eagles	Carolina League	A
1964	21	Asheville Tourists	Southern League	AA
1965	22	Columbus Jets	International League	AAA
1966	23	Columbus Jets	International League	AAA
1968	25	York Pirates	Eastern League	AA
1969	26	Columbus Jets	International League	AAA
1969	26	Pittsburgh Pirates	National League	MLB
1970	27	Columbus Jets	International League	AAA
1970	27	Pittsburgh Pirates	National League	MLB
1971	28	Charleston Charlies	International League	AAA
1972	29	Omaha Royals	American Association	AAA
1973	30	Omaha Royals	American Association	AAA
1974	31	Omaha Royals	American Association	AAA

Hiraldo (Chico) Ruiz Sablón

Known in Cuba as Hiraldo Sablón and in the United States as Chico Ruiz, poses a challenge to those looking for the record of this player born in the town of Santo Domingo in the Matanzas Province in Cuba on December 12, 1938.

During the 1960-61 season this switch hitter played third base and came to bat 164 times hitting .274, with the team he played during all of his three seasons in Cuba (batting .267). He would be part of the team during the 1960 Caribbean Series, playing two games and hitting .500, coming to the plate twice.

Sablón Ruiz left from La Habana on the 5th of November, 1961 to go to Miami, Florida on his way to join the Cincinnati Reds according to immigration records.

He played the better part of 14 seasons, 1958-71, including eight in the major leagues. While in the majors, he played in seven positions showing his fielding versatility but mostly at second and third base.

Hiraldo Sablón Ruiz's last season came in 1971 playing for the California Angels, hitting .263 in 31 games. He passed away in a tragic auto accident on February 9, 1972 on his way to San Diego, California from Los Angeles.

Additional sources:

Echevarria Roberto González The Pride of Havana A history of Cuban Baseball page 356.

Torres, Angel. *La Leyenda del Beisbol Cubano.* Miami, Florida: Review Printers, 1996.

Year	Age	Tm	Lg	Lev
1958	19	Geneva Redlegs	New York-Pennsylvania League	D
1959	20	Visalia Redlegs	California League	C
1960	21	Columbia Reds	South Atlantic League	A
1961	22	Indianapolis Indians	American Association	AAA

Year	Age	Tm	Lg	Lev
1962	23	San Diego Padres	Pacific Coast League	AAA
1963	24	San Diego Padres	Pacific Coast League	AAA
1964	25	San Diego Padres	Pacific Coast League	AAA
1964	25	Cincinnati Reds	National League	MLB
1965	26	Cincinnati Reds	National League	MLB
1966	27	Cincinnati Reds	National League	MLB
1967	28	Cincinnati Reds	National League	MLB
1968	29	Cincinnati Reds	National League	MLB
1969	30	Cincinnati Reds	National League	MLB
1970	31	California Angels	American League	MLB
1971	32	Salt Lake City Angels	Pacific Coast League	AAA
1971	32	California Angels	American League	MLB

Hernan Valdés Vila

Another player who played partially with the Habana Lions, but also played for Cinfuegos, had a low batting average of .207 in 111 times at bat. During his two seasons in the Cuban League, he played for both teams, but his batting average would not rise significantly.

Born on July 31, 1937, he played a total of five seasons in the U.S. minors and, although his batting average was .308, it did not appear to impress management sufficiently enough to enable him to rise in the ranks of the minor system beyond the lower levels.

Though he played for the Wilson team of the Class B of the Carolina league in 1961, he ultimately stayed in Cuba following the end of the season.

Additional source: Iván Davis, telephone interview with author, January 31, 2018.

Year	Age	Tm	Lg	Lev
1957	19	Michigan City White Caps	Midwest League	D
1958	20	Missoula Timberjacks	Pioneer League	C
1959	21	Fox Cities Foxes	Illinois-Indiana-Iowa League	B
1959	21	Charlotte Hornets	South Atlantic League	A
1960	22	Charlotte Hornets	South Atlantic League	A
1961	23	Des Moines Demons	Illinois-Indiana-Iowa League	B
1961	23	Charlotte Hornets	South Atlantic League	A
1961	23	Wilson Tobs	Carolina League	B

Outfielders

Ultus Alvarez Suárez

He played seven seasons for Cienfuegos as an outfielder with a batting average of .250. During the 1960-61, was in line with his .243 average for those years. Alvarez played twice in the Caribbean Series, for a total of eight games and in the 1956 through the 1958 seasons, the Cuban Sugar Kings team.

Outside of the Cuban League, Ultus Alvarez played a total of thirteen seasons, reaching the AAA level but not the majors. He played for two teams in the Mexican League in 1963 and, before ending his playing career, in 1964. His batting average in the minors was a robust .278 playing mostly the outfield, although, he would see some action at first base.

Although his birthday is reflected as being 1933 and 1934 in different publications, his immigration record from March of 1958 shows his birthday as 1932 and the birth place as Las Villas even though the permanent address was Cumanayagua. His playing record in the U.S. after the 1960-61 season ended, through 1964, shows his having stayed in the U.S. He passed away in Miami Florida on August 6, 2010.

Year	Age	Tm	Lg	Lev
1952	19	Hornell Dodgers	Pennsylvania-Ontario-New York League	D
1953	20	Thomasville Dodgers	Georgia-Florida League	D
1954	21	Newport News Dodgers	Piedmont League	B
1954	21	Pueblo Dodgers	Western League	A
1955	22	Columbia Reds	South Atlantic League	A
1955	22	Nashville Volunteers	Southern Association	AA
1956	23	Havana Sugar Kings	International League	AAA
1957	24	Havana Sugar Kings	International League	AAA
1958	25	Havana Sugar Kings	International League	AAA
1958	25	Savannah Redlegs	South Atlantic League	A
1959	26	Nashville Volunteers	Southern Association	AA
1960	27	Nashville Volunteers	Southern Association	AA
1961	28	Jersey City Jerseys	International League	AAA
1962	29	Jacksonville Suns	International League	AAA
1963	30	Puebla Pericos	Mexican League	AA
1963	30	Mexico City Tigres	Mexican League	AA
1964	31	Orlando Twins	Florida State League	A

Andrés Antonio (Tony) González González

One of the better-known players of that era, centerfielder Tony González, had an outstanding last season in Cuba with a batting average of .290 for 217 times at bat. During his four seasons in Cuba, all with Cienfuegos, his batting average was .277, and he had a .429 average in the Caribbean Series. His record was equally good playing during the 1958 and 1959 seasons with the Cuban Sugar Kings for 284 games with a .285 hitting average. He played in all seven games in the Little World Series, batting .320 in 25 times at the plate.

Beyond his seasons in the Cuban League he played twice in the Puerto Rican winter league, as well as in Mexico and in Japan, for one season each, towards the end of his 16-season career. Twelve of these seasons were in the major leagues--nine with the Philadelphia Phillies. He also managed the Tampico Single A team in Mexico where his team had a record of 71 wins and 55 losses.

Tony González, a member of the Cuban Baseball Hall of Fame in Miami, Florida, came to the U.S. following the 60-61 season, reporting to the Philadelphia Phillies where he would play his second season in the majors. Currently, he lives in Miami, Florida. A more complete biography is available through the SABR BioProject.

Additional source: Costello, Rory and Ramírez, José SABR.org BioProject Tony González.

Year	Age	Tm	Lg	Lev
1957	20	Bradford Beagles/ Hornell Redlegs	New York-Pennsylvania League	D
1957	20	Wausau Lumberjacks	Northern League	C
1958	21	Havana Sugar Kings	International League	AAA
1959	22	Havana Sugar Kings	International League	AAA
1960	23	Cincinnati Reds	National League	MLB
1960	23	Philadelphia Phillies	National League	MLB
1961	24	Philadelphia Phillies	National League	MLB
1962	25	Philadelphia Phillies	National League	MLB

Year	Age	Tm	Lg	Lev
1963	26	Philadelphia Phillies	National League	MLB
1964	27	Philadelphia Phillies	National League	MLB
1965	28	Philadelphia Phillies	National League	MLB
1966	29	Philadelphia Phillies	National League	MLB
1967	30	Philadelphia Phillies	National League	MLB
1968	31	Philadelphia Phillies	National League	MLB
1969	32	San Diego Padres	National League	MLB
1969	32	Atlanta Braves	National League	MLB
1970	33	Atlanta Braves	National League	MLB
1970	33	California Angels	American League	MLB
1971	34	California Angels	American League	MLB
1972	35	Hiroshima Toyo Carp	Japan Central League	Fgn
1972	35	Jalisco Charros	Mexican League	AAA
1973	36	Reading Phillies	Eastern League	AA

Roman Mejías Gómez

Mejías played with the Almendares, Habana and the Cienfuegos teams in Cuba for a total of seven seasons, starting in 1954 hitting .276 in 408 games and 1454 times at bat. During his last season, his batting average was a robust .289 in 253 times at the plate. Twice playing in the Caribbean Series, he played a total of 10 games batting .256.

His career outside of Cuba spanned 14 seasons, from 1953 through 1966, including one year in the Japan Central League. He played in the majors for the Pittsburgh Pirates for six seasons, from 1955 through 1961, for Houston in 1962, and the Boston Red Sox in 1963 and 64. Mejías is a member of the Cuban Baseball Hall of Fame in Miami, Florida.

Following the end of the 60-61 season, Mejías secured a visa in Mexico and arrived in the U.S. on February 28, 1961. He played only four games in April and May for the Pirates, and the rest of the season found him in Columbus in the International league, before he returned to the majors the following year with Houston.

His immigration record showed a birth year of 1925, unlike those found in publications showing 1930.

His stay in Boston had a personal significance. The management of the Red Sox led by owner Tom Yawkey, worked with the U.S. State Department and the Red Cross to reunite him with his wife, Nicolasa, his two children, and his two sisters on March 16, 1963.

Additional source: Briley Ron, Costello Rory and Nowlin Bill SABR.org BioProject Román Mejías.

Year	Age	Tm	Lg	Lev
1953	22	Batavia Clippers	Pennsylvania-Ontario-New York League	D
1954	23	Waco Pirates	Big State League	B
1955	24	Pittsburgh Pirates	National League	MLB
1956	25	Hollywood Stars	Pacific Coast League	Opn
1957	26	Columbus Jets	International League	AAA

Year	Age	Tm	Lg	Lev
1957	26	Pittsburgh Pirates	National League	MLB
1958	27	Pittsburgh Pirates	National League	MLB
1959	28	Pittsburgh Pirates	National League	MLB
1960	29	Columbus Jets	International League	AAA
1960	29	Pittsburgh Pirates	National League	MLB
1961	30	Columbus Jets	International League	AAA
1961	30	Pittsburgh Pirates	National League	MLB
1962	31	Houston Colt .45's	National League	MLB
1963	32	Boston Red Sox	American League	MLB
1964	33	Boston Red Sox	American League	MLB
1965	34	Toronto Maple Leafs	International League	AAA
1966	35	Sankei Atoms	Japan Central League	Fgn

Juan Antonio Vistuer

Vistuer played a total of seven seasons in Cuba as a member of all four teams, finishing with Cienfuegos, and hitting a weak .202. But he was able to be a member of two Caribbean Series with Almendares and with Cienfuegos. He also played for the Havana Cubans in 1952. In 1957, he appeared in six games with the Cuban Sugar Kings. This was the only team with whom he reached the AAA level with during his career, from 1951 through 1961.

Following the end of the last professional season in Cuba, he like many other players, secured a visa from Mexico and he arrived in the U.S. on March 24, 1961. Fernandina Beach, located outside of Jacksonville, Florida was his destination before reporting to the Minnesota Twins organization, where he would play his last season for the Wilson Class B team of the Carolina league.

However, after the 1961 season, he returned to Cuba and became an instructor, having studied Physical Education in the USSR as part of the new baseball system in the island.

Vistuer (along with Gilberto Torres) became a member of the Cuban National Baseball Commission headed at the time by Juan Ealo de la Herrán and later on, in 1971, by then Commissioner Napoleón Quevedo. As reported by the Bohemia magazine in 1984, he visited the Soviet Union where he "studied physical education and returned to Cuba to assist with the new baseball".

Ultimately, Vistuer left Cuba and moved to Mexico where he passed away, as reported, on January 14, 1998, in Monterrey, Mexico.

Additional sources:

elfinanciaro.com.mx
El Sol de Mexico December 4, 2016.
Echevarria Roberto González The Pride of Havana A History of Cuban Baseball Oxford University Press New York, Oxford 1999 Page 370
Ecured.cu/Federacion_Cubana_de_Beisbol

Year	Age	Tm	Lg	Lev
1951	20	Sherman-Denison Twins	Big State League	B
1951	20	Geneva Robins	Border League	C
1951	20	Chickasha Chiefs	Sooner State League	D
1951	20	Big Spring Broncs	Longhorn League	C
1952	21	Havana Cubans	Florida International League	B
1952	21	Big Spring Broncs	Longhorn League	C
1953	22	Charlotte Hornets	Tri-State League	B
1954	23	Rock Hill Chiefs	Tri-State League	B
1955	24	High Point-Thomasville Hi-Toms	Carolina League	B
1955	24	Charlotte Hornets	South Atlantic League	A

Year	Age	Tm	Lg	Lev
1956	25	Mexico City Diablos Rojos	Mexican League	AA
1957	26	Veracruz Aguila	Mexican League	AA
1957	26	Havana Sugar Kings	International League	AAA
1957	26	Mexico City Diablos Rojos	Mexican League	AA
1958	27	Monterrey Sultanes	Mexican League	AA
1959	28	Monterrey Sultanes	Mexican League	AA
1960	29	Wilson Tobs	Carolina League	B
1960	29	Charlotte Hornets	South Atlantic League	A
1961	30	Wilson Tobs	Carolina League	B

Mario Zambrano Montes De Oca

His one season in Cuba came during this last season where he distinguished himself with a .272 batting average in 162 times at bat as an outfielder for the champions of the Cienfuegos squad. He began his professional career in 1958 playing for the Palatka Redlegs, where he also played the following year in 1959. He played professional baseball through the 1962 season, in the Carolina League, and for the Cuban Sugar Kings in 1960 for only two games. While he never actually rose beyond the B level, his batting average during those five seasons in the minors was .308

Zambrano was born on March 4, 1938 in Central Unión and stayed in Cuba until he was able to secure a visa through Toronto, Canada. This enabled him to travel to the U.S. through Jacksonville, Florida on March of 1962. His playing career reflects his stay in the U.S. following the end of the 1960-61 season in Cuba.

Year	Age	Tm	Lg	Lev
1958	20	Palatka Redlegs	Florida State League	D
1958	20	Gainesville G-Men	Florida State League	D
1958	20	Orlando Flyers	Florida State League	D
1959	21	Palatka Redlegs	Florida State League	D
1960	22	Havana Sugar Kings/ Jersey City Jerseys	International League	AAA
1960	22	Topeka Reds	Illinois-Indiana-Iowa League	B
1960	22	Missoula Timberjacks	Pioneer League	C
1961	23	Topeka Reds	Illinois-Indiana-Iowa League	B
1962	24	Raleigh Capitals	Carolina League	B

Chapter 6

ALMENDARES

The Almendares team ownership turned a page for the better in 1944 when sports people from the Vedado Tennis Club took control of the team. Board members included Mario Mendoza, president; Doctor Julio Sanguily, treasurer; Doctor Juan Portela, secretary and members at large Luis Aizcorbe, José Gómez Mena, Raúl Perera, Indalecio Pertierra, Julio Pertierra, Generoso Castro, Eugenio Sardiñas, Martín Menocal and Monchy de Arcos. The latter being its General Manager.

Additional source:

The kingdom of baseball http://thekingdomofbaseball.proboards.com/thread/1861/tendremos-reescribir-historia-baseball-cubano#ixzz4Jb9tiDqL

Manager

The Field Manager was Regino José (Reggie) Otero Gómez. He was joined by coaches Juan Ealo and Reinaldo Cordero.

Regino Otero

Otero was born in La Habana on September 7, 1915. He had been a Cuban baseball player with a long career in the minor leagues in the United States from 1936 to 1953. During his 17 seasons, he appeared in 1749 games and had a .303 batting average. He played briefly with the Chicago Cubs in 1945. He appeared in 14 games for the Cubs

and had a .391 batting average. He also played 13 years in the Cuban League, from 1936 to 1953. After his playing career ended, he managed in Cuba, Mexico and Venezuela including the Havana Sugar Kings from 1954 through mid-1956. He led the Industriales de Valencia in the Venezuelan League to three titles, and the Leones del Caracas to four titles. His seven championships are the most in the league's history. He also served as a coach for the Cincinnati Reds from 1959 to 1965, and was a member of the Cleveland Indians' coaching staff in 1966. In 1967, he became a scout, working for Cleveland and the Los Angeles Dodgers into the 1980s. Regino Otero is a member of the Cuban Baseball Hall of Fame in Miami, Florida.

An interesting story came out of an interview with Otero (see source cited below). He was asked why he put Orlando Peña on the mound against Cienfuegos during that pivotal game to win a championship during the 1960-61 season knowing that Otero could use his young pitcher Marcelino López who seemed to have a strong hold on the Almendares team. Otero's simple reply was that this game was of so much importance that he went with the most experienced arm thrower. Almendares lost the game.

After the 1960-1961 season ended, Regino Otero arrived in the U.S. on March 3rd, 1961 with a visa obtained in Mexico and reported to the Cincinnati Reds team where he served as a coach.

Otero died of a heart attack on October 21, 1988 in Hialeah Florida and is buried at the Vista Memorial Gardens in Miami.

Additional sources:

Nuevo Herald Angel Torres
Miguelito de la Hoz, telephone interview with author, February 1, 2018.
His managing career in the U.S. minors and Mexico is shown below:

Year	Age	Tm	Lg	Lev	Aff	G	W	L	W-L%
1951	35	Portsmouth	PIED	B	1 of 1	142	74	67	.525
1952	36	Portsmouth	PIED	B	1 of 1	135	71	64	.526
1954	38	Havana	IL	AAA	1 of 1	157	78	77	.503
1955	39	Havana	IL	AAA	CIN 1 of 1	156	87	66	.569
1956	40	Havana	IL	AAA	CIN 1 of 2	154	72	82	.468
1957	41	Monterrey	MEX	AA	1 of 1	122	60	60	.500
1958	42	Monterrey	MEX	AA	1 of 2	123	56	64	.467
7 Seasons						989	498	480	.509

His playing career is shown below:

Year	Age	Tm	Lg	Lev	Aff
1936	20	York White Roses/ Trenton Senators	New York-Pennsylvania League	A	
1936	20	Albany Senators	International League	AA	WSH
1937	21	Trenton Senators	New York-Pennsylvania League	A	WSH
1938	22	St. Augustine Saints	Florida State League	D	

Year	Age	Tm	Lg	Lev	Aff
1939	23	Greenville Spinners	South Atlantic League	B	WSH
1940	24	Greenville Spinners	South Atlantic League	B	WSH
1941	25	Springfield Nationals	Eastern League	A	
1942	26	Utica Braves	Canadian-American League	C	
1943	27	Voluntarily Retired			
1944	28	Los Angeles Angels	Pacific Coast League	AA	CHC
1945	29	Los Angeles Angels	Pacific Coast League	AA	CHC
1945	29	Chicago Cubs	National League	MLB	CHC
1946	30	Los Angeles Angels	Pacific Coast League	AAA	CHC
1947	31	Los Angeles Angels	Pacific Coast League	AAA	CHC
1948	32	Portsmouth Cubs	Piedmont League	B	
1949	33	Portsmouth Cubs	Piedmont League	B	
1950	34	Portsmouth Cubs	Piedmont League	B	
1951	35	Portsmouth Cubs	Piedmont League	B	
1952	36	Portsmouth Cubs	Piedmont League	B	
1953	37	Springfield Cubs	International League	AAA	CHC

Pitchers

Vicente Amor Alvarez

Amor was born in La Habana on August 9, 1932 or 33. He pitched in Cuba for a total of six seasons, five with the Habana Lions, and the last one with Almendares where he participated in eleven games and sported an ERA of 3.75. His record over the six seasons included 38 wins, 28 losses and an ERA of 2.98. He was named Rookie of the Year in 1954-55. Although he did not pitch during the 1959-60 season, he played for the Cuban Sugar Kings for five seasons where he entered in 146 games, with a record of 31-30 and a 3.92 ERA.

He played in the U.S. from 1950, at the tender age of 17, through 1959. He reached the majors on two occasions, once with the Cubs in 1955, and later with Cincinnati in 1957 where he had a combined record of one win and three losses. He was selected as a member of the Cuban Baseball Hall of Fame in Miami, Florida.

He travelled to the U.S. on March 17, of 1960 as a "ball player" from La Habana to Miami to join the Marlins. But the record does not reflect he made the team. Vicente later lived in Hialeah, Florida, where he owned a business producing electrical signs. Last reported he was still living in the Miami, Florida area, remaining in the U.S. See source cited below.

Additional source: José (Chamby) Campos, telephone interview with author, January 26 and 27, 2018.

Year	Age	Tm	Lg	Lev
1950	17	Big Spring Broncs	Longhorn League	D
1950	17	Donna-Weslaco Twins	Rio Grande Valley League	C
1951	18	Sherman-Denison Twins	Big State League	B
1952	19	St. Petersburg Saints	Florida International League	B
1952	19	Paris Indians	Big State League	B
1952	19	Texarkana Bears	Big State League	B
1953	20	St. Petersburg Saints	Florida International League	B
1954	21	Oklahoma City Indians	Texas League	AA
1955	22	Havana Sugar Kings	International League	AAA
1955	22	Chicago Cubs	National League	MLB
1956	23	Havana Sugar Kings	International League	AAA

Year	Age	Tm	Lg	Lev
1956	23	Tulsa Oilers	Texas League	AA
1957	24	Havana Sugar Kings	International League	AAA
1957	24	Cincinnati Redlegs	National League	MLB
1958	25	Havana Sugar Kings	International League	AAA
1959	26	Havana Sugar Kings	International League	AAA

Andrés Ayón Bron

He played with Almendares during his last season out of the total of four he played in Cuba. The other three seasons he played for the Tigres de Marianao. His 60-61 record showed a total of 28 appearances at the mound with eight complete games, 11 wins, 12 losses and a 3.77 ERA. He won a total of 17 games and lost 18 with a 3.47 ERA during the four seasons but had a better record with the Cuban Sugar Kings teams that he joined in 1959 and 60 where his ERA was 3.00.

His playing career outside of Cuba spanned for 21 seasons from 1957 through 1979, mostly in Mexico after the 1964 season. He won 65 games and lost 50 in the U.S. minor leagues and managed a Triple A Team (Sabinas) in the Mexican League in 1971 with a record of 62 wins and 83 losses.

Following the end of the 1960-61 season, Ayón came to the U.S. via Mexico on March 17, 1961 to join the Jersey City team. He left his son behind, who was also named Andrés, who was born on January 8, 1961. When he returned to Cuba, his son was able to travel to the U.S. on March 27, 1962 from La Habana but, ironically, Andrés, the father, was not able to leave Cuba until November 1, 1962 after securing a visa from Toronto, Canada. It was noted that Ayón would travel between Cuba, the U.S. and Mexico regularly after his 1962 arrival to the U.S. See source cited below.

Additional source: José (Chamby) Campos, telephone interview with author, January 30, 2018.

Year	Age	Tm	Lg	Lev
1957	20	Wausau Lumberjacks	Northern League	C
1958	21	Visalia Redlegs	California League	C
1959	22	Havana Sugar Kings	International League	AAA
1959	22	Savannah Reds	South Atlantic League	A
1959	22	Topeka Hawks	Illinois-Indiana-Iowa League	B
1960	23	Havana Sugar Kings/ Jersey City Jerseys	International League	AAA
1961	24	Jersey City Jerseys	International League	AAA
1962	25	Macon Peaches	South Atlantic League	A
1963	26	Macon Peaches	South Atlantic League	AA
1964	27	Puebla Pericos	Mexican League	AA
1965	28	Puebla Pericos	Mexican League	AA
1966	29	Puebla Pericos	Mexican League	AA
1967	30	Jalisco Charros	Mexican League	AAA
1968	31	Seattle Angels	Pacific Coast League	AAA
1968	31	Jalisco Charros	Mexican League	AAA
1969	32	Jalisco Charros	Mexican League	AAA
1970	33	Jalisco Charros	Mexican League	AAA
1971	34	Sabinas Piratas	Mexican League	AAA
1971	34	Saltillo Saraperos	Mexican League	AAA
1972	35	Saltillo Saraperos	Mexican League	AAA
1973	36	Saltillo Saraperos	Mexican League	AAA
1973	36	Puebla Pericos	Mexican League	AAA
1975	38	Cordoba Cafeteros	Mexican League	AAA
1976	39	Nuevo Laredo Tecolotes	Mexican League	AAA
1977	40	Nuevo Laredo Tecolotes	Mexican League	AAA
1979	42	Nuevo Laredo Tecolotes	Mexican League	AAA

Miguel Angel (Mike) Cuellar Santana

Among the better-known players with a well-deserved reputation and an excellent screw ball and change-up is "Mike" Cuellar. He pitched for the only team he would play for during his five seasons in Cuba. This was the Almendares, and ending his career in his homeland with a 3.12 ERA in 112.1 innings, 70 strike outs, 42 walks and a 6-6 record. His five-season record reflected a 3.09 ERA during 96 games. He played in the 1959 Caribbean Series, winning the one game he would appear in, with two strike outs and three walks. He was a member of the 1957-1960 Cuban Sugar Kings, appearing in 146 games, with a 37-39 record and a 2.86 ERA including the Little World Series where he appeared in four games.

Outside of Cuba, he played a total of 21 seasons, winning 248 games, after he was signed by the Cincinnati Reds as an amateur free agent in 1957. He had drawn attention with a no-hitter he pitched for an army team in 1955 while serving in the Cuban army during the regime of Fulgencio Batista, the former dictator and head of the Cuban government. He played two seasons in Mexico, 1962 and 1979 and 15 seasons in the major leagues where he won a total of 185 games. He earned a Cy Young Award in 1969 while pitching for the

Baltimore Orioles winning 23 games only to win 24 the following season.

At the end of the 1960-61 season he arrived in the U.S. via Mexico on April 1961 to join the Jersey City team. In April of 62 he flew in from Caracas, Venezuela and played during that season preparing to join the Monterrey Sultanes team in Mexico. Cuellar was recognized as a member of the Cuban Baseball of Fame in Miami, Florida for all that he contributed to baseball during his career.

Miguel Cuellar was born in Santa Clara on May 8, 1936 died at the age of 72 on April 2, 2010 in Orlando Florida. He is buried in the Woodland Cemetery in that city.

Year	Age	Tm	Lg	Lev
1957	20	Havana Sugar Kings	International League	AAA
1958	21	Havana Sugar Kings	International League	AAA
1959	22	Havana Sugar Kings	International League	AAA
1959	22	Cincinnati Redlegs	National League	MLB
1960	23	Havana Sugar Kings/ Jersey City Jerseys	International League	AAA
1961	24	Indianapolis Indians	American Association	AAA
1961	24	Jersey City Jerseys	International League	AAA
1961	24	Syracuse Chiefs	International League	AAA
1962	25	Monterrey Sultanes	Mexican League	AA
1963	26	Knoxville Smokies	South Atlantic League	AA
1963	26	Jacksonville Suns	International League	AAA
1964	27	Jacksonville Suns	International League	AAA
1964	27	St. Louis Cardinals	National League	MLB
1965	28	Jacksonville Suns	International League	AAA
1965	28	Houston Astros	National League	MLB
1966	29	Houston Astros	National League	MLB

Year	Age	Tm	Lg	Lev
1967	30	Houston Astros	National League	MLB
1968	31	Houston Astros	National League	MLB
1969	32	Baltimore Orioles	American League	MLB
1970	33	Baltimore Orioles	American League	MLB
1971	34	Baltimore Orioles	American League	MLB
1972	35	Baltimore Orioles	American League	MLB
1973	36	Baltimore Orioles	American League	MLB
1974	37	Baltimore Orioles	American League	MLB
1975	38	Baltimore Orioles	American League	MLB
1976	39	Baltimore Orioles	American League	MLB
1977	40	California Angels	American League	MLB
1979	42	Coatzacoalcos Azules	Mexican League	AAA

Iván Davis Mata

Some publications show his name as Isaac, but he reaffirmed that his name was indeed Iván during our interview.

Iván played only one season in Cuba, 1960-61. He appeared in five games for a total of 8.2 innings and had a 4.15 ERA. Outside of Cuba, he played a total of three seasons with four different teams affiliated with the Cincinnati Reds, including the Palatka Redlegs in 1959 and 1960 earning a total of 21 wins and 20 losses. During his playing days for the Redlegs, Davis was a member of the 1960 championship team of the Florida State League that had a regular season record of 81 and 56 while playing in the Azalea Bowl. The park had an attendance of 17,330, but that season their average was only 253. The photo included in this book, courtesy of Iván Davis, shows some of his fellow players. Another of his fellow players was the Cuban, Elio Ribet Jr. (not in the picture) who drowned on July 27, 1960. This story will be told further on in this book.

Following the 60-61 season, Davis played with Topeka and Columbia but, ultimately, he stayed in Cuba with his wife for reasons he referred to as "mistakes of the young." While in Cuba, he became an umpire for 25 years including the International Tournaments. He moved to the U.S. permanently in 1993.

Additional source: Iván Davis, telephone interviews with author, October 24, 2016, January 31 2018, and February 2, 2018.

Year	Age	Tm	Lg	Lev
1959	19	Geneva Redlegs	New York-Pennsylvania League	D
1959	19	Palatka Redlegs	Florida State League	D
1960	20	Palatka Redlegs	Florida State League	D
1961	21	Topeka Reds	Illinois-Indiana-Iowa League	B
1961	21	Columbia Reds	South Atlantic League	A

Julio (Valdés) Guerra

Julio Guerra played a total of five seasons in Cuba, all with the Almendares team, appearing in 39 games, with a record of 3 wins and 8 losses. During the last season, he went to the mound on eight different occasions, but had only one win and had an 8.59 ERA.

His career outside of Cuba went on for seven seasons, including the 1962 season in Mexico, where he played for two teams. He never made it to the majors, playing from 1957 through 1963, winning 56 games and losing 63 in the minors.

His playing career in 1961 and the 1963 season suggests he stayed in the U.S. where he died. Immigration records during that time were not available, but his stay in the U.S. was further confirmed (see source cited below).

Additional source: Andrés Pascual, telephone interview with author, February 5, 2018.

Year	Age	Tm	Lg	Lev
1957	20	Cocoa Indians	Florida State League	D
1958	21	Burlington Indians	Carolina League	B
1958	21	Reading Indians	Eastern League	A
1958	21	San Diego Padres	Pacific Coast League	AAA
1959	22	Reading Indians	Eastern League	A
1960	23	Reading Indians	Eastern League	A
1961	24	Burlington Indians	Carolina League	B
1961	24	Durham Bulls	Carolina League	B
1962	25	San Luis Potosi Tuneros	Mexican Center League	C
1962	25	Mexico City Tigres	Mexican League	AA
1963	26	Charlotte Hornets	South Atlantic League	AA

René (Látigo) Gutiérrez Valdés

Látigo was one of my favorite players as a young fan because of his unusual (whip-like) wind-up. He played with the Habana Lions during the last season of his eight in the Cuban League. He also played for

Cienfuegos and Marianao earning a combined record of 34 and 38 in 213 games and striking out 346 batters, while walking 294. During his time with the Almendares squad in this last season, he pitched but in two games with a total of 6.1 innings. He was part of the 1956 Caribbean Series with Cienfuegos pitching in two games and winning one with ten strikeouts and two walks.

He played professional baseball outside of Cuba from 1952 through the 1964 season including one season in Mexico. He made the majors in 1957 with the Brooklyn Dodgers where he played five games and had a record of one win and one loss. His minor league combined record included 152 wins and a 3.60 ERA.

His birthday is a subject of speculation, but his immigration travel record from Cuba in February of 1959 to join the Dodger organization, had his birthday listed as being in 1928.

Following the end of the Cuban 60-61 season, he played in the U.S. and Mexico. He passed away on March 15, 2008 in Miami Florida.

Year	Age	Tm	Lg	Lev
1952	23	Juarez Indios	Arizona-Texas League	C
1953	24	Juarez Indios	Arizona-Texas League	C
1954	25	Pueblo Dodgers	Western League	A
1954	25	Bakersfield Indians	California League	C
1955	26	St. Paul Saints	American Association	AAA
1956	27	Portland Beavers	Pacific Coast League	Opn
1957	28	Montreal Royals	International League	AAA
1957	28	Brooklyn Dodgers	National League	MLB
1958	29	Montreal Royals	International League	AAA
1959	30	Montreal Royals	International League	AAA
1960	31	Montreal Royals	International League	AAA
1961	32	Spokane Indians	Pacific Coast League	AAA
1962	33	Monterrey Sultanes	Mexican League	AA

Year	Age	Tm	Lg	Lev
1963	34	Monterrey Sultanes	Mexican League	AA
1964	35	Yucatan Venados	Mexican Southeast League	A

José Ramón López Hevia

López played only two seasons in Cuba, both with Almendares appearing in a total of 17 games. During the last season he went to the mound three times for a total of 4.1 innings. However, he had a career in baseball starting in 1958 with the North Platte Class D team of the Nebraska State League, through 1974 in Mexico, winning 34 and losing 48 games in the minors.

He played in Mexico most seasons following the 1962 season and had a brief call-up to the majors with the California Angels in 1967, playing seven innings in four games while being the losing pitcher in one contest.

At the end of the 1960-61 season in Cuba, López Hevia secured a visa from Mexico and traveled to the U.S. on March 9, 1961. He passed away on September 4, 1982 in Miami, Florida and his remains were placed in the Woodland Memorial Park of that city.

Year	Age	Tm	Lg	Lev
1958	25	North Platte Indians	Nebraska State League	D-
1958	25	Cocoa Indians	Florida State League	D
1959	26	Minot Mallards	Northern League	C
1960	27	Minot Mallards	Northern League	C
1960	27	Burlington Indians	Carolina League	B
1960	27	Reading Indians	Eastern League	A
1961	28	Reading Indians	Eastern League	A
1962	29	Charleston Indians	Eastern League	A
1963	30	Monterrey Sultanes	Mexican League	AA
1964	31	Monterrey Sultanes	Mexican League	AA

Year	Age	Tm	Lg	Lev
1965	32	Monterrey Sultanes	Mexican League	AA
1966	33	Monterrey Sultanes	Mexican League	AA
1966	33	California Angels	American League	MLB
1967	34	Seattle Angels	Pacific Coast League	AAA
1968	35	Monterrey Sultanes	Mexican League	AAA
1969	36	Monterrey Sultanes	Mexican League	AAA
1970	37	Monterrey Sultanes	Mexican League	AAA
1971	38	Reynosa Broncs	Mexican League	AAA
1972	39	Yucatan Leones	Mexican League	AAA
1973	40	Tampico Alijadores	Mexican League	AAA
1974	41	Veracruz Aguila	Mexican League	AAA

Marcelino López Pons

He played only one season in Cuba, at the age of 16, for the Almendares Club. He went to the mound 18 times, won three games and lost 6, with a 3.40 ERA in 76.1 innings. His control over the eventual champions Cienfuegos is referenced within the information about the Almendares skipper Regino Otero.

Outside of Cuba, Marcelino López played for sixteen seasons, from 1960 through 1976, winning 80 games. He scored 31 wins during his eight years in the majors, including the opening game at the Anaheim Stadium on April 19, 1966 against Tommy John. He also played in the Venezuelan League in 1965-66 where he was the ERA leader with 1.51.

Following the end of the 60-61 season, even though he played in Williamsport Grays of the Easter League, he returned to Cuba. He later departed from La Habana on March 9, 1962, securing a visa out of Toronto, Canada as part of the Philadelphia organization and applied for U.S. citizenship at the District Court in Miami in 1973 with Pedro Ramos and Gabriel A. Martínez serving as his witnesses.

He was born on September 7, 1943 in La Habana, passed away on November 29, 2001 in Hialeah Florida and is interred in the Vista Memorial Gardens of the same city.

Additional source: Miguelito de la Hoz, telephone interview with author, February 1, 2018.

Year	Age	Tm	Lg	Lev
1960	16	Tampa Tarpons	Florida State League	D
1961	17	Williamsport Grays	Eastern League	A
1962	18	Buffalo Bisons	International League	AAA
1963	19	Arkansas Travelers	International League	AAA
1963	19	Philadelphia Phillies	National League	MLB
1964	20	Chattanooga Lookouts	Southern League	AA
1965	21	California Angels	American League	MLB
1966	22	California Angels	American League	MLB
1967	23	FIL Orioles	Florida Instructional League	WRk
1967	23	California Angels	American League	MLB
1967	23	Baltimore Orioles	American League	MLB

Year	Age	Tm	Lg	Lev
1968	24	Miami Marlins	Florida State League	A
1968	24	Elmira Pioneers	Eastern League	AA
1969	25	Rochester Red Wings	International League	AAA
1969	25	Baltimore Orioles	American League	MLB
1970	26	Baltimore Orioles	American League	MLB
1971	27	Milwaukee Brewers	American League	MLB
1972	28	Portland Beavers	Pacific Coast League	AAA
1972	28	Cleveland Indians	American League	MLB
1973	29	Oklahoma City 89ers	American Association	AAA
1973	29	Hawaii Islanders	Pacific Coast League	AAA
1974	30	Charleston Charlies	International League	AAA
1974	30	Veracruz Aguila	Mexican League	AAA
1974	30	Tampico Alijadores	Mexican League	AAA
1974	30	Coahuila Mineros	Mexican League	AAA
1976	32	Columbus Astros	Southern League	AA

Lázaro Ramón Gonzalo (Cholly) Naranjo

Cholly, as he is known, was another player who also was a member of the Habana Lions during that last season. He pitched in eleven games, including one complete game, with a record of 2-2 in 35.2 innings.

He played nine seasons in Cuba, all eight plus years with Almendares, pitching in 152 games with 234 strike outs, 196 walks and a 3.60 ERA. He played twice in the Caribbean Series with Almendares, appearing in three games with a 1-0 record and an outstanding 1.64 ERA. In 1953, he played for the Havana Cubans during 29 games, striking out 83 batters and walking 60 while winning 8 games, losing 6, with a 3.77 ERA.

Outside of Cuba his playing career spanned from 1952 through 1961, winning 72 games in the minors as he pursued his baseball career and ultimately reached the major leagues with the Pittsburgh Pirates in 1956 for a brief period where he had a 1-2 record.

A memorable experience for Cholly took place in 1954 when the U.S. President Ike Eisenhower opened the season throwing the first baseball that was caught by Johnny Sain. According to a newspaper report, the President then made a second throw that was caught by Cholly Naranjo who promptly threw it back to the President, who caught it and in turn threw it back to Cholly. It was said to be an unprecedented move by a President playing catch with a player, and an experience that Cholly would never forget.

Following the end of the 1961 season, Cholly Naranjo obtained a visa via Mexico and travelled to the U.S. on March 28, 1961 where he played for Jacksonville and Houston before deciding it was time to retire due to arm problems, and so he returned to Cuba. He stayed in Cuba for 30 years, working for the Habana's Sports City as an athletic teacher. Later, in 1991, he came back to the U.S. but returned to Cuba in 1993. He once again returned in 1995 to the U.S. and resides in Miami Florida till the present day.

Additional sources:

Ramírez, José SABR.org BioProject Cholly Naranjo
Starts and Stripes on April 14, 1954 Volume 12 Number 359
Cholly Naranjo, personal interview with author, February 2016

Year	Age	Tm	Lg	Lev
1952	17	Chattanooga Lookouts	Southern Association	AA
1952	17	Richmond Colts	Piedmont League	B
1953	18	Havana Cubans	Florida International League	B
1953	18	Chattanooga Lookouts	Southern Association	AA
1954	19	Charlotte Hornets	South Atlantic League	A
1954	19	Chattanooga Lookouts	Southern Association	AA
1955	20	Lincoln Chiefs	Western League	A
1955	20	Hollywood Stars	Pacific Coast League	Opn
1956	21	Hollywood Stars	Pacific Coast League	Opn
1956	21	Pittsburgh Pirates	National League	MLB
1957	22	Columbus Jets	International League	AAA
1958	23	Columbus Jets	International League	AAA
1959	24	Columbus Jets	International League	AAA
1959	24	Nashville Volunteers	Southern Association	AA
1960	25	Nashville Volunteers	Southern Association	AA
1961	26	Jacksonville Jets	South Atlantic League	A
1961	26	Houston Buffs	American Association	AAA

Carlos Alberto (Patato) Pascual Lus

Patato Pascual, the brother of Camilo Pascual, played seven seasons in the Cuban League between Habana and Almendares, for a total of 80 games, sporting a 12-5 record and a 2.92 ERA.

During his last season he played in only seven games, for 30 innings, and had a 3.15 ERA with a 0-0 record. His career in Cuba also included playing as an amateur for the Unión Atlética team.

During the two Caribbean Series he played, he had 1-2 record. He also played for the Havana Cubans during the 1951, 52, and 53 seasons, in 72 games, with a record of 28-25, 234 strike outs and a 2.91 ERA. In 1954, he played for the Cuban Sugar Kings in eight games, winning one.

A versatile player, he played the infield for the Havana Cubans and the Cuban Sugar Kings and had a .250 batting average with both teams.

Outside of Cuba, *Patato* Pascual had a career spanning from 1949 through 1962. As a pitcher he had a 40-32 record and a batting average of .323 in the minors. He reached the major leagues with the Washington Senators in 1950 where he had a record of one win and one loss with one hit in four times at bat.

He managed in the Venezuelan League where he won a series with the Navegantes de Magallanes.

In 1977, Pascual managed the Wisconsin Rapids Single A team in the Midwest league, a team affiliated with the Minnesota Twins and had a record of 66 wins and 72 losses. He also became a scout with the New York Mets where he is given credit for discovering Dwight Gooden. He like other former players founded a very successful baseball academy. One of his many recognitions took place as he was inducted in the Cuban Professional Baseball Hall of Fame.

At the end of the 60-61 season, he played for the Florida League Fort Walton Team in both 1961 and 1962 and his permanent parole into the U.S. came in November of 1962 as he travelled from the Dominican Republic.

Born in La Habana on March 13, 1931, Pascual passed away on May 12, 2011 in Miami Florida, and his remains are interred in the Miami Memorial Park.

Additional source: cubanbaseball.com

Year	Age	Tm	Lg	Lev
1949	18	Big Spring Broncs	Longhorn League	D
1950	19	Havana Cubans	Florida International League	B
1950	19	Big Spring Broncs	Longhorn League	D
1950	19	Washington Senators	American League	MLB
1951	20	Havana Cubans	Florida International League	B
1952	21	Havana Cubans	Florida International League	B
1953	22	Havana Cubans	Florida International League	B
1953	22	Seattle Rainiers	Pacific Coast League	Opn
1954	23	Havana Sugar Kings	International League	AAA
1955	24	Yucatan Leones	Mexican League	AA
1955	24	Hobbs Sports	Longhorn League	C
1956	25	Hobbs Sports	Southwestern League	B
1957	26	Midland/Lamesa Indians	Southwestern League	B
1958	27	Fox Cities Foxes	Illinois-Indiana-Iowa League	B
1958	27	Charlotte Hornets	South Atlantic League	A
1959	28	Fox Cities Foxes	Illinois-Indiana-Iowa League	B
1960	29	Fort Walton Beach Jets	Alabama-Florida League	D
1961	30	Fort Walton Beach Jets	Alabama-Florida League	D
1962	31	Fort Walton Beach Jets	Alabama-Florida League	D

Orlando Gregorio Peña Guevara

Orlando Peña had a great command of the fork ball. He pitched in 27 games during the 1960-61 season and had nine complete games. To go along with his 10-6 record, he struck out 77 players and walked 28, with a 3.73 ERA. He became the eventual losing pitcher in Cuba's last game against Pedro Ramos. His six seasons in the Cuban League were with the Almendares team where he won 42 games against 29 losses and had a very strong 2.77 ERA. He also played in six games in two Caribbean Series, winning two games. In three seasons with the Cuban Sugar Kings during 1957, 1958 and 1960, he participated in 134 games, winning 36 against 31 losses, striking out 341 players, with 152 walks and a 3.14 ERA.

Outside of Cuba, this right-hander played from 1955, where he won 21 games in his first season with only 8 losses, through 1979, winning a total of 204 during his 22 seasons. He played 14 years in the major leagues and had a record of 56-77, with a 3.11 ERA.

At the end of the 1960-61 season, Peña a member of the Cuban Baseball Hall of Fame in Miami, Florida, was among those players who secured a visa from Mexico, arriving in the U.S. on March 3,

1961. Born on November 17, 1933 in Victoria de las Tunas, he applied to become a U.S. Citizen in 1969 in the Miami District Court.

Year	Age	Tm	Lg	Lev
1955	21	Daytona Beach Islanders	Florida State League	D
1956	22	High Point-Thomasville Hi-Toms	Carolina League	B
1957	23	Havana Sugar Kings	International League	AAA
1958	24	Havana Sugar Kings	International League	AAA
1958	24	Cincinnati Redlegs	National League	MLB
1959	25	Cincinnati Redlegs	National League	MLB
1960	26	Havana Sugar Kings/ Jersey City Jerseys	International League	AAA
1960	26	Cincinnati Reds	National League	MLB
1961	27	Jersey City Jerseys	International League	AAA
1961	27	Toronto Maple Leafs	International League	AAA
1962	28	Toronto Maple Leafs	International League	AAA
1962	28	Kansas City Athletics	American League	MLB
1963	29	Kansas City Athletics	American League	MLB
1964	30	Kansas City Athletics	American League	MLB
1965	31	Kansas City Athletics	American League	MLB
1965	31	Detroit Tigers	American League	MLB
1966	32	Detroit Tigers	American League	MLB
1967	33	Detroit Tigers	American League	MLB
1967	33	Cleveland Indians	American League	MLB
1968	34	Portland Beavers	Pacific Coast League	AAA
1968	34	Seattle Angels	Pacific Coast League	AAA
1969	35	Omaha Royals	American Association	AAA
1970	36	Pittsburgh Pirates	National League	MLB

Year	Age	Tm	Lg	Lev
1971	37	Rochester Red Wings	International League	AAA
1971	37	Miami Orioles	Florida State League	A
1971	37	Baltimore Orioles	American League	MLB
1972	38	Miami Orioles	Florida State League	A
1972	38	Rochester Red Wings	International League	AAA
1973	39	Baltimore Orioles	American League	MLB
1973	39	St. Louis Cardinals	National League	MLB
1974	40	St. Louis Cardinals	National League	MLB
1974	40	California Angels	American League	MLB
1975	41	Tucson Toros	Pacific Coast League	AAA
1975	41	California Angels	American League	MLB
1979	45	Miami Amigos	Inter-American League	AAA

Catchers

Enrique Roberto (Hank) Izquierdo Valdéz

He played a total of seven seasons in the Cuban League, for Cienfuegos and Almendares. This weak hitting catcher had a total of 126 times at bat during the last professional season in his home country. Izquierdo was the batter that hit a grounder to second base, closing the game that gave Cienfuegos the Championship during that last season, becoming the last out of the professional Baseball Cuban League. That last out prevented Paulino Casanova from coming to the plate for the first time in the Cuban League since he was ready to pinch hit for the pitcher.

Izquierdo, born in 1931, came to the Cuban League as a second baseman in the Pedro Betancourt Amateur League, but was soon changed to a catcher due to his ability with the glove.

He played for the Cuban Sugar Kings from 1957 through 1960, including five games in the Little World Series, where he batted .222, and also played in the 1959 Caribbean Series that Almendares won in Venezuela.

This resourceful and versatile player was also an infielder and an outfielder in addition to being a catcher. He had a long 23-year career, finishing in the Mexican League for his last five years when he played at the triple A level. He reached the majors with the Minnesota Twins in 1967, batting .269 in 16 games. His batting average in the minors was an improved .253, given his average in Cuba.

Izquierdo managed for six seasons in the Mexican League at the Triple A level from 1970 through 1976 ending with a record of 423 wins and 413 losses.

As the Cuban season ended in February of 1961, Izquierdo secured the Mexican visa that brought him to the U.S. on March 20, 1961, when he reported to the Cincinnati organization. He would see little time at the game that year and returned to Cuba, only to leave again, this time traveling directly from La Habana in June of the same year. He played a total of 28 games for Jersey City in 1961 and did not play again until 1963. He became a U.S. Citizen in 1969, with Carlos *Patato* Pascual serving as one of the witnesses. He was inducted to the Cuban Professional Baseball Hall of Fame in 1997.

Sadly, he was shot in the stomach during a robbery and succumbed to that injury a long time later, dying in West Palm Beach on August 1, 2015

Additional sources:

Omelis Hongamen e-mail correspondence.
CNN ireport.com August 1, 2015
Andrés Pascual, eltubeyero22.files.wordpress.com/2015/08

Year	Age	Tm	Lg	Lev
1951	20	Galveston White Caps	Gulf Coast League	B
1952	21	Galveston White Caps	Gulf Coast League	B
1953	22	Galveston White Caps	Gulf Coast League	B
1954	23	Winston-Salem Twins	Carolina League	B

Year	Age	Tm	Lg	Lev
1955	24	Keokuk Kernels	Illinois-Indiana-Iowa League	B
1956	25	Indianapolis Indians	American Association	AAA
1956	25	San Antonio Missions	Texas League	AA
1956	25	Mobile Bears	Southern Association	AA
1957	26	Havana Sugar Kings	International League	AAA
1958	27	Havana Sugar Kings	International League	AAA
1959	28	Havana Sugar Kings	International League	AAA
1960	29	Havana Sugar Kings/ Jersey City Jerseys	International League	AAA
1961	30	Jersey City Jerseys	International League	AAA
1963	32	Orlando Twins	Florida State League	A
1964	33	Charlotte Hornets	Southern League	AA
1965	34	Charlotte Hornets	Southern League	AA
1966	35	Denver Bears	Pacific Coast League	AAA
1966	35	Charlotte Hornets	Southern League	AA
1967	36	Denver Bears	Pacific Coast League	AAA
1967	36	Minnesota Twins	American League	MLB
1968	37	Oklahoma City 89ers	Pacific Coast League	AAA
1969	38	Oklahoma City 89ers	American Association	AAA
1970	39	Veracruz Aguila	Mexican League	AAA
1971	40	Veracruz Aguila	Mexican League	AAA
1972	41	Yucatan Leones	Mexican League	AAA
1973	42	Yucatan Leones	Mexican League	AAA
1974	43	Veracruz Aguila	Mexican League	AAA

Orlando de Jesús McFarlane Quesada

McFarlane played three seasons in Cuba with the Almendares squad including the last season. His career went beyond Cuba, and he played a total of 14 seasons, from 1958 through 1971, with a batting average of .285 in the U.S. minors, where he played 1st and 3rd base, in addition to catcher. He reached the major leagues in 1962 for a total of five seasons, hitting .240.

Following the end of the 60-61 season in Cuba, McFarlane came to stay in the U.S., based on his career record. He played in Ashville during the 1961 season. Further confirmation is shown in his marriage record from Henderson County in North Carolina as he married a Dorothy Wilkins from Ashville North Carolina on December 16, 1961. They were divorced in 1966. Orlando McFarlane passed away in the city of Ponce in Puerto Rico on June 18, 2007.

Year	Age	Tm	Lg	Lev
1958	20	Salem Rebels	Appalachian League	D-
1959	21	Dubuque Packers	Midwest League	D
1959	21	Grand Forks Chiefs	Northern League	C

Year	Age	Tm	Lg	Lev
1960	22	Burlington Bees	Illinois-Indiana-Iowa League	B
1961	23	Asheville Tourists	South Atlantic League	A
1962	24	Columbus Jets	International League	AAA
1962	24	Pittsburgh Pirates	National League	MLB
1963	25	Columbus Jets	International League	AAA
1964	26	Pittsburgh Pirates	National League	MLB
1965	27	Hawaii Islanders	Pacific Coast League	AAA
1965	27	Asheville Tourists	Southern League	AA
1966	28	Detroit Tigers	American League	MLB
1967	29	California Angels	American League	MLB
1968	30	Seattle Angels	Pacific Coast League	AAA
1968	30	California Angels	American League	MLB
1969	31	Hawaii Islanders	Pacific Coast League	AAA
1969	31	Tidewater Tides	International League	AAA
1970	32	Tidewater Tides	International League	AAA
1971	33	Mexico City Diablos Rojos	Mexican League	AAA

Infielders

Edmundo (Sandy) Amorós Isasis

Very few Cuban players are better known that “Sandy” Amorós. During his eleven seasons in Cuba he played for both the Habana and Almendares teams. In 699 games, he had a batting average of .281 and was named the Rookie of the Year for the 1950-51 season. He played in four Caribbean Series for a total of 22 games and had an outstanding .354 batting average.

During his last season in Cuba, his average of .288 came during 226 appearances at the plate.

He reached the majors in 1952 with the Brooklyn Dodgers, the team where he played most of his games in the major leagues. During his seven seasons in the majors, his average was .255, but his ability with the glove has been amply documented and is worthy of research by readers who wish to gain the true significance of his contributions in the major leagues. Amorós is a member of the Cuban Baseball Hall of Fame in Miami, Florida.

Following the end of the last season, Amorós chose to remain in Cuba although he did play in Denver in 1961 and Mexico in 1962. Soon after, he settled down in Cuba in a ranch he owned.

It was reported he was offered a job managing a team by Fidel Castro in 1962, but he declined and his assets, including his ranch, were taken away by the Castro government.

He left Cuba in 1967 penniless and did menial jobs dying at the age of 62 on June 27, 1992 in Miami, Florida.

Additional source: Nicholas Dawidoff. “The Struggles Of Sandy A,” *Sports Illustrated*, July 10, 1989.

Year	Age	Tm	Lg	Lev
1952	22	St. Paul Saints	American Association	AAA
1952	22	Brooklyn Dodgers	National League	MLB
1953	23	Montreal Royals	International League	AAA
1954	24	Montreal Royals	International League	AAA
1954	24	Brooklyn Dodgers	National League	MLB

Year	Age	Tm	Lg	Lev
1955	25	Brooklyn Dodgers	National League	MLB
1956	26	Brooklyn Dodgers	National League	MLB
1957	27	Brooklyn Dodgers	National League	MLB
1958	28	Montreal Royals	International League	AAA
1959	29	Montreal Royals	International League	AAA
1959	29	Los Angeles Dodgers	National League	MLB
1960	30	Los Angeles Dodgers	National League	MLB
1960	30	Detroit Tigers	American League	MLB
1961	31	Denver Bears	American Association	AAA
1962	32	Mexico City Diablos Rojos	Mexican League	AA

Miguel Angel de la Hoz Piloto

Better known as Miguelito de la Hoz, as a teenager in Cuba, and even today, he had a very steady .277 batting average in 242 times at bat during that last season in Cuba. He played a total of four seasons in his home country, all for Almendares, as delivered a .265 average at the plate over the course of 499 appearances. He told me during our interview how the Cuban League paid established players $1350 per month during the baseball season, by agreement with Major League Baseball. He signed originally for $350 a month a very good salary in those days.

In 1957, at the age of 18, he was interested in pursuing a baseball career, but his mother did not want him to sign the baseball contract being offered. His father said, “Do what you want. Play ball or, if you wish, go to the University and pursue a higher education.” He signed the baseball contract on September 29, 1957 because, as he recalled he received a bonus of ten thousand dollars. Monchy de Arcos asked him at the time, as a suggestion, if he might want to secure a visa for his parents so they could go to the U.S. and see him play. He did and secured a “Tourist” visa for them, a decision that would be of greater significance later on. On a personal note, De La Hoz, though born in La Habana had an uncle on his mother’s side, by the name of Restituto Piloto, who was a bus driver in my hometown of Aguacate where my father owned one of the buses.

Miguelito’s career outside of Cuba began in 1958, at the age of 19, with an affiliate of the Cleveland Indians. He played a total of 13 seasons, ending in 1970 with a combined batting average of .285, even though, during the seven seasons in the minors, he batted .301. His nine seasons in the major leagues ended in 1969, with a batting average of .255. De La Hoz is a member of the Cuban Baseball of Fame in Miami, Florida.

When he decided to leave Cuba, his parents told him, “Don’t tell anyone you are leaving.” As we have learned, there was an arrangement between Major League Baseball and Mexico to allow Cuban players to play in Mexico but, in reality, it was a way to secure a visa to enter the U.S. Monchy de Arcos of the Cleveland Indians was the one person who knew when they would leave Cuba and was in charge of notifying them of the date.

At the appointed date and time, De la Hoz went to the Mexican Embassy in Habana, secured a visa, which was waiting for him, and left for Mexico City. He left without a suitcase and with only $5 dollars in his pocket, as many did in those days did, including this author. He remembers that, at the time, Fidel Castro sent a representative, a Capitán Moro, to tell him that, upon return from Mexico, "You have a job with the Revolution." Of course, by then De la Hoz knew he would not be going back. Prior to taking off for Mexico he bought a package of Bacardi rum as a gift to coaches in the U.S., but when he arrived in Mexico, the customs agent would not let him get through unless he surrendered the Bacardi, and so he did.

De La Hoz remembers talking to Pitcher Orlando Peña on the plane and, upon arrival at the Mexico City airport, a station wagon was waiting to take him to Hotel Virreyes where other players, like José Valdivielso, Orlando McFarlane, and Orlando Peña were also staying. They went to the American Embassy and that night they went out to eat as their journey was almost at the end. And yet some would say was just beginning. The next day he traveled to the U.S., arriving on March 3, 1961.

His career went on from there. A month later, in April of 1961, he was back with the Cleveland Indians for his second tour in the major leagues. In the winter of 61-62, he played in Puerto Rico, where he was the batting champion and, when he returned to Miami, where he had a house with Monchy de Arcos, his father called him and told him that the son of a mutual acquaintance was going to Miami from Cuba and had a message for him. The message he received was "Don't return to Cuba." His parents arrived in the U.S. soon thereafter.

Miguel de la Hoz became a naturalized U.S. citizen in 1971 in the U.S. District Court in Miami and lives today in Miami, Florida. During our interview, he reflected on the current migration of Cubans through a number of different countries such Ecuador, Colombia, Panamá, Nicaragua and Mexico as a continuing sad condition for the Cuban people that does not seem to have an end.

Additional source: Miguel de la Hoz, telephone interview with author, November 12, 2016.

Year	Age	Tm	Lg	Lev
1958	19	Minot Mallards	Northern League	C
1959	20	Reading Indians	Eastern League	A
1959	20	San Diego Padres	Pacific Coast League	AAA
1960	21	Toronto Maple Leafs	International League	AAA
1960	21	Mobile Bears	Southern Association	AA
1960	21	Cleveland Indians	American League	MLB
1961	22	Cleveland Indians	American League	MLB
1962	23	Jacksonville Suns	International League	AAA
1962	23	Cleveland Indians	American League	MLB
1963	24	Cleveland Indians	American League	MLB
1964	25	Milwaukee Braves	National League	MLB
1965	26	Milwaukee Braves	National League	MLB
1966	27	Atlanta Braves	National League	MLB
1967	28	Atlanta Braves	National League	MLB
1968	29	Richmond Braves	International League	AAA
1969	30	Indianapolis Indians	American Association	AAA
1969	30	Richmond Braves	International League	AAA
1969	30	Cincinnati Reds	National League	MLB
1970	31	Indianapolis Indians	American Association	AAA

Humberto (Chico) Fernández Pérez

This veteran of ten seasons in the Cuban League played for Cienfuegos and the Habana teams prior to Almendares. His overall record during a total of 567 games included a batting average of .257. In the last season, playing shortstop for the Almendares *Alacranes* (Scorpions),

his average dipped to .235 for 213 times at the plate. He also played during the 1956 Caribbean Series for Cienfuegos in six games batting a healthy .286.

Outside of Cuba he played from 1951 through 1968 in the U.S., Mexico and Japan, including eight seasons in the majors, with a batting average of .240 in 856 games, mostly at short stop though he would play at second and third for a few games during that time.

Even though research did not unveil his leaving Cuba in 1961, his playing career shows his having played for the Detroit Tigers of the American League starting on April 11 of that year and thereafter, through 1968, for the Tacoma Cubs of the Pacific Coast League. Fernández was elected as a member of the Cuban Baseball Hall of Fame in Miami, Florida.

According to Roberto González Echevarría's book, Fernández lost an apartment house he had built for his parents under the Urban Reform legislation of the time.

Humberto Fernández was born on March 2, 1932 in La Habana and passed away on June 11, 2016 in Sunrise City in Broward County in Florida.

Additional source: González Echevarría, Roberto. *The Pride of Havana: A History of Cuban Baseball* (New York: Oxford University Press, 1999) page 351

Year	Age	Tm	Lg	Lev
1951	19	Billings Mustangs	Pioneer League	C
1952	20	Miami Sun Sox	Florida International League	B
1953	21	Montreal Royals	International League	AAA
1954	22	Montreal Royals	International League	AAA
1955	23	Montreal Royals	International League	AAA
1956	24	Montreal Royals	International League	AAA
1956	24	Brooklyn Dodgers	National League	MLB
1957	25	Philadelphia Phillies	National League	MLB
1958	26	Philadelphia Phillies	National League	MLB
1959	27	Philadelphia Phillies	National League	MLB
1960	28	Detroit Tigers	American League	MLB
1961	29	Detroit Tigers	American League	MLB
1962	30	Detroit Tigers	American League	MLB
1963	31	Seattle Rainiers	Pacific Coast League	AAA
1963	31	Detroit Tigers	American League	MLB
1963	31	New York Mets	National League	MLB
1964	32	Indianapolis Indians	Pacific Coast League	AAA
1964	32	Syracuse Chiefs	International League	AAA
1965	33	Hanshin Tigers	Japan Central League	Fgn
1966	34	Reynosa Broncs	Mexican League	AA
1967	35	Tacoma Cubs	Pacific Coast League	AAA
1968	36	Tacoma Cubs	Pacific Coast League	AAA

Gabriel Antonio (Tony) Martínez Díaz

During the last season, his second, in Cuba, Martínez came to the plate 83 times, played the infield for Almendares, and had a batting average of .265. He had come to the plate only ten times the previous season.

He played in the U.S. from 1960 through 1968 which included part of four seasons for the Cleveland Indians in the major leagues batting a low .171.

Following the end of the 60-61 season, Martínez came to the U.S. via Mexico arriving on March 9, 1961. He also traveled from Panama on February 5, 1962 where he stated that his permanent address was in Panama City and in San Juan Puerto Rico. He became a U.S. Citizen in 1971 in the Miami District Court. Martínez passed away on August 24, 1991 and is buried in the Vista Memorial Garden Cemetery of the same city.

Year	Age	Tm	Lg	Lev
1960	20	Minot Mallards	Northern League	C
1961	21	Reading Indians	Eastern League	A
1962	22	Jacksonville Suns	International League	AAA
1963	23	Jacksonville Suns	International League	AAA
1963	23	Cleveland Indians	American League	MLB
1964	24	Portland Beavers	Pacific Coast League	AAA
1964	24	Cleveland Indians	American League	MLB
1965	25	Jacksonville Suns	International League	AAA
1965	25	Portland Beavers	Pacific Coast League	AAA

Year	Age	Tm	Lg	Lev
1965	25	Cleveland Indians	American League	MLB
1966	26	Tulsa Oilers	Pacific Coast League	AAA
1966	26	FIL Cardinals	Florida Instructional League	WRk
1966	26	Cleveland Indians	American League	MLB
1967	27	Tulsa Oilers	Pacific Coast League	AAA
1967	27	Jacksonville Suns	International League	AAA
1968	28	Modesto Reds	California League	A

José Rivero

Rivero would play but three seasons in the Cuban League, all with Almendares, with a total of 52 times at bat, hitting .135. During the last season he did not have a hit during his only two times at the plate.

According to immigration records, Rivero's date of birth was March 10, 1939. He left Cuba, boarding in La Habana, on March 25, 1962 to join the Cleveland Indians organization even though there is no record that can be found showing that he played outside of Cuba. According to Iván Davis, he also travelled back to Cuba only to come back to the U.S. around 2013 or 2014.

Additional source: Iván Davis, telephone interview with author, October 24, 2016.

Antonio Nemesio (Tony) Taylor Sánchez

An outstanding second baseman, Taylor played seven seasons in the Cuban League, hitting an average of .275 in 409 games and 1460 appearances at the plate. In his last season in Cuba, his average of .280 also showed some punch, with six triples, 9 doubles and six homeruns to go along with his speed in stealing 22 bases. He played in the 1959 Caribbean Series in six games and had a .346 batting average.

During his 23 seasons in the U.S., he played a total of 19 in the majors where he hit .261, mostly with the Philadelphia Phillies and was named to an All Star game. From 1982 through 1986 he managed five teams in the minors, winning 285 games and losing 416. His record led to his induction in the Cuban Baseball Hall of Fame in Miami, Florida. A more complete biography can be found in the SABR bio project, showing the full life of this Jamaican-descent player born in the Alava Sugar Mill in the Matanzas Province.

He left Cuba in March of 1961 via Mexico accompanied by his wife and his 2 month-old baby daughter.

Additional source: Costello Rory and Ramírez José SABR.org Bio-Project. Tony Taylor.

Year	Age	Tm	Lg	Lev
1954	18	Texas City/Thibodaux Pilots	Evangeline League	C
1955	19	St. Cloud Rox	Northern League	C
1956	20	Danville Leafs	Carolina League	B
1957	21	Dallas Eagles	Texas League	AA
1958	22	Chicago Cubs	National League	MLB
1959	23	Chicago Cubs	National League	MLB
1960	24	Chicago Cubs	National League	MLB
1960	24	Philadelphia Phillies	National League	MLB
1961	25	Philadelphia Phillies	National League	MLB
1962	26	Philadelphia Phillies	National League	MLB
1963	27	Philadelphia Phillies	National League	MLB

Year	Age	Tm	Lg	Lev
1964	28	Philadelphia Phillies	National League	MLB
1965	29	Philadelphia Phillies	National League	MLB
1966	30	Philadelphia Phillies	National League	MLB
1967	31	Philadelphia Phillies	National League	MLB
1968	32	Philadelphia Phillies	National League	MLB
1969	33	Philadelphia Phillies	National League	MLB
1970	34	Philadelphia Phillies	National League	MLB
1971	35	Philadelphia Phillies	National League	MLB
1971	35	Detroit Tigers	American League	MLB
1972	36	Detroit Tigers	American League	MLB
1973	37	Detroit Tigers	American League	MLB
1974	38	Philadelphia Phillies	National League	MLB
1975	39	Philadelphia Phillies	National League	MLB
1976	40	Philadelphia Phillies	National League	MLB

Outfielders

Pedro Almenares Alarcón

While not playing in Cuba during the 1958-59 and 1959-60 seasons, Almenares returned for the last season of the league, came to bat only nine times and hit but .111. His overall record during six seasons in Cuba included a robust .272 batting average in 515 times at the plate.

Outside of Cuba, he played from 1952 through 1961, including seven seasons in the minors where he hit for an average of .297 and four seasons, 1958-61, in Mexico.

Born in Manzanillo, in the eastern part of Cuba, on May 5, 1927. Following the end of the 1960-61 season Almenares returned to Cuba and became party to the first National Series in Cuba. He contributed to the construction of the Bobby Salamanca baseball stadium in the town of San Miguel de Padrón.

Additional sources:
cubanosfamosos.com
Ecured

Year	Age	Tm	Lg	Lev
1952	19	Sheboygan Indians	Wisconsin State League	D
1953	20	Great Falls Electrics	Pioneer League	C
1954	21	Elmira Pioneers	Eastern League	A
1955	22	Pueblo Dodgers	Western League	A
1955	22	St. Paul Saints	American Association	AAA
1956	23	St. Paul Saints	American Association	AAA
1956	23	Macon Dodgers	South Atlantic League	A
1957	24	Pueblo Dodgers	Western League	A
1958	25	Nogales Mineros	Arizona-Mexico League	C
1958	25	Nuevo Laredo Tecolotes	Mexican League	AA
1958	25	Monterrey Sultanes	Mexican League	AA
1959	26	Monterrey Sultanes	Mexican League	AA
1960	27	Monterrey Sultanes	Mexican League	AA
1960	27	Poza Rica Petroleros	Mexican League	AA
1961	28	Puebla Pericos	Mexican League	AA

Carlos Paula Conill

The very popular Paula played nine seasons in the Cuban League, all for Almendares, hitting .250 during his last season there. His overall batting average was .265 in 1135 times at bat. He played twice in the Caribbean series, in five different games. He also played for the Cuban Sugar Kings in 1959, in 88 games with a .312 batting average.

Joe Cambria who scouted in Cuba for nearly 30 years was responsible for signing over 400 players, including Carlos Paula. Heading into the 1954 Spring Training, Washington Senators' scout Joe Cambria touted Paula as "a player who can do everything well enough to be in the majors." He will have "the best throwing arm in the outfield, is a terror on the bases, and can hit big league pitching." Manager Bucky Harris, to whom Paula was nothing more than a rumor, responded, "If this fellow is such a great hitter, then how come he hit only .309 in the Big State League?" See the source of articles below, which are also worthy of reading if only to show the prejudice and bias of that time which provides a sad glimpse to the treatment many of these black players endured during those days.

Playing from 1952 through 1960, Paula, a member of the Cuban Baseball Hall of Fame in Miami, Florida, spent seven seasons in the minors hitting .310. His last season in the Mexican League, in 1960, he batted .339. He spent three seasons in the majors where his batting average was .271

In 1954, the Senators had not yet integrated. The press anticipated the Senators' color line would be broken in 1954, but not by Paula. Cuban Angel Scull, as the *Sporting News* reported, was "assured of an outfield berth and will be the first Negro ever to play for the Nats." But in camp, Paula began to turn heads. Sportswriter Shirley Povich, who sent daily dispatches to the *Post* from camp, wrote that Paula "fingers the bat like a toothpick" and that he played center field "as if he belonged." Even Bucky Harris warmed up to the prospect, saying, "He can whack that ball. He has that size, and he gets some beautiful extra leverage into his swing. And he isn't simply fast for a big man. He's fast for a man of any size." It should be noted that Scull never appeared in a major league game. Records have not been found of

Paula's whereabouts after the last season when he did not seem to have returned to baseball at the age of 32.

Carlos Paula passed away on April 25, 1983 and is buried at Mt. Nebo in Miami, Florida.

Additional sources:

BL-9972.95 (National Baseball Hall of Fame
baseballhall.org/discover by Larry Brunt
José (Chamby) Campos, personal interview with author, January 26, 2018.

Year	Age	Tm	Lg	Lev
1952	24	Decatur Commodores	Mississippi-Ohio Valley League	D
1953	25	Paris Indians	Big State League	B
1953	25	Decatur Commodores	Mississippi-Ohio Valley League	D
1954	26	Charlotte Hornets	South Atlantic League	A
1954	26	Washington Senators	American League	MLB
1955	27	Washington Senators	American League	MLB
1956	28	Miami Marlins	International League	AAA
1956	28	Denver Bears	American Association	AAA
1956	28	Louisville Colonels	American Association	AAA
1956	28	Washington Senators	American League	MLB
1957	29	Minneapolis Millers	American Association	AAA
1958	30	Sacramento Solons	Pacific Coast League	AAA
1959	31	Sacramento Solons	Pacific Coast League	AAA
1959	31	Havana Sugar Kings	International League	AAA
1960	32	Mexico City Tigres	Mexican League	AA

Leopoldo Jesús Posada Hernández

Leo Posada played five seasons in Cuba, for both the Habana and the Almendares teams hitting an average .270 in 167 games and 419 times at the plate.

During the 60-61 season Orestes Miñoso was President of the players' association and Camilo Pascual was the Treasurer. They held a meeting of all the players on the El Cerro baseball field and agreed to reduce salaries from approximately $2000 to $1500, $1500 to $1100/$1200 due to lack of funds to finish the season. Salaries during the Cuban league season were paid monthly for basically 3-4 months. If you played in the U.S. at the Triple A level you would get approximately $700, and at the AA level, $600. Reserves were paid $200. They were not in the playing roster but would practice with the team. See source cited below.

For Posada's last season in Cuba his batting average was .274 in 208 times at bat. Posada has indicated that nobody knew the end was imminent until a representative of the Cuban Government, Felipe Guerra Matos, met with the players and told them professional baseball would be ending that season. Matos was at the time responsible for the direction of sports in general *(Dirección General de Deportes)* which preceded INDER (Institute for Sports, Physical Education and Recreation).

Posada's playing career outside of the Cuban League spanned from 1954 through 1969 including 16 seasons in the minors, hitting .288, one season in Mexico, and three seasons in the majors hitting .256 for the Kansas City Athletics. His first home run was off Jim Perry.

Posada also managed for nine different seasons, leading his teams to a combined record of 478 wins and 633 losses.

Posada told his story of leaving Cuba via Mexico arriving in the U.S. on March 3, 1961 to join the Kansas City Athletics where he had a contract to play baseball. Camilo Pascual and José Ramón López were among those travelling with him. As with many other players, he had been counseled by family members, his father and mother-in-law, that leaving Cuba was the proper action. His wife followed two weeks later.

When they arrived in Mexico they got some money, all their expenses were paid, and lodging at the Virreyes Hotel was arranged and paid for. Next day they went to the U.S. embassy, got a visa and left that afternoon for the U.S.

On a personal level Posada has no family left in Cuba and has celebrated 61 years of marriage with his dear wife. He is most proud of having been the only Cuban to have been both an Olympian bicycle star and a Major League Baseball Player. He takes great satisfaction that he wore #19 with Kansas City and his nephew Jorge was #20 with the New York Yankees.

Additional sources:

Leopoldo Posada, telephone interview with author,
November 12, 2016
Pascual Andrés El Ultimo Campenato de Beisbol professional Cubano eltubeyero22 November 20, 2011
Starts and Stripes September 30, 1960 page 199

Year	Age	Tm	Lg	Lev
1954	18	Lake Charles Lakers	Evangeline League	C
1954	18	Odessa Oilers	Longhorn League	C
1954	18	Corpus Christi Clippers	Big State League	B
1955	19	Corpus Christi Clippers	Big State League	B
1956	20	Corpus Christi Clippers	Big State League	B
1957	21	Columbia Gems	South Atlantic League	A
1957	21	Abilene Blue Sox	Big State League	B
1957	21	Little Rock Travelers	Southern Association	AA
1958	22	Rochester/Winona A's	Illinois-Indiana-Iowa League	B
1959	23	Shreveport Sports	Southern Association	AA
1960	24	Shreveport Sports	Southern Association	AA
1960	24	Kansas City Athletics	American League	MLB
1961	25	Shreveport Sports	Southern Association	AA
1961	25	Kansas City Athletics	American League	MLB
1962	26	Toronto Maple Leafs	International League	AAA
1962	26	Kansas City Athletics	American League	MLB
1963	27	Hawaii Islanders	Pacific Coast League	AAA
1963	27	Monterrey Sultanes	Mexican League	AA
1963	27	Toronto Maple Leafs	International League	AAA
1964	28	San Antonio Bullets	Texas League	AA
1965	29	Amarillo Sonics	Texas League	AA
1966	30	Amarillo Sonics	Texas League	AA
1967	31	Oklahoma City 89ers	Pacific Coast League	AAA
1968	32	Cocoa Astros	Florida State League	A
1969	33	Cocoa Astros	Florida State League	A

Angel Scull Sáez

After playing in the Amateur Pedro Betancourt League, Scull played ten seasons in the Cuban League and had a batting average of .277. During the 1960-61 season, he had 258 appearances at the plate and a .260 batting average.

He played in the Caribbean Series in 1954 and 55 with Almendares for twelve games with a .306 batting average in 49 times at the plate. With the Havana Cubans in 1952, he led the league in stolen bases with 54 and had triples while batting .274. Two years later, he joined the Cuban Sugar Kings, playing a total of 492 games and a .264 batting average, and led the all-time list of stolen bases with 72. On April 9, 1952 he broke the racial barriers in the Florida International League along with Silvio García and George Handy.

His accomplishments led to his induction into the Cuban Baseball Hall of Fame in 1997 in Miami Florida.

Angel Scull played in the U.S. and Mexico for nineteen seasons, from the 1951 through 1969. He played from 1963 on in the Mexican League and had a batting average of .282 in the minors. He also managed for one season in the Mexican League in 1978 and his teams' record was 33 wins and 32 losses.

Larry Brunt's article relates that the press concluded that the Washington Senators' color barrier would be broken in 1954 by Scull. The baseball card company, Topps, included a baseball card of Scull in its 1954 set (see below) but he never made it.

One theory is that Carlos Paula got hot during the spring and another claim was that Scull got hurt. Either way, Scull never played in the majors despite his good seasons in the minors.

Immigration records show that he came to the U.S. on March 19, 1962. He played for Syracuse during the 1961 season and for the Atlanta Crackers in 1962, so it is clear he stayed in the U.S. following the end of the Cuban League. Angel Scull Sáez passed away on February 14, 2005 in Miami, Florida.

Additional source: baseballhall.org/discover by Larry Brunt

Year	Age	Tm	Lg	Lev
1951	22	Wellsville Rockets	Pennsylvania-Ontario-New York League	D
1952	23	Fort Lauderdale Braves/ Key West Conchs	Florida International League	B
1952	23	Havana Cubans	Florida International League	B
1953	24	Charleston Senators	American Association	AAA
1954	25	Havana Sugar Kings	International League	AAA
1955	26	Havana Sugar Kings	International League	AAA
1956	27	Havana Sugar Kings	International League	AAA
1957	28	Havana Sugar Kings	International League	AAA
1958	29	Toronto Maple Leafs	International League	AAA
1959	30	Toronto Maple Leafs	International League	AAA
1959	30	Montreal Royals	International League	AAA
1960	31	Montreal Royals	International League	AAA
1961	32	Syracuse Chiefs	International League	AAA
1962	33	Atlanta Crackers	International League	AAA
1962	33	Vancouver Mounties	Pacific Coast League	AAA
1963	34	Poza Rica Petroleros	Mexican League	AA

Year	Age	Tm	Lg	Lev
1964	35	Poza Rica Petroleros	Mexican League	AA
1965	36	Poza Rica Petroleros	Mexican League	AA
1966	37	Poza Rica Petroleros	Mexican League	AA
1967	38	Poza Rica Petroleros	Mexican League	AAA
1968	39	Campeche Pirates	Mexican Southeast League	A
1968	39	Poza Rica Petroleros	Mexican League	AAA
1969	40	Campeche Shrimpers	Mexican Southeast League	A

José Ramón Villar Lamazares

Born in Manguito, Matanzas on September 2, 1939, Villar played outfield for Almendares as well as first base during three seasons in Cuba. He had a batting average of .240, but his average during the 1960-61 season was higher, reaching .260 in 154 times at bat.

His playing career outside of Cuba was in the U.S. minor league system from 1959 through the 1967 season in Class D and Single A teams batting .270 during those nine seasons.

He left Cuba via Mexico and arrived in the U.S. on March 9, 1961. He subsequently returned to Cuba and ultimately boarded a flight from Habana in March 1962, on his way to join the Jacksonville club. Later that same year on November 12, he traveled from Santo Domingo in the Dominican Republic to join the Cleveland Indians organization. His baseball career record shows him staying in the U.S.

Year	Age	Tm	Lg	Lev
1959	20	Selma Cloverleafs	Alabama-Florida League	D
1960	21	Selma Cloverleafs	Alabama-Florida League	D
1961	22	Reading Indians	Eastern League	A
1962	23	Charleston Indians	Eastern League	A

Year	Age	Tm	Lg	Lev
1963	24	Grand Forks Chiefs	Northern League	A
1964	25	Burlington Indians	Carolina League	A
1964	25	Raleigh Cardinals	Carolina League	A
1965	26	Raleigh Cardinals	Carolina League	A
1965	26	Rock Hill Cardinals	Western Carolinas League	A
1966	27	St. Petersburg Cardinals	Florida State League	A
1967	28	Cedar Rapids Cardinals	Midwest League	A

Chapter 7

HABANA

Manager

Fermín Guerra

Born Fermín Romero Guerra, but known as "Mike" Guerra, in La Habana on October 11, 1912, Guerra played in the majors for the Philadelphia Athletics, for Washington and for the Boston Red Sox from September 1937 through the 1951 season. But his playing career began in 1936 and ended in 1955. During his nine seasons in the majors, his batting average was .242 and his minor league average was .275, also during nine seasons.

His career in Cuba as a player for the Habana, Marianao and Almendares spanned over twenty seasons hitting for an average of .250 in over 2800 games. As a manager, his record over the twelve seasons was 389 wins and 380 losses. He also managed the Almendares team in the Caribbean series in 1949 and 50 winning a total of 9 games and losing three while earning a first place in 1949. Guerra played and managed the Havana Cubans in 1952 and the Cuban Sugar Kings in 1954.

He led the Habana Lions from the 1958-59 season through its last, the 1960-61 season, with a record 32 wins and 34 losses during that last season. His winningest pitcher during that last season was Luis Tiant Jr. who had ten victories and went on to earn the Rookie of the Year award.

Guerra was also a full-time scout for the Detroit Tigers in Cuba, an appointment that was published in Stars and Stripes. See source cited below.

His SABR biography shows how, in 1962, during the first National Series after the Castro revolution, he managed the Occidentales squad. Fidel Castro took some swings in the batter's box to open the series. Guerra's team went 18-9 to win the Series, but Guerra himself "would soon fall from favor," according to Peter C. Bjarkman's source cited below. "[He] was later sent to pick potatoes in Camagüey because of his resistance to the regime." See González Echevarría, source cited below. Guerra did get a second chance at managing in the Castro era, in the Sixth National Series, in 1967. Apparently, he incurred the regime's displeasure by listening to the Voice of America radio. See source cited below. As late as 1977, Guerra was living on Calle Cristina in La Habana, but no longer working for INDER, Cuba's Institute for Sports, Physical Education and Recreation. The *retirado*, or retired as he entered on his Hall of Fame questionnaire, may have obscured a lack of employment due to political differences with the regime.)

Fermín Guerra was deservedly elected to the Cuban Baseball Hall of Fame in 1969, in Miami.

Two days before his 80th birthday, after a long struggle with heart disease, Guerra died at Mount Sinai Medical Center in Miami Beach. It was October 9, 1992. He was survived by his wife and daughters and his remains were buried at the Flagler Memorial Park in Miami, Florida.

Additional sources:

Bjarkman Peter C., A History of Cuban Baseball, 1864-2006, (Jefferson, NC: McFarland and Company, 2007), p. 241.

González Echevarría Roberto. The Pride of Havana: A History of Cuban Baseball (New York: Oxford University Press, 1999) page 266.

Nowlin Bill SABR BioProject "Fermín Guerra"
(http://sabr.org/bioproj/person)

Nuevo Herald Angel Torres

Stars and Stripes November 29, 1959, page 19

Year	Age	Tm	Lg	Lev
1936	23	York White Roses/Trenton Senators	New York-Pennsylvania League	A
1936	23	Albany Senators	International League	AA
1937	24	Salisbury Indians	Eastern Shore League	D
1937	24	Washington Senators	American League	MLB
1938	25	Charlotte Hornets	Piedmont League	B
1938	25	Salisbury Indians	Eastern Shore League	D
1939	26	Greenville Spinners	South Atlantic League	B
1940	27	Springfield Nationals	Eastern League	A
1941	28	Charlotte Hornets	Piedmont League	B
1941	28	Greenville Spinners	South Atlantic League	B
1941	28	Springfield Nationals	Eastern League	A
1942	29	Chattanooga Lookouts	Southern Association	A1
1943	30	Puebla Angeles	Mexican League	Ind
1944	31	Washington Senators	American League	MLB
1945	32	Washington Senators	American League	MLB
1946	33	Washington Senators	American League	MLB
1947	34	Philadelphia Athletics	American League	MLB
1948	35	Philadelphia Athletics	American League	MLB
1949	36	Philadelphia Athletics	American League	MLB
1950	37	Philadelphia Athletics	American League	MLB
1951	38	Boston Red Sox	American League	MLB
1951	38	Washington Senators	American League	MLB
1952	39	Havana Cubans	Florida International League	B
1954	41	Havana Sugar Kings	International League	AAA
1955	42	Yucatan Leones	Mexican League	AA

Pitchers

Eduardo Bauta Galvez

During Bauta's last season in Cuba, he appeared in 24 games, including two complete games, with 4 win and 4 loss record. His 3.53 ERA was quite a bit higher than his ERA of 2.70 for his three seasons in the Cuban League.

His overall career outside of Cuba started in 1956 in the Midwest league and ended in 1974. He pitched in the Mexican League for the Poza Rica Petroleros. He won 70 games and lost 49 during his 13 seasons in the minors and reached the majors with the St. Louis Cardinals and New York Mets for five seasons, earning a 6-6 record.

A review of his immigration records does not show him leaving Cuba after the last season in 60-61, but his playing career during that season with Portland and St. Louis and thereafter confirms that he left Cuba and stayed in the U.S.

Year	Age	Tm	Lg	Lev
1956	21	Clinton Pirates	Midwest League	D
1957	22	Grand Forks Chiefs	Northern League	C
1958	23	Lincoln Chiefs	Western League	A
1959	24	Salt Lake City Bees	Pacific Coast League	AAA
1960	25	Columbus Jets	International League	AAA
1960	25	St. Louis Cardinals	National League	MLB
1961	26	Portland Beavers	Pacific Coast League	AAA
1961	26	St. Louis Cardinals	National League	MLB
1962	27	Atlanta Crackers	International League	AAA
1962	27	St. Louis Cardinals	National League	MLB
1963	28	St. Louis Cardinals	National League	MLB
1963	28	New York Mets	National League	MLB
1964	29	Buffalo Bisons	International League	AAA
1964	29	New York Mets	National League	MLB
1965	30	Buffalo Bisons	International League	AAA
1965	30	Rochester Red Wings	International League	AAA
1967	32	Williamsport Mets	Eastern League	AA
1967	32	Jacksonville Suns	International League	AAA
1968	33	Visalia Mets	California League	A
1969	34	Poza Rica Petroleros	Mexican League	AAA
1970	35	Poza Rica Petroleros	Mexican League	AAA
1971	36	Poza Rica Petroleros	Mexican League	AAA
1972	37	Eugene Emeralds	Pacific Coast League	AAA
1972	37	Poza Rica Petroleros	Mexican League	AAA
1973	38	Poza Rica Petroleros	Mexican League	AAA
1973	38	Eugene Emeralds	Pacific Coast League	AAA
1974	39	Poza Rica Petroleros	Mexican League	AAA

Silvio Alberto Castellanos Correa

Castellanos was born in the city of Cienfuegos on February 17, 1936, a date shown on his 1959 immigration record as he was on his way to report to the Washington organization in Orlando Florida. He played for the Habana Lions during his three seasons in Cuba winning 33 games with a 4.26 ERA. During his last season, his ERA climbed to 4.54 and ended the season with a record of 3 wins and 2 losses in 12 games.

His professional career outside of Cuba began in 1957 with the Charlotte Class A team. From 1960 through 1963 he played for Veracruz, an AA team in the Mexican League, winning 14 games during the team's championship season. His minor league record included 13 wins and 17 losses, appearing in 102 games.

His July 10, 1960 travel record shows him arriving in Texas from Mexico and indicating a permanent address in Veracruz, Mexico and a U.S. address in San Antonio, Texas. Following his career in Mexico, Castellanos became the manager of the Honduras Armed Forces team and he ultimately died in that country.

Additional source: Andrés Pascual, telephone interview with author, February 5, 2018.

Year	Age	Tm	Lg	Lev
1957	21	Charlotte Hornets	South Atlantic League	A
1958	22	Missoula Timberjacks	Pioneer League	C
1959	23	Missoula Timberjacks	Pioneer League	C
1959	23	Fox Cities Foxes	Illinois-Indiana-Iowa League	B
1960	24	Veracruz Aguilas	Mexican League	AA
1961	25	Veracruz Aguilas	Mexican League	AA
1962	26	Veracruz Aguilas	Mexican League	AA
1963	27	Veracruz Aguilas	Mexican League	AA

Julio (Jiquí) Moreno González

Moreno had an excellent ERA of 2.03 for his last season. His win and loss record was 3 and 5 in 17 appearances. He played a total of 12 seasons in Cuba, participating in 231 games, with a 40-52 record and a 3.78 ERA. During his three Caribbean Series with Habana, he played in four games and had a 3.21 ERA. Playing four seasons with the Havana Cubans during 1947-50, in 79 games he had a solid record of 50 wins and 16 losses with a 2.24 ERA. During 1954 and 1955 he also played for the Cuban Sugar Kings in 66 games, winning 11 and losing 9.

His overall record and contributions to the game would earn him induction into the Cuban Baseball Hall of Fame in Miami, Florida in 1983.

His career outside of Cuba began in the Mexican Independent League in 1945 and ended in Mexico in 1966. Playing a total of eight seasons in the minors, he won a total of 66 games and lost 33, with a 3.17 ERA. In the Mexican League, his record was 12-31. Moreno played during four seasons in the majors for the Washington Senators earning 50 victories against 53 losses and a 4.25 ERA.

In 1960, Jiqui Moreno managed the Puebla Team in Mexico leading his team to a 63 win and 80 loss record.

Unable to find a record of his leaving Cuba, but playing in Mexico after the 1960-61 season, may suggest he never left. . However, his 1973 U.S. Citizenship papers in the Miami District Court shows his permanent Residence status in the U.S. since 1963. Moreno died in Miami Florida on January 2, 1987 and is buried at the Miami Woodland Cemetery. A more complete story about Moreno can be found in the SABR biography cited below.

Additional source: Costello, Rory. *"Julio Moreno"* SABR Bio Project (http://sabr.org/bioproj/person)

Year	Age	Tm	Lg	Lev
1945	24	Veracruz Azules	Mexican League	Ind
1946	25	Havana Cubans	Florida International League	C
1947	26	Havana Cubans	Florida International League	C
1948	27	Havana Cubans	Florida International League	C
1949	28	Havana Cubans	Florida International League	B
1950	29	Havana Cubans	Florida International League	B
1950	29	Washington Senators	American League	MLB
1951	30	Washington Senators	American League	MLB
1952	31	Washington Senators	American League	MLB
1953	32	Chattanooga Lookouts	Southern Association	AA
1953	32	Washington Senators	American League	MLB
1954	33	Havana Sugar Kings	International League	AAA
1955	34	Havana Sugar Kings	International League	AAA
1956	35	Yucatan Leones	Mexican League	AA
1957	36	Yucatan Leones	Mexican League	AA
1958	37	Nuevo Laredo Tecolotes	Mexican League	AA
1959	38	Nuevo Laredo Tecolotes	Mexican League	AA
1960	39	Puebla Pericos	Mexican League	AA
1961	40	Puebla Pericos	Mexican League	AA
1962	41	Jacksonville Suns	International League	AAA
1962	41	Puebla Pericos	Mexican League	AA
1963	42	Puebla Pericos	Mexican League	AA
1964	43	Puebla Pericos	Mexican League	AA

Year	Age	Tm	Lg	Lev
1965	44	Puebla Pericos	Mexican League	AA
1966	45	Puebla Pericos	Mexican League	AA

Gustavo Muñiz

For his last and sixth season in the Cuban League (all with the Habana Lions), Muñiz had a 0-1 record with a 3.46 ERA, in 17 games. His career in Cuba earned him a 6-5 record, with a 2.54 ERA. Unable to find his U.S. records, Muñiz played in the U.S. until 1962 and thus one can ascertain he stayed in this country.

Additional sources:

Omelis Hongamen, telephone interview with author.
Iván Davis, telephone interview with author, January 31, 2018.

Fernando Pedro (Trompoloco) Rodríguez Borrego

Trompoloco played seven seasons in the Cuban League with all four teams of the time, winning 12 and losing 10, in 110 games. During his last professional season, he had a 4-1 record in 28 games with a 2.47 ERA.

He also played in 1959 at the Caribbean Series with Almendares, appearing in one game, striking out one batter and walking one. Playing for the Havana Cubans during the 1947, 47, 51 and 52 seasons, he won 32 games and lost 36 in 100 games, and had a 2.88 ERA.

Beginning in 1945 through the 1962 season, he played professional baseball outside of Cuba, including three seasons in the Mexican League with two brief appearances in the majors. Though he did not win a game during his eight appearances in the majors, his minor league record was 146 wins and 140 losses.

His record in the U.S. went beyond the end of the 1960-61 season. He played in Mexico at the age of 37-38, which leaves open the question whether he stayed in Cuba for a time.

He passed away on June 11, 2009 in Miami, Florida. An immigration record from 1960 shows that Rodríguez was returning to the U.S. with a status as a Permanent Resident (Form I 151) thus reflecting his residence in the United States. His date of birth of May 20, 1924, listed on the form, is not consistent with other publications.

Year	Age	Tm	Lg	Lev
1945	21	Kingsport Cherokees	Appalachian League	D
1945	21	Williamsport Grays	Eastern League	A
1946	22	Pensacola Fliers	Southeastern League	B
1946	22	Havana Cubans	Florida International League	C
1947	23	Havana Cubans	Florida International League	C
1948	24	Big Spring Broncs	Longhorn League	D
1948	24	Sherman-Denison Twins	Big State League	B
1949	25	Big Spring Broncs	Longhorn League	D
1949	25	Abilene Blue Sox	West Texas-New Mexico League	C
1950	26	Abilene Blue Sox	West Texas-New Mexico League	C
1951	27	Havana Cubans	Florida International League	B
1952	28	Havana Cubans	Florida International League	B
1953	29	Midland Indians	Longhorn League	C
1954	30	Greenville Spinners	Tri-State League	B
1955	31	Greenville Spinners	Tri-State League	B
1956	32	Nuevo Laredo Tecolotes	Mexican League	AA
1956	32	Minneapolis Millers	American Association	AAA
1956	32	Dallas Eagles	Texas League	AA
1957	33	Minneapolis Millers	American Association	AAA

Year	Age	Tm	Lg	Lev
1958	34	Portland Beavers	Pacific Coast League	AAA
1958	34	Buffalo Bisons	International League	AAA
1958	34	Chicago Cubs	National League	MLB
1959	35	Buffalo Bisons	International League	AAA
1959	35	Montreal Royals	International League	AAA
1959	35	Philadelphia Phillies	National League	MLB
1960	36	St. Paul Saints	American Association	AAA
1961	37	Mexico City Diablos Rojos	Mexican League	AA
1962	38	Mexico City Diablos Rojos	Mexican League	AA

Minervino (Minnie) Alejandro Rojas Landin

Rojas appeared for the first and only time in the Cuban League in three games for a total of 2.2 innings during the last season at 28 years of age, even though his age is listed as 26, born in 1933, when he played for the Artesia Class D affiliate of the San Francisco Giants during its 1960 season.

Rojas left Cuba arriving in the U.S. on March 11, 1962. He had a minor league career which fluctuated between the U.S. and Mexico, from 1960 through 1969, in which he earned a record of 34 wins and 24 losses. He saved his best performance for the major leagues where he played for three seasons starting in 1966 and earned an overall record of 23-16 with 43 saves and 3.00 ERA. He earned the American League Fireman of the Year Award in 1967, leading the league with 27 saves.

Unfortunately, Rojas developed arm trouble and was never the same after the 1968 season, even though he tried to make a return by pitching for the Hawaii Islanders and in the Mexican League in 1969.

The following year, Rojas was involved in an auto accident in Florida that kept him partially paralyzed and unable to walk. The accident also killed his two daughters, but his wife, whom he had married in 1966, and his son survived.

Rojas died in Los Angeles on March 23, 2002, at the age of 68 and his remains are interred at the California Inglewood Cemetery.

Year	Age	Tm	Lg	Lev
1960	26	Artesia Giants	Sophomore League	D
1961	27	Fresno Giants	California League	C
1962	28	El Paso Sun Kings	Texas League	AA
1963	29	Tacoma Giants	Pacific Coast League	AAA
1963	29	El Paso Sun Kings	Texas League	AA
1964	30	Jalisco Charros	Mexican League	AA
1964	30	Mexico		
1965	31	Jalisco Charros	Mexican League	AA
1965	31	Mexico		
1966	32	Seattle Angels	Pacific Coast League	AAA

Year	Age	Tm	Lg	Lev
1966	32	California Angels	American League	MLB
1967	33	California Angels	American League	MLB
1968	34	California Angels	American League	MLB
1969	35	Hawaii Islanders	Pacific Coast League	AAA
1969	35	Jalisco Charros	Mexican League	AAA

Diego Pablo Seguí González

Seguí played two seasons in Cuba both with the Habana Lions, with a record of 1-5 and a 2.45 ERA. The 26 games he appeared in accounted for most of his record since he appeared in only one game during his previous season, 1958-59.

His career outside of Cuba included eight seasons in the Venezuelan League winning 97 games and losing 52 (see source cited below). He played in the U.S. and Mexico from 1958 and 1985, including fifteen seasons in the majors, winning 92 games and losing 111, with

71 saves and a 3.81 ERA. His seven seasons in the minors brought an additional 55 wins and 48 losses to his record.

His accomplishments on the baseball diamond earned him the induction into the Cuban Baseball Hall of Fame in Miami in 1997.

His record clearly shows his leaving Cuba after the last season, although, one record found has him travelling from Nicaragua to the U.S. on February 24, 1962 with a visa secured in Toronto, Canada. His destination was recorded as the Kansas City organization in Kansas, even though he had played the previous season for the Hawaii team in the Pacific Coast League, a Kansas City affiliate.

Additional source: Gutiérrez, Daniel; González, Javier (2006); *Records de la Liga Venezolana de Béisbol Profesional* LVBP

Year	Age	Tm	Lg	Lev
1958	20	Tucson Cowboys	Arizona-Mexico League	C
1959	21	Pocatello A's	Pioneer League	C
1960	22	Sioux City Soos	Illinois-Indiana-Iowa League	B
1961	23	Hawaii Islanders	Pacific Coast League	AAA
1962	24	Kansas City Athletics	American League	MLB
1963	25	Kansas City Athletics	American League	MLB
1964	26	Kansas City Athletics	American League	MLB
1965	27	Kansas City Athletics	American League	MLB
1966	28	Hawaii Islanders	Pacific Coast League	AAA
1966	28	Vancouver Mounties	Pacific Coast League	AAA
1966	28	Washington Senators	American League	MLB
1967	29	Vancouver Mounties	Pacific Coast League	AAA
1967	29	Kansas City Athletics	American League	MLB
1968	30	Oakland Athletics	American League	MLB
1969	31	Seattle Pilots	American League	MLB
1970	32	Oakland Athletics	American League	MLB

Year	Age	Tm	Lg	Lev
1971	33	Oakland Athletics	American League	MLB
1972	34	Oakland Athletics	American League	MLB
1972	34	St. Louis Cardinals	National League	MLB
1973	35	St. Louis Cardinals	National League	MLB
1974	36	Boston Red Sox	American League	MLB
1975	37	Boston Red Sox	American League	MLB
1976	38	Hawaii Islanders	Pacific Coast League	AAA
1977	39	Seattle Mariners	American League	MLB
1978	40	Cordoba Cafeteros	Mexican League	AAA
1979	41	Cordoba Cafeteros	Mexican League	AAA
1980	42	Reynosa Broncos	Mexican League	AAA
1980	42	Reynosa Broncos	Mexican League (6 team season)	AAA
1981	43	Reynosa Broncos	Mexican League	AAA
1982	44	Reynosa Broncos	Mexican League	AAA
1983	45	Yucatan Leones	Mexican League	AAA
1984	46	Leon Bravos	Mexican League	AAA
1985	47	Monclova Acereros	Mexican League	AAA

Luis Clemente Tiant Jr. Vega

One of the most effective and popular Cuban born players, Luis Tiant Jr. played only one season in the Cuban League and earned the Rookie of the Year award for that last professional season. Tiant played in 30 games and completed nine of his starts, Tiant would go on to win 10 games, while losing eight. He pitched in 158.2 innings, striking out 115 and walking 90, with a 2.72 ERA.

He played a total of 23 seasons, in the majors, minors and the Mexican League.

His career outside of Cuba was no less than his outstanding beginning in Mexico. He was signed by Berto Avila who had been his father's bullpen catcher. Avila and Carlos Alberto González, who was the umpire-in-chief, had gone to Cuba looking for players, saw him pitch, and signed him to a contract even though he was under 17 years old, his father did the formal signing. As a newcomer, he did not know any of his teammates including the four Cubans on the team. Playing for the Mexico City Tigers, he won 17 games and loss 7, at the age of nineteen. All he wanted was to play professional baseball and have the opportunity to reach the majors. So, the only solution in his mind at the time was to leave Cuba, go to Mexico and see what could happen.

He left Cuba on May 25, 1961 thinking it would be for only three months, but instead, his absence lasted 46 years. Like many players at the time, you did not know who to trust, nor did you speak to anyone about it. He does not remember other players saying anything at the time. Leaving Cuba at the end of the 60-61 season, he went to Mexico to continue playing there, but the letter from his father, referred to below, changed those plans forever. He played in Mexico where he met and married his wife María, on August 12, 1961. Tiant wanted to return to Cuba to spend his honeymoon but his father, also a well-known former Cuban Pitcher, wrote him a letter the week before they were to leave indicating that professional baseball was no longer allowed. His mother, however, would visit him in Mexico in 1968. Tiant and his family lived in Mexico full time until 1974 when he moved permanently to the U.S.

His minor league record during the five seasons he played, shows he won 52 games, lost 30 and had a 3.07 ERA while completing 47 games. It was during that time, while he played in Caguas Puerto Rico, that his contract was bought by the Cleveland Indians from the Mexican League. During his nineteen seasons in the majors, Tiant won 229 games, the most of any Cuban pitcher to date, and lost 172, with a 3.30 ERA, completing 187 games. His first game was against the Yankees winning 3-0 with 11 strike outs, allowing 4 hits, in front of 30,061 fans. He was selected on three occasions to the All Star team. His lack of induction into the Hall of Fame in Cooperstown continues to be a subject of much argument as fans, especially in Boston, have continued to feel he is deserving of that honor for his performance on the mound throughout his stellar career.

Playing in the U.S., Tiant would experience continuing racism in West Virginia and South Carolina. An impact of a cultural and language barrier which at one point, due to his limited vocabulary, had him eating mostly scrambled eggs and salad for a month. He also recalls about the early days, not being allowed to eat with his teammates, and being called names, or being told they all looked like monkeys, which ended only when he left and went to his room and cried.

In 1962 he was assigned to the team in Jacksonville but pitched for only one inning giving up a walk due to a bad elbow. Coincidentally this author was outside of the same city during that time at a Cuban refugee camp for boys brought to the U.S. through the "Pedro Pan" program.

During the 1968 season, Tiant had the ERA record with 21 wins, and 9 shutouts. But his parents were away. He recalls how a letter from his dad where he wrote "you don't care anymore," made him cry. He would learn later on, that when they watched him on Cuban television, his mother would touch the screen to make some kind of *contact* with her son. This is a poignant example of the suffering that these players endured during that period in their young lives. A much-publicized story about his parents coming to see him tells how then Senator George McGovern brought a letter from Massachusetts

Senator Edward Brooke Jr. to Fidel Castro requesting his approval for his parents to travel. Happily, they did and were able to see him play in the majors. His father, who died in 1976, never returned to Cuba and his mother sadly passed away two days later while waiting for her husband's memorial service.

Today, Tiant continues to live with his wife María and his children while working for the Boston Red Sox, among other business ventures, doing community work and supporting a number of charities. He can be easily found during Spring Training with the Red Sox in Ft. Myers Florida and before Red Sox games in Boston, typically surrounded by fans of all ages.

Additional sources:

Hock Jonathan, "The Lost Son of Havana"
Hockfilms New York. 2009
Nowlin Bill, Tan Cecilia eds.
SABR the Red Sox team that saved baseball
Luis Tiant Jr, interviews with author.

Year	Age	Tm	Lg	Lev
1959	18	Mexico City Tigres	Mexican League	AA
1960	19	Mexico City Tigres	Mexican League	AA
1961	20	Mexico City Tigres	Mexican League	AA
1962	21	Charleston Indians	Eastern League	A
1962	21	Jacksonville Suns	International League	AAA
1963	22	Burlington Indians	Carolina League	A
1964	23	Portland Beavers	Pacific Coast League	AAA
1964	23	Cleveland Indians	American League	MLB
1965	24	Cleveland Indians	American League	MLB
1966	25	Cleveland Indians	American League	MLB
1967	26	Cleveland Indians	American League	MLB

Year	Age	Tm	Lg	Lev
1968	27	Cleveland Indians	American League	MLB
1969	28	Cleveland Indians	American League	MLB
1970	29	Minnesota Twins	American League	MLB
1971	30	Richmond Braves	International League	AAA
1971	30	Louisville Colonels	International League	AAA
1971	30	Boston Red Sox	American League	MLB
1972	31	Boston Red Sox	American League	MLB
1973	32	Boston Red Sox	American League	MLB
1974	33	Boston Red Sox	American League	MLB
1975	34	Boston Red Sox	American League	MLB
1976	35	Boston Red Sox	American League	MLB
1977	36	Boston Red Sox	American League	MLB
1978	37	Boston Red Sox	American League	MLB
1979	38	New York Yankees	American League	MLB
1980	39	New York Yankees	American League	MLB
1981	40	Portland Beavers	Pacific Coast League	AAA
1981	40	Pittsburgh Pirates	National League	MLB
1982	41	Tabasco Plataneros	Mexican League	AAA
1982	41	California Angels	American League	MLB
1983	42	Mexico City Diablos Rojos	Mexican League	AAA
1983	42	Yucatan Leones	Mexican League	AAA

René (Látigo) Gutiérrez Valdés

Látigo, one of my favorite players as a young fan for his unusual (whip-like wind-up, played with Almendares during that last season, his eighth in the Cuban League. He also played for Cienfuegos and Marianao, with a combined record of 34 wins and 38 losses in 213 games and striking out 346 batters while walking 294. During his

time with the Habana Lions he played in 28 games winning five, and losing 6 during 56.2 innings, with a 5.09 ERA.

He was part of the 1956 Caribbean Series with Cienfuegos, pitching in two games and winning one with ten strikeouts and two walks.

He played professional baseball outside of Cuba from 1952 through the 1964 season including one season in Mexico. He made the majors in 1957 with the Brooklyn Dodgers for five games, where he had a record of 1-1. His minor league combined record included 152 wins and a 3.60 ERA.

His birthday is a subject of speculation, but his official travel papers from Cuba in February of 1959 to join the Dodger organization, had his birthday listed as 1928.

Following the end of the Cuban 60-61 season he played in the U.S. and Mexico. He passed away on March 15, 2008 in Miami, Florida.

Year	Age	Tm	Lg	Lev
1952	23	Juarez Indios	Arizona-Texas League	C
1953	24	Juarez Indios	Arizona-Texas League	C
1954	25	Pueblo Dodgers	Western League	A
1954	25	Bakersfield Indians	California League	C

Year	Age	Tm	Lg	Lev
1955	26	St. Paul Saints	American Association	AAA
1956	27	Portland Beavers	Pacific Coast League	Opn
1957	28	Montreal Royals	International League	AAA
1957	28	Brooklyn Dodgers	National League	MLB
1958	29	Montreal Royals	International League	AAA
1959	30	Montreal Royals	International League	AAA
1960	31	Montreal Royals	International League	AAA
1961	32	Spokane Indians	Pacific Coast League	AAA
1962	33	Monterrey Sultanes	Mexican League	AA
1963	34	Monterrey Sultanes	Mexican League	AA
1964	35	Yucatan Venados	Mexican Southeast League	A

Lázaro Ramón Gonzalo (Cholly) Naranjo

Another player who also played for Almendares during that last season pitched for the Lions in nine games and had a record of 2-2 in 30 innings.

Cholly as he was known, played nine seasons in Cuba, 8 plus with Almendares, pitching in a 152 games with 234 strikeouts, 196 walks and a 3.60 ERA. He played twice in the Caribbean Series with Almendares during 3 games, with a 1-0 record and an outstanding 1.64 ERA. In 1953, he played for the Havana Cubans during 29 games, striking out 83 batters and walking 60 while winning 8 games, losing 6 with a 3.77 ERA.

Outside of Cuba his playing career spanned from 1952 through 1961, winning 72 games in the minors as he pursued his professional career and, ultimately, reached the major leagues with the Pittsburgh Pirates in 1956 for a brief period where he had a 1-2 record.

A memorable experience for Cholly took place in 1954 as then President Ike Eisenhower opened the season throwing the first baseball that was caught by Johnny Sain. According to Stars and Stripes, the President then made a second throw that was caught by Naranjo who promptly threw it back to the President who caught it and then proceeded to throw it back to Cholly. It was said to be an unprecedented move of the President playing catch with a player, and an experience that Cholly would never forget.

Following the end of the 1961 season, Cholly Naranjo obtained a visa via Mexico travelling to the U.S. on March 28, 1961 where he played for Jacksonville and Houston before concluding it was time to retire due to arm problems and so he returned to Cuba. He stayed for 30 years, working at the Habana's Sports City as an athletic teacher. Later, in 1991, he came back to the U.S., but returned to Cuba in 1993. He once again returned in 1995 to the U.S., until the present time.

Additional sources:

Cholly Naranjo, personal interview with author, February 2016.
Ramírez José SABR BioProject Cholly Naranjo
Stars and Stripes April 14, 1954 Volume 12 Number 359

Year	Age	Tm	Lg	Lev
1952	17	Chattanooga Lookouts	Southern Association	AA
1952	17	Richmond Colts	Piedmont League	B
1953	18	Havana Cubans	Florida International League	B
1953	18	Chattanooga Lookouts	Southern Association	AA
1954	19	Charlotte Hornets	South Atlantic League	A
1954	19	Chattanooga Lookouts	Southern Association	AA
1955	20	Lincoln Chiefs	Western League	A
1955	20	Hollywood Stars	Pacific Coast League	Opn
1956	21	Hollywood Stars	Pacific Coast League	Opn
1956	21	Pittsburgh Pirates	National League	MLB
1957	22	Columbus Jets	International League	AAA
1958	23	Columbus Jets	International League	AAA
1959	24	Columbus Jets	International League	AAA
1959	24	Nashville Volunteers	Southern Association	AA
1960	25	Nashville Volunteers	Southern Association	AA
1961	26	Jacksonville Jets	South Atlantic League	A
1961	26	Houston Buffs	American Association	AAA

Catchers

Roberto (Musulungo) Gutiérrez Herrera

His name appears in some quarters as Roberto Herrera, but he is also shown as Roberto Gutiérrez leading to some confusion and making the research on him somewhat challenging.

However, Musulungo was a nickname that was given to him by a friend who told him he looked like another friend whom they also called Musulungo. Thereafter, they began calling him Musulungo, and still to this day (see source cited below).

Musulungo played five seasons for both Almendares and the Habana teams with a low batting average of .198 in 263 appearances at the plate. A scout who wished to sign Musulungo was faced with the fact that a decision to do so required his mother's approval. According to Gutierrez she took almost two months to make the decision (see source cited below). During the last season, he came to bat 124 times and hit a bit higher than his average with .226.

His career outside of Cuba spanned from 1956 in Gainesville of the Florida League through 1975, which included seven seasons in the minors, where he hit .263, and almost exclusively in Mexico from 1965 on. During the 1967, 68, 1970 and 71 seasons he played in the Venezuelan League, batting .306.

Towards the end of his playing career, in 1975, Musulungo became an umpire for 24 years.

He has not returned to Cuba leaving after the 60-61 season, and has indicated that there is no particular reason to return, and that his children also have no interest in doing so.

He lives in Miami with his son Roberto. Ricky Gutierrez, a former major league player is his other son.

Additional sources:

ElUniversal.com
Ecured.com
EcuRed Antonio Guerra Silva

Year	Age	Tm	Lg	Lev
1956	17	Gainesville G-Men	Florida State League	D
1957	18	Daytona Beach Islanders	Florida State League	D
1958	19	Hobbs Cardinals	Sophomore League	D
1958	19	Stockton Ports	California League	C
1959	20	Winnipeg Goldeyes	Northern League	C
1960	21	Dallas-Fort Worth Rangers	American Association	AAA
1960	21	Columbus Jets	International League	AAA

Year	Age	Tm	Lg	Lev
1961	22	Columbus Jets	International League	AAA
1961	22	San Juan/Charleston Marlins	International League	AAA
1962	23	Rochester Red Wings	International League	AAA
1962	23	Atlanta Crackers	International League	AAA
1963	24	Erie Sailors	New York-Pennsylvania League	A
1963	24	Auburn Mets	New York-Pennsylvania League	A
1964	25	Asheville Tourists	Southern League	AA
1965	26	Reynosa Broncs	Mexican League	AA
1966	27	Reynosa Broncs	Mexican League	AA
1966	27	Charlotte Hornets	Southern League	AA
1967	28	York White Roses	Eastern League	AA
1968	29	Puebla Pericos	Mexican League	AAA
1969	30	Puebla Pericos	Mexican League	AAA
1970	31	Yucatan Leones	Mexican League	AAA
1971	32	Yucatan Leones	Mexican League	AAA
1972	33	Yucatan Leones	Mexican League	AAA
1973	34	Yucatan Leones	Mexican League	AAA
1974	35	Tampico Alijadores	Mexican League	AAA
1975	36	Coahuila Mineros	Mexican League	AAA

Rafael Miguel (Son) Noble Magee

Noble played a total of 16 seasons in the Cuban League, mostly with the Cienfuegos squad. His career began in his native Province of Oriente, playing for the Mineros. Soon after, he was signed by the Habana Lions, playing his first game in 1942. After playing for Cienfuegos he returned to play for the Lions in his last season hitting a low .171 in

123 times at bat. His overall record showed 2773 times at bat, hitting a more acceptable .256 batting average. His defensive skills made up for whatever weaknesses he had at the plate, since he possessed a great arm and ability with the glove. An interesting detail about Noble is that he played for the first televised game in Cuba on October 31, 1959, between Cienfuegos and Habana.

Playing in three Caribbean Series, he excelled at the plate hitting .314 in 35 times at bat. He first played in 1956 where he was named the Most Valuable Player and was the batting leader. He then went back in 1958 with the Marianao team, followed by the 1960 series with Cienfuegos. All three tournaments were won by the Cuban squad. He played two seasons for the Cuban Sugar Kings in 1954, hitting for an average of .271 in 772 times at the plate.

In the U.S., he played in the Negro League during the 1940s with the New York Cubans from 1945 through 1948. In 1950 he played for the Oakland Triple A team, slamming 15 home runs and batting .316. He was also part of a major brawl where he suffered a broken nose. His minor league career went on for a total of twelve seasons, hitting .274. He made it to the major leagues with the New York Giants during three different seasons with a batting average of .218. Rafael Noble was inducted into the Cuban Baseball Hall of Fame in Miami, Florida.

Noble arrived in the U.S. on April 8, 1961 from Mexico to play what would be his last professional season at the age of 42 with the Houston Triple A team of the Chicago Cubs. However, he returned to Cuba after playing only five games and became a coach in Cuba, a job that disappeared after two years. He stayed in his home country until 1971 and then moved to New York City while his daughter, Daisy, stayed behind in Cuba. In New York he purchased a liquor store which he kept until his death that was brought about by complications of his diabetic condition. Born in 1919, he passed away on May 9, 1998 at the age of 79.

Additional sources:

Betancourt Hernández Aldo, *Historia de mi Pueblo*
Self Published 2008,
Costello, Rory SABR.org BioProject, Ray Noble
Romero Esteban, *Un grande de la receptoría*
by Esteban Romero SwingCompleto,
http://thekingdomofbaseball.proboards.com/thread/1861/tendremos-reescribir-historia-baseball-cubano?page=4#ixzz4LStUnyCg

Year	Age	Tm	Lg	Lev
1945	26	New York Cubans	Negro National League	NgM
1946	27	New York Cubans	Negro National League	NgM
1947	28	New York Cubans	Negro National League	NgM
1948	29	New York Cubans	Negro National League	NgM
1949	30	Jersey City Giants	International League	AAA
1950	31	Oakland Oaks	Pacific Coast League	AAA
1951	32	New York Giants	National League	MLB
1952	33	Oakland Oaks	Pacific Coast League	Opn
1952	33	New York Giants	National League	MLB
1953	34	Minneapolis Millers	American Association	AAA
1953	34	New York Giants	National League	MLB
1954	35	Havana Sugar Kings	International League	AAA
1955	36	Havana Sugar Kings	International League	AAA
1956	37	Columbus Jets	International League	AAA
1957	38	Buffalo Bisons	International League	AAA
1958	39	Buffalo Bisons	International League	AAA
1959	40	Houston Buffs	American Association	AAA
1960	41	Houston Buffs	American Association	AAA
1961	42	Houston Buffs	American Association	AAA

Infielders

Juan Francisco (Panchón) Herrera Villavicencio

Panchón Herrera was this author's favorite player in the Cuban League growing up. I was honored to be asked by SABR to pencil his biography for the BioProject, which is the source for most of this modest effort.

Herrera played seven seasons in Cuba with the Cienfuegos and the Habana teams hitting .254, with 42 home runs, 49 doubles and 10 triples. He was clearly a slugger, though he showed good running skills, stealing 24 bases during that time. During his last season in Cuba, his batting average was a robust .290, hitting ten home runs with 41 runs batted in. His performance earned him a well-deserved induction into the Cuban Baseball Hall of Fame in Miami in 1997.

Outside of Cuba, he played during 22 different seasons, from 1955 through 1974, fourteen in the minors, hitting 239 home runs, 752 RBIs, and batting .291. He had three seasons in the majors, for the Philadelphia Phillies, batting .271 with 31 homeruns and 128 RBIs. He also played five seasons in the Mexican League. During three seasons in 1969, 72 and 74, Herrera managed teams in the U.S. and Mexico with a record 176 wins and 208 losses.

Late in life he spent time driving children to school and was said to be loved by all of them.

He left Cuba in 1961, securing a visa with the assistance of the Philadelphia team, with fellow players Tony Taylor, and Marcelino López.

Panchón was born in 1934 and passed away in Miami, Florida on April 28, 2005.

Additional sources:

Omelis Hongamen, telephone interview with author.
Ramírez José SABR BioProject *"Pancho Herrera"* (http://sabr.org/bioproj/person)

Year	Age	Tm	Lg	Lev
1955	21	Schenectady Blue Jays	Eastern League	A
1955	21	Syracuse Chiefs	International League	AAA
1956	22	Schenectady Blue Jays	Eastern League	A
1957	23	Miami Marlins	International League	AAA
1958	24	Miami Marlins	International League	AAA
1958	24	Philadelphia Phillies	National League	MLB
1959	25	Buffalo Bisons	International League	AAA
1960	26	Philadelphia Phillies	National League	MLB
1961	27	Philadelphia Phillies	National League	MLB
1962	28	Buffalo Bisons	International League	AAA
1963	29	Columbus Jets	International League	AAA
1964	30	Columbus Jets	International League	AAA
1965	31	Columbus Jets	International League	AAA
1966	32	Columbus Jets	International League	AAA
1966	32	Syracusc Chicfs	International League	AAA
1967	33	Dallas-Fort Worth Spurs	Texas League	AA

Year	Age	Tm	Lg	Lev
1967	33	Reynosa Broncs	Mexican League	AAA
1968	34	Ciudad Del Carmen Cameroneros	Mexican Southeast League	A
1968	34	Miami Marlins	Florida State League	A
1969	35	Ciudad Del Carmen Cameroneros	Mexican Southeast League	A
1969	35	Miami Marlins	Florida State League	A
1970	36	Saltillo Saraperos	Mexican League	AAA
1972	38	Key West Conchs	Florida State League	A
1974	40	Tampico Alijadores	Mexican League	AAA

Cristobal Rigoberto (Minnie) Mendoza Carreras

An infielder for the Habana Lions, Mendoza played two seasons, hitting .284 in 88 times at bat. During the last season in Cuba his average of .297 came during 74 times at the plate. He played four games for the 1956 Cuban Sugar Kings, with only eleven times at bat.

Mendoza was signed with the Cincinnati Reds in 1954, playing professionally through the 1973 season. During his 19-year minor league career he hit for average, at a .290 clip but, nevertheless, was not able to make it to the majors except for one season with the Minnesota Twins in 1970 for only sixteen games, hitting .188 at the age of 36 years old. Mendoza managed during three different seasons, two in Mexico and one in the Florida Single A League, where his teams had a 250-393 win and loss record.

He was known to help his fellow Cuban players by cooking meals for them and planning social gatherings, all of which had a profound and positive effect on those arriving without family or friends and on limited assistance while trying to cope with a new culture and environment.

Upon leaving Cuba in 1961, his father told him, "You don't have no future here. You better leave. It's the best thing for your family.

As soon as possible, and that is what I did". He never saw his father, Ricardo, again. He died in 1969. Mendoza had also left behind his wife, Julia, and daughter, and did not see them again until 1964, in Nicaragua, and then in the U.S., in Charlotte, in 1965, when they arrived from Spain. He returned to Cuba in 1979 to visit his mother and five siblings, and in 1984 for his mother's funeral. He would not be the only Cuban, in and out of baseball that returned home during those difficult moments and experiences, given the political realities and government controls existing at the time, and that still exist today.

A final note; his date of birth during his travel from La Habana to Fernandina Beach to join the Charlotte squad was listed as December 3, 1934. This differs from the November 16, 1933 date found in other publications.

Additional sources:

Tony Oliva by Thom Henninger, University of Minnesota Press Minneapolis London 2015 page 7

Tony Oliva by Thom Henninger, University of Minnesota Press Minneapolis London page 196-7

Year	Age	Tm	Lg	Lev
1954	20	Nogales Yaquis	Arizona-Texas League	C
1954	20	Miami Beach Flamingos/ Greater Miami Flamingos	Florida International League	B
1955	21	Portsmouth Merrimacs	Piedmont League	B
1956	22	Havana Sugar Kings	International League	AAA
1956	22	Nuevo Laredo Tecolotes	Mexican League	AA
1957	23	Albuquerque Dukes	Western League	A
1957	23	Wausau Lumberjacks	Northern League	C
1958	24	Missoula Timberjacks	Pioneer League	C
1959	25	Missoula Timberjacks	Pioneer League	C
1960	26	Charlotte Hornets	South Atlantic League	A

Year	Age	Tm	Lg	Lev
1961	27	Charlotte Hornets	South Atlantic League	A
1962	28	Vancouver Mounties	Pacific Coast League	AAA
1963	29	Charlotte Hornets	South Atlantic League	AA
1964	30	Charlotte Hornets	Southern League	AA
1965	31	Charlotte Hornets	Southern League	AA
1966	32	Charlotte Hornets	Southern League	AA
1967	33	Charlotte Hornets	Southern League	AA
1968	34	Charlotte Hornets	Southern League	AA
1969	35	Denver Bears	American Association	AAA
1970	36	Evansville Triplets	American Association	AAA
1970	36	Minnesota Twins	American League	MLB
1971	37	Charlotte Hornets	Dixie Association	AA
1972	38	Charlotte Hornets	Southern League	AA
1973	39	Monterrey Sultanes	Mexican League	AAA

Ramón Patricio (Witty) Witremundo Ramos Quintana

This third baseman for the Lions hit a weak .224 during his last and eighth professional season in Cuba in 143 times at bat. Having played for Almendares, and Marianao previously, his batting average was equally low, hitting .212. He played during two Caribbean Series, in 1957 and 58, batting .200 in 20 times at bat.

His average was higher when he played for the Triple A Cuban Sugar Kings in 1957 and 58, hitting .241 in 580 times at the plate. Quintana's career in the minors began in 1951 and ran through the 1959 season when his batting average was .262 in 1056 games.

Following the end of the 60-61 season in Cuba, he played in Mexico through 1964 and stayed in that country. He passed away on February 16, 2003.

Additional source: Iván Davis, telephone interview with author, January 31, 2018.

Year	Age	Tm	Lg	Lev
1951	18	Galveston White Caps	Gulf Coast League	B
1951	18	Big Spring Broncs	Longhorn League	C
1952	19	Big Spring Broncs	Longhorn League	C
1953	20	Wichita Indians	Western League	A
1953	20	Anderson Rebels	Tri-State League	B
1954	21	San Antonio Missions	Texas League	AA
1955	22	San Antonio Missions	Texas League	AA
1956	23	San Antonio Missions	Texas League	AA
1956	23	Vancouver Mounties	Pacific Coast League	Opn
1957	24	Havana Sugar Kings	International League	AAA
1958	25	Savannah Redlegs	South Atlantic League	A
1958	25	Havana Sugar Kings	International League	AAA
1958	25	Nashville Volunteers	Southern Association	AA
1959	26	Monterrey Sultanes	Mexican League	AA
1959	26	Savannah Reds	South Atlantic League	A
1960	27	Veracruz Aguilas	Mexican League	AA
1961	28	Veracruz Aguilas	Mexican League	AA
1962	29	Veracruz Aguilas	Mexican League	AA
1963	30	Veracruz Aguilas	Mexican League	AA
1964	31	Veracruz Aguilas	Mexican League	AA

Héctor Antonio Rodríguez Ordenana

The Cuban League had the benefit that last season of having Rodríguez play eighteen of his nineteen seasons in Cuba. Primarily with the Almendares team, this slick fielder shortstop batted .262 in his last season in 260 times at bat, consistent with his .263 batting average for

all those nineteen seasons. He was named the Rookie of the Year for the 1942-43 season.

He played in four Caribbean Series with 83 times at bat and batted a robust .361 average.

His career outside of Cuba ran the gamut. He started in 1943, playing in Mexico, only to join the New York Cubans in the Negro League the following year, and then returned to Mexico until 1951. He then entered the U.S. minors at the age of 31 and had a .281 batting average. By the next year, at age 32, he played in the majors for the Chicago White Sox in 124 games and batted .265. His career spanned 23 seasons including also managing in the Mexican League from 1964 through 1976, with his teams having a record of 468 wins and 416 losses.

It is not surprising to note that he was inducted into the Cuban Baseball of Fame in 1983.

Rodríguez left Cuba via Mexico, arriving in Los Angeles on March 23, 1961 on his way to join the San Diego baseball team. In 1970, at the Miami District Court, the city in which he lived, Hector Rodríguez became a U.S. citizen. Naturalization papers signed by Rodríguez show a different date of birth-August 20, 1923)-and a different city (Guanajay, Pinar del Rio)-that is different than published elsewhere-June 13, 1920, in the town of Alquizar.

Hector Rodríguez passed away on September 1, 2003 in Cancun, Quintana Roo in Mexico.

Year	Age	Tm	Lg	Lev
1943	23	Mexico City Diablos Rojos	Mexican League	Ind
1944	24	New York Cubans	Negro National League	NgM
1945	25	Tampico Alijadores	Mexican League	Ind
1946	26	Tampico Alijadores	Mexican League	Ind
1947	27	Tampico Alijadores	Mexican League	Ind
1948	28	Veracruz Azules	Mexican League	Ind
1948	28	Tampico Alijadores	Mexican League	Ind
1949	29	San Luis Potosi Tuneros	Mexican League	Ind
1950	30	Veracruz Azules	Mexican League	Ind
1951	31	Montreal Royals	International League	AAA
1951	31	San Luis Potosi Tuneros	Mexican League	Ind
1952	32	San Luis Potosi Tuneros	Mexican League	Ind
1952	32	Chicago White Sox	American League	MLB
1953	33	Syracuse Chiefs	International League	AAA
1954	34	Toronto Maple Leafs	International League	AAA
1955	35	Toronto Maple Leafs	International League	AAA
1956	36	Toronto Maple Leafs	International League	AAA
1957	37	Toronto Maple Leafs	International League	AAA
1958	38	Toronto Maple Leafs	International League	AAA
1959	39	Toronto Maple Leafs	International League	AAA
1960	40	San Diego Padres	Pacific Coast League	AAA
1961	41	San Diego Padres	Pacific Coast League	AAA

Year	Age	Tm	Lg	Lev
1962	42	Mexico City Diablos Rojos	Mexican League	AA
1963	43	Mexico City Diablos Rojos	Mexican League	AA
1964	44	Campeche Pirates	Mexican Southeast League	A
1966	46	Tabasco Plataneros	Mexican Southeast League	A

Octavio Victor (Cuqui/Cookie) Rojas Rivas

In that last season in Cuba, Cuqui Rojas started out playing with Cienfuegos but was traded early on, and played most of his 43 games with the Lions, leading the league with a .322 batting average in 264 times at bat. This sure-handed second baseman played four seasons in Cuba, primarily with Cienfuegos, batting .285 with 134 singles. He played in the 1960 Caribbean Series in two games and seven times at bat, hitting .429.

During 1959 and 1960, he played for the Cuban Sugar Kings where his average was a low .229. He also played in the Little World Series in 1959 with no hits in three times at the plate.

Outside of the Cuban League, Rojas played from 1956 through the 1977 season. In his seven seasons in the minors, he batted .255, playing in 785 games. His major league career went on for sixteen seasons, playing in 1822 games while hitting .263. He was selected for the 1965, 1971, 72 and 73 All Star Teams where he had a home run and two RBIs in three times at bat. A major accomplishment in his career was to be named the manager of a major league baseball team, which he did for three different seasons with California, Florida and Toronto ending with a 235 win and 251 loss record. He was recognized as a member of the Cuban Baseball Hall of Fame in Miami, Florida and in 2011 was inducted into the Hispanic Heritage Baseball Museum Hall of Fame.

Octavio Rojas told me in our interview how-in yet another version of the same story- at the Tropical Park players were gathered together and told there would be no professional baseball in Cuba early on, and so players knew that 60-61 would be the last professional season in Cuba. His own choice was stated as a simple choice, since he wanted to play professional baseball and that was no longer possible in his native country. His nickname "Cuqui" (given by his mother) was anglicized to Cookie (both pronounced the same way) and he is currently known by both.

He, like many others, left in 1961 via Mexico preceded by his pregnant wife with their daughter in February even though a different report indicates that he returned to Cuba "to collect his pregnant wife and young child…" As with most players, the adaptation process to a new country, culture and language was very difficult (see source cited below). Others that did not leave at the time, like Tony Castaño and Fermín Guerra, were said to have family and or business responsibilities that kept them there for a longer period of time. Rojas lives today in the Southwest Florida area.

Additional sources:

Octavio Rojas, telephone interview with author, November 30, 2016.

Harris John R. and Burbridge Jr. John J. The Short but Exciting Life of the Havana Sugar Kings The National Pastime SABR 2016
Cardona, Joe and González Ralf "Major League Cuban" a co-production of South Florida PBS and Royal Palms Films 2017.

Year	Age	Tm	Lg	Lev
1956	17	West Palm Beach Sun Chiefs	Florida State League	D
1957	18	Wausau Lumberjacks	Northern League	C
1958	19	Savannah Redlegs	South Atlantic League	A
1959	20	Havana Sugar Kings	International League	AAA
1960	21	Havana Sugar Kings/ Jersey City Jerseys	International League	AAA
1961	22	Jersey City Jerseys	International League	AAA
1962	23	Dallas-Fort Worth Rangers	American Association	AAA
1962	23	Cincinnati Reds	National League	MLB
1963	24	Philadelphia Phillies	National League	MLB
1964	25	Philadelphia Phillies	National League	MLB
1965	26	Philadelphia Phillies	National League	MLB
1966	27	Philadelphia Phillies	National League	MLB
1967	28	Philadelphia Phillies	National League	MLB
1968	29	Philadelphia Phillies	National League	MLB
1969	30	Philadelphia Phillies	National League	MLB
1970	31	St. Louis Cardinals	National League	MLB
1970	31	Kansas City Royals	American League	MLB
1971	32	Kansas City Royals	American League	MLB
1972	33	Kansas City Royals	American League	MLB
1973	34	Kansas City Royals	American League	MLB
1974	35	Kansas City Royals	American League	MLB
1975	36	Kansas City Royals	American League	MLB

Year	Age	Tm	Lg	Lev
1976	37	Kansas City Royals	American League	MLB
1977	38	Kansas City Royals	American League	MLB

Lázaro (Chico) Terry

Terry played four seasons in the Cuban League, all with the Habana Lions, starting in 1953, hitting .211 in only 57 times at bat. The 60-61 season was not substantially different as he came to the plate only 24 times but was able to have a very good average (.292).

Playing outside of Cuba, he began his career in 1953 with the Ogden Reds of the Pioneer League and ended in 1962 in the Mexican League. His batting average in the minors was .286 reaching the Triple A level in 1959 and 1960 where he batted .271 for the Indianapolis Indians.

After the end of the 60-61 season, he played in Mexico in 1961 and 62, which simply means he went on with his professional career during that time but ultimately stayed in Cuba. See source cited below.

Additional source: Iván Davis, telephone interview with author, January 31, 2018.

Year	Age	Tm	Lg	Lev
1953	20	Ogden Reds	Pioneer League	C
1954	21	Columbia Reds	South Atlantic League	A
1954	21	Ogden Reds	Pioneer League	C
1955	22	Ogden Reds	Pioneer League	C
1956	23	Syracuse Chiefs	Eastern League	A
1957	24	Port Arthur/Temple Redlegs	Big State League	B
1957	24	Durham Bulls	Carolina League	B
1958	25	Albuquerque Dukes	Western League	A
1959	26	Charleston ChaSox	South Atlantic League	A

Year	Age	Tm	Lg	Lev
1959	26	Indianapolis Indians	American Association	AAA
1960	27	Indianapolis Indians	American Association	AAA
1961	28	Monterrey Sultanes	Mexican League	AA
1962	29	Monterrey Sultanes	Mexican League	AA

Outfielders

Alberto Asdrubal Baró Hernández

Born in Mayarí, Holguín, on November 28, 1928, Baró played a total of nine seasons in Cuba for the Almendares, Marianao and Habana teams. He came to the plate 914 times, hitting .248. In his last professional season in Cuba, he came to bat only 22 times, hitting a low .136, which would reflect a similar average in his three appearances during the Caribbean Series in 1954, 57 and 58 (.148). His years with the Cuban Sugar Kings in 1954-56 were more rewarding at the plate with a .289 batting average. During an interview with Ben Strauss, (see source cited below) Baró, said there was a song written about him with one line declaring, "Some men can give you beautiful children, but only Baró can give you a hit."

In 1947, he was a member of the Jalsia club of the Pedro Betancourt League. He then moved to the Matanzas team in the Santa Clara Central League in Cuba, where he was the batting leader, hitting over .400. In 1951 he played in the California League for the Santa Barbara Dodgers, where he batted a strong .300 and continued his career through the minors and the Mexican League, ending in 1963. During his playing time in the minor leagues he hit for average with .294, playing mostly at the Double and Triple A level.

His travel record to the U.S. in March of 1959 to join the Houston Oilers shows a date of birth of November 26, 1926 which differs from other publications citing November 21, 1928.

Baró stayed in Cuba, but also played in Mexico after the end of the 1960-61 season. There he played through the 1964 season, ending his active career as a player with the Campeche team. In 1964 he became the hitting coach for the Azucareros in the IV National Series in Cuba and later became the manager during the V Series.

He passed away in La Habana Cuba on November 18, 2014.

Additional sources:

In Havana, Remembering a Minor League Championship by Ben Strauss March 23, 2013 Asdrúbal Baró: Un pelotero admirado y querido by Jorge Rivas Trabajadores 20 November 2014.

Year	Age	Tm	Lg	Lev
1951	24	Santa Barbara Dodgers	California League	C
1952	25	Santa Barbara Dodgers	California League	C
1953	26	Miami Sun Sox	Florida International League	B
1954	27	Charleston Senators	American Association	AAA
1954	27	Havana Sugar Kings	International League	AAA
1955	28	Havana Sugar Kings	International League	AAA
1956	29	Havana Sugar Kings	International League	AAA
1956	29	Omaha Cardinals	American Association	AAA
1957	30	Omaha Cardinals	American Association	AAA
1957	30	Houston Buffaloes	Texas League	AA
1958	31	San Antonio Missions	Texas League	AA
1958	31	Houston Buffaloes	Texas League	AA
1959	32	San Antonio Missions	Texas League	AA
1959	32	Omaha Cardinals	American Association	AAA
1959	32	Poza Rica Petroleros	Mexican League	AA
1959	32	Nuevo Laredo Tecolotes	Mexican League	AA
1960	33	Veracruz Aguilas	Mexican League	AA
1961	34	Veracruz Aguilas	Mexican League	AA
1962	35	Veracruz Aguilas	Mexican League	AA

Year	Age	Tm	Lg	Lev
1963	36	Veracruz Aguilas	Mexican League	AA
1964	37	Campeche Pirates	Mexican Southeast League	A

Pedro D. Cardenal

For his last professional season in Cuba, Cardenal had a batting average of .272 in 213 times at bat. This was similar to his average for all seven seasons he played in his country. When playing those seasons for Cienfuegos and Habana, he came to bat 1229 times, hitting .262. In 1956 he played in the Caribbean Series but had no hits in six times at bat.

His career outside of Cuba began in 1953 for a total of eight seasons in the minors, hitting .299. In addition, he played a total of six seasons in Mexico, from the 1959 through the 1964 season.

From all accounts it appears that the brother of major league player José Cardenal stayed in Mexico after his career ended, passing away in an auto accident.

As a final note, travel records continue to shift in this particular case. On his arrival to the U.S. on March 23, 1958, his birthday is listed as December 23, 1933. This is two years older than it appears elsewhere. And the place of birth is also listed as Matanzas, not La Habana.

Year	Age	Tm	Lg	Lev
1953	17	Sherman-Denison Twins	Sooner State League	D
1954	18	Duluth Dukes	Northern League	C
1955	19	Winnipeg Goldeyes	Northern League	C
1956	20	Winnipeg Goldeyes	Northern League	C
1957	21	Columbus Foxes	South Atlantic League	A
1957	21	Winston-Salem Red Birds	Carolina League	B
1958	22	Winston-Salem Red Birds	Carolina League	B

Year	Age	Tm	Lg	Lev
1958	22	York White Roses	Eastern League	A
1959	23	Nuevo Laredo Tecolotes	Mexican League	AA
1960	24	Puebla Pericos	Mexican League	AA
1961	25	Puebla Pericos	Mexican League	AA
1962	26	Puebla Pericos	Mexican League	AA
1963	27	Puebla Pericos	Mexican League	AA
1964	28	Campeche Pirates	Mexican Southeast League	A
1964	28	Puebla Pericos	Mexican League	AA

Daniel Morejón Torres

A strong batting average during his last professional season in Cuba batting .289, Morejón came to bat 256 times. This was his fourth season in the Cuba League, starting in 1956, hitting .281 with 798 appearances at the plate. He was named the Rookie of the year during the 1956-57 season when he batted .330.

He played for the Cuban Sugar Kings for six seasons, from 1954 through 1960, hitting .260 with 1767 times at bat. He led the Little World Series in 1959, playing in all seven games with 6 runs, 11 hits, 2 doubles, 7 RBIs and a .407 batting average, and driving in the winning run in Games 6 and 7 for the Kings.

Daniel Morejón began his career outside of Cuba in 1954 with the Portsmouth team in the Piedmont League. He remained in the minor league system through the 1963 season, hitting .275 in 1299 games. An exception to this was 1958 where he had a 12-game appearance in the major leagues with the Cincinnati Reds hitting only .192. He played in the Mexican league for nine seasons, from 1964 through the 1972 season. His contributions to the game led to his induction as a member of the Cuban Baseball Hall of Fame in Miami, Florida.

He left Cuba via Mexico arriving to the U.S. on March 17, 1961. However he seems to have returned to Cuba after the season ended, for he traveled from La Habana to Managua, Nicaragua on November 12, 1961, only to return to the U.S. the following February 6, 1962 to join the Jacksonville Suns.

Again it is worth noting that his travel papers from all those years reflect a date of birth of 1928, a couple of years older than those shown elsewhere.

Morejón passed away on April 27, 2009 in Miami Florida where he had worked for thirty years at the end of his career maintaining the baseball fields at Tropical Park.

Additional source: hitzoneinc.com.

Year	Age	Tm	Lg	Lev
1954	23	Portsmouth Merrimacs	Piedmont League	B
1954	23	Miami Beach Flamingos/ Greater Miami Flamingos	Florida International League	B
1954	23	Havana Sugar Kings	International League	AAA
1955	24	High Point-Thomasville Hi-Toms	Carolina League	B
1956	25	Havana Sugar Kings	International League	AAA
1956	25	Savannah Redlegs	South Atlantic League	A
1957	26	Havana Sugar Kings	International League	AAA
1958	27	Havana Sugar Kings	International League	AAA
1958	27	Cincinnati Redlegs	National League	MLB
1959	28	Havana Sugar Kings	International League	AAA
1960	29	Havana Sugar Kings/ Jersey City Jerseys	International League	AAA
1961	30	Jersey City Jerseys	International League	AAA
1962	31	Jacksonville Suns	International League	AAA
1963	32	Jacksonville Suns	International League	AAA
1964	33	Puebla Pericos	Mexican League	AA

Year	Age	Tm	Lg	Lev
1965	34	Puebla Pericos	Mexican League	AA
1966	35	Puebla Pericos	Mexican League	AA
1967	36	Reynosa Broncs	Mexican League	AAA
1968	37	Reynosa Broncs	Mexican League	AAA
1969	38	Reynosa Broncs	Mexican League	AAA
1970	39	Saltillo Saraperos	Mexican League	AAA
1971	40	Saltillo Saraperos	Mexican League	AAA
1972	41	Cordoba Cafeteros	Mexican League	AAA

Hilario (Sandy) Valdespino Borroto

Valdespino played his third and last season in Cuba coming to bat 247 times and hitting .300. His three season totals included a .275 batting average, and he was named the Rookie of the Year in 1959-60.

His playing career in the U.S. and Mexico began in 1957 and ended in 1974. He batted .284 in the U.S. minors and played a total of seven seasons in the majors in 382 games hitting .230. He participated in the 1965 World Series with the Minnesota Twins, going 3 for 5.

As with many players, the language barrier and different foods posed problems, especially during those early years when he went into the minor leagues at the age of 18 years old.

A goal about coming to the U.S. to play baseball was to be able to help his mother, but sadly she died during that first year. Valdespino never returned to Cuba but sends help to members of his family. (Source cited below.)

Giving his playing career, he came and stayed in the U.S. following the end of the 1960-61 season but research has not led to identifying the actual travel dates. Valdespino became a coach for the West Haven Yankees in 1977 and the Rochester Red Wings in 1985.

Additional source: Henninger Thom, Tony Oliva University of Minnesota Press Minneapolis London 2015 page 26.

Year	Age	Tm	Lg	Lev
1956	17	Did Not Play		
1957	18	Midland/Lamesa Indians	Southwestern League	B
1958	19	Fox Cities Foxes	Illinois-Indiana-Iowa League	B
1958	19	Missoula Timberjacks	Pioneer League	C
1959	20	Charlotte Hornets	South Atlantic League	A
1960	21	Charleston Senators	American Association	AAA
1961	22	Syracuse Chiefs	International League	AAA
1961	22	Indianapolis Indians	American Association	AAA
1962	23	Dallas-Fort Worth Rangers	American Association	AAA
1962	23	Vancouver Mounties	Pacific Coast League	AAA

Year	Age	Tm	Lg	Lev
1963	24	Dallas-Fort Worth Rangers	Pacific Coast League	AAA
1964	25	Atlanta Crackers	International League	AAA
1965	26	Minnesota Twins	American League	MLB
1966	27	Denver Bears	Pacific Coast League	AAA
1966	27	Minnesota Twins	American League	MLB
1967	28	Minnesota Twins	American League	MLB
1968	29	Richmond Braves	International League	AAA
1968	29	Atlanta Braves	National League	MLB
1969	30	Oklahoma City 89ers	American Association	AAA
1969	30	Houston Astros	National League	MLB
1969	30	Seattle Pilots	American League	MLB
1970	31	Omaha Royals	American Association	AAA
1970	31	Portland Beavers	Pacific Coast League	AAA
1970	31	Milwaukee Brewers	American League	MLB
1971	32	Omaha Royals	American Association	AAA
1971	32	Kansas City Royals	American League	MLB
1972	33	Omaha Royals	American Association	AAA
1973	34	Monterrey Sultanes	Mexican League	AAA
1973	34	Ciudad Juarez Indios	Mexican League	AAA
1974	35	Poza Rica Petroleros	Mexican League	AAA

Luis Zayas Travieso

Born August 25, 1936, in La Habana, Zayas played professional baseball in Cuba during three seasons starting in 1951. His first-year stats are incomplete, and his .221 batting average is based on his last two seasons. During his last season with the Lions he batted .235 in 119 times at bat.

He played for the Cuban Sugar Kings in 1958 with 228 times at bat, hitting .219. "I think I must have had 20 girl friends that year." Luis Zayas, believed to be the only other former Sugar King living in Cuba. He later said, "We had a slogan around the team that said, 'One step from the big leagues,' and we believed it". (See source cited below.)

He played five seasons in the U.S. in the minor league system, starting in 1955, and batting .306. In 1960, he travelled to Miami and San Antonio in an attempt to join the Los Angeles Dodgers organization. But he spent most of his career in the Mexican League, for nine seasons through 1966. It is said he stayed in that country after the Cuban Revolution since it was believed that players who remained in the U.S. after the Revolution were blacklisted in Cuba. Those active in Mexico were given a chance to wind out their careers and return to their home country.

"The door was open to the big leagues, and I had to give that up, which was very, very difficult. But I knew that I could not live anywhere but Cuba." He added that a Ku Klux Klan rally he witnessed during a season in Savannah, Georgia also weighed on him.

He later managed in Cuba. He guided the Metropolitanos team to a 28-21 record in 1977-1978. He led the Isla de la Juventud squad to a 12-39 record in 1979-1980, the team's third season. He was also a technical commissioner in Cuban baseball into the 21st Century and married at Estadio Latinoamericano in 2001.

In 2009, he participated in a US-Cuban Old Time Senior Softball Tournament coined "softball diplomacy" by some of the players. The game was organized in part by a relative by marriage of this author. It prompted Zayas, then 72 years old to be quoted as saying, "The people have nothing to do with the government". "We, the people, are open." Efforts like this have gone on for some time, but as it has become clear, for real change to take place, efforts, and compromises at different levels beyond the baseball diamond need to take place.

Zayas, 75, who was a coach for the Cuban National team until 2012, lives only blocks from the pile of concrete that is Estadio

Latinoamericano, once the home of the Sugar Kings and the stadium where Industriales, Havana's National Series team, now plays. Zayas makes frequent trips to the stadium during the season.

Additional sources:

Strauss Ben Remembering a Minor League Championship Correspondence with Cuban baseball researcher Rogelio Manzano New York Times March 23, 2013
Baseball Guides from 1956, 1958, 1960, 1964 and 1967
Schworm Peter In Cuba, diamond diplomacy Senior softballers from Bay State find the bases for understanding in Havana Boston.com November 24, 2009

Year	Age	Tm	Lg	Lev
1955	17	Mexico City Diablos Rojos	Mexican League	AA
1955	17	Nogales Yaquis	Arizona-Mexico League	C
1956	18	Nogales Diablos Rojos	Arizona-Mexico League	C
1957	19	Wenatchee Chiefs	Northwest League	B
1957	19	Clovis Redlegs	Southwestern League	B
1958	20	Savannah Redlegs	South Atlantic League	A
1958	20	Havana Sugar Kings	International League	AAA
1959	21	Monterrey Sultanes	Mexican League	AA
1959	21	Montreal Royals	International League	AAA
1960	22	Mexico City Tigres	Mexican League	AA
1961	23	Mexico City Tigres	Mexican League	AA
1962	24	Mexico City Tigres	Mexican League	AA
1963	25	Mexico City Tigres	Mexican League	AA
1963	25	Reynosa Broncs	Mexican League	AA
1964	26	Reynosa Broncs	Mexican League	AA

Year	Age	Tm	Lg	Lev
1965	27	Campeche Pirates	Mexican Southeast League	A
1966	28	Campeche Pirates	Mexican Southeast League	A

Chapter 8

MARIANAO

The Marianao ownership was made up from 1948-49 by a group composed of Doctor Alfredo Pequeño and José Rodríguez. When first founded in 1922-23, the club was known as the *Elefantes* de Marianao, but was better known as the *Monjes Grises*, the Gray Monks, in the 1930s.[49] and their name was changed to the "Tigres" (the Tigers) in 1948.[50]

Manager

José María (Cuso) Fernández

Born on July 6, 1896 in Guanabacoa Cuba, Fernández got his third and last manager's job in Cuba's professional baseball league in 1960-1961, its final campaign. He guided Marianao to a 31-35 season, last place, but only four games out in what was a close race. Among his players were Miguel (Mike) Fornieles, José Tartabull, Juan Delis, Orestes (Minnie) Miñoso, Zoilo Versalles, José Valdivielso and Julio Becquer, all of whom had the opportunity to play in an integrated majors, which Fernández could not. His overall managerial record in Cuba included 58 wins and 63 losses.

His career in the U.S. began in 1916 in the Negro Leagues and went on for 35 years. He played as a catcher, and at first base. He managed the New York Cubans from 1938 through 1950, leading them to the National League Championship of the Negro League, beating the American League Champions Cleveland Buckeyes in 1947.

His playing career in Cuba started at the age of 19, from 1915-1916 through the 1942-43 season, and had a batting average of .273

over the 27 seasons. Cuso Fernández was elected to the Cuban Baseball Hall of Fame in Miami in 1983.

At the end of the 1960-61 season, Cuso remained in Cuba and, when the Cuban *Serie Nacional* started in 1962, following the end of professional baseball, Fernández managed Habana to a last-place and a 10-17 record. He died on July 20, 1972 in Cuba.

Additional sources:

http://thekingdomofbaseball.proboards.com/thread/1861/tendremos-reescribir-historia-baseball-cubano#ixzz4JbAVg7iP
Baseball Reference
Negro League Baseball Museum e-museum

Year	Age	Tm	Lg
1916	20	New York Cuban Stars	Independent Negro
1917	21	New York Cuban Stars	Independent Negro
1918	22	New York Cuban Stars	Independent Negro
1919	23	New York Cuban Stars	Independent Negro
1920	24	Havana Cuban Stars (East)	Independent Negro
1921	25	All-Cubans	Independent Negro
1922	26	Cuban Stars East	Independent Negro
1923	27	Cuban Stars East	Eastern Colored League
1924	28	Cuban Stars East	Eastern Colored League
1925	29	Cuban Stars East	Eastern Colored League
1926	30	Cuban Stars East	Eastern Colored League
1927	31	Cuban Stars East	Eastern Colored League
1928	32	Cuban Stars East	Eastern Colored League
1929	33	Cuban Stars West	Negro National League
1929	33	Cuban Stars East	American Negro League
1930	34	Chicago American Giants	Negro National League

Year	Age	Tm	Lg
1931	35	Cuban Stars East	American Negro League
1931	35	Cuban House of David	Independent Negro
1932	36	Cuban Stars East	East-West League
1933	37	Cuban Stars West	Independent Negro
1934	38	Cuban Stars East	Independent Negro
1935	39	The Cuban Stars	Independent Negro
1935	39	Cuban Stars East	Independent Negro
1938	42	New York Cubans	Independent Negro
1939	43	New York Cubans	Negro National League
1940	44	New York Cubans	Negro National League
1941	45	New York Cubans	Negro National League
1942	46	New York Cubans	Negro National League
1944	48	New York Cubans	Negro National League

Pitchers

Fidel Alvarez Sánchez

He was said to have a great curve ball (see source cited below). Alvarez, known as Gallego, played a total of three seasons in Cuba, all with the *Tigres* squad where he had a combined 2-3 record.

During the last season, he appeared in 21 games, completing only one, and had a 3.73 ERA while winning one game and losing one.

This righty pitched outside of Cuba from 1953, starting with the Class C Artesia Drillers of the Longhorn League at the age of 19, and played from 1956 through 1963 with the exception of one season in the Mexican League. His four-season minor league record was 66-42 with a 4.16 ERA.

Research did not yield his travelling to the U.S. following the end of the 1960-61 season but given his playing in Mexico through the end of his career in 1973, one can readily assume that he stayed in Mexico and did not return to Cuba.

Additional source: Octavio Cuqui Rojas, telephone interview with author, November 30.2016.

Year	Age	Tm	Lg	Lev
1953	19	Artesia Drillers	Longhorn League	C
1954	20	Port Arthur Sea Hawks	Evangeline League	C
1955	21	Lafayette Oilers	Evangeline League	C
1955	21	Port Arthur Sea Hawks	Big State League	B
1956	22	Nuevo Laredo Tecolotes	Mexican League	AA
1956	22	Roswell Rockets	Southwestern League	B
1956	22	Victoria Eagles	Big State League	B
1957	23	Nuevo Laredo Tecolotes	Mexican League	AA
1958	24	Monterrey Sultanes	Mexican League	AA
1959	25	Monterrey Sultanes	Mexican League	AA
1960	26	Monterrey Sultanes	Mexican League	AA
1961	27	Poza Rica Petroleros	Mexican League	AA
1961	27	Monterrey Sultanes	Mexican League	AA
1962	28	Poza Rica Petroleros	Mexican League	AA
1963	29	Poza Rica Petroleros	Mexican League	AA
1964	30	Jalisco Charros	Mexican League	AA
1964	30	Veracruz Aguilas	Mexican League	AA
1965	31	Veracruz Aguilas	Mexican League	AA
1965	31	Puerto Mexico Portenos	Mexican Southeast League	A
1968	34	Monterrey Sultanes	Mexican League	AAA
1972	38	Tampico Stevedores	Mexican League	AAA
1973	39	Tampico Alijadores	Mexican League	AAA

Rodolfo (Rudy) Arias Martínez

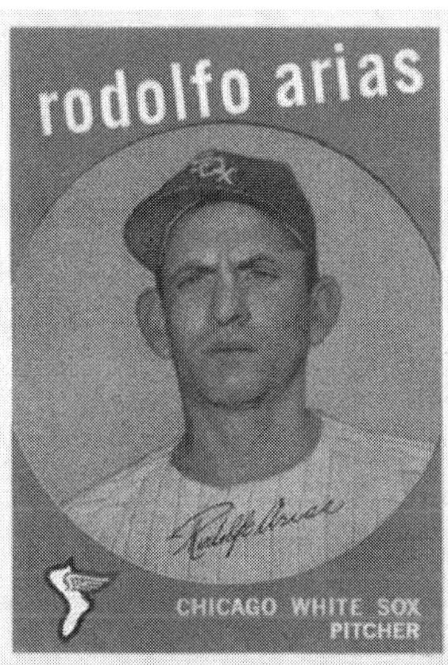

The subject of a SABR biography, Rodolfo Arias played a total of six seasons in Cuba, five of which with the Tigres of Marianao. Appearing in 124 games, and a record of 28-29 with an ERA of 2.73, Arias had a winning record that last season of 10-9 and a 2.69 ERA. On January 17, he pitched 18 innings, but lost the game after Daniel Morejón had a single with runner at 2nd base. The eventual recipient of the Rookie of the Year Award, Luis Tiant, was the winning pitcher in relief.

He appeared in the 1957 and 58 Caribbean Series in two games and played with the Cuban Sugar Kings in 1958 in 43 games with a 7-7 record. On August 17 of that season, he pitched the only No-Hit No-Run game in the history of the franchise.

Outside of Cuba he played for a total of eleven seasons, from 1953 through 1966. His minor league record was 82-68 for nine seasons, playing in Mexico to complete his career. He played for the Chicago White Sox during the 1956 season, winning 2 games without a loss and had a 4.09 ERA.

He played for the Jersey City team following the end of the 1960-61 season but returned to Cuba in 1961 after hearing rumors that Cuba was starting the professional Cuban league again. While practicing baseball in Cuba, he tore a tendon and, soon after, learned that the rumor he had heard was in fact false. Wanting to play professional baseball, he left again from La Habana. He arrived in Miami in April of 1962 after having secured a visa in Toronto on his way to join the San Diego organization.

Rodolfo Arias passed away on January 12, 2018 in Miami, Florida, spending his last few days in the hospital with respiratory problems. His son Rodolfo and daughter Olga as well as many members of the family, were present during the wake, including former major leaguer Cholly Naranjo and this author. He was buried on January 22nd at the Woodland Cemetery in Miami alongside his wife Olga who had passed away in 2010.

Additional sources:

Ramírez, José *"Rudy Arias"* SABR Bio Project (http://sabr.org/bioproj/person)

GO-GO to Glory The 1959 Chicago White Sox edited by Don Zminda 2009 SABR.t

Year	Age	Tm	Lg	Lev
1953	22	Madisonville Miners	Kentucky-Illinois-Tennessee League	D
1954	23	Waterloo White Hawks	Illinois-Indiana-Iowa League	B
1955	24	Colorado Springs Sky Sox	Western League	A
1955	24	Amarillo Gold Sox	West Texas-New Mexico League	B
1956	25	Colorado Springs Sky Sox	Western League	A
1956	25	Toronto Maple Leafs	International League	AAA

Year	Age	Tm	Lg	Lev
1957	26	Colorado Springs Sky Sox	Western League	A
1958	27	Havana Sugar Kings	International League	AAA
1959	28	Chicago White Sox	American League	MLB
1960	29	Miami Marlins	International League	AAA
1960	29	San Diego Padres	Pacific Coast League	AAA
1961	30	Jersey City Jerseys	International League	AAA
1962	31	Columbus Jets	International League	AAA
1962	31	Macon Peaches	South Atlantic League	A
1962	31	San Diego Padres	Pacific Coast League	AAA
1965	34	Poza Rica Petroleros	Mexican League	AA
1966	35	Poza Rica Petroleros	Mexican League	AA

Pedro Alfonso Carrillo

Carrillo had a difficult year on the mound during his last and fifth season in Cuba, with an ERA of 9.00 in eleven games, and losing two games without a win. His combined record over the five seasons playing for Habana, Cienfuegos and Marianao in 44 game appearances earned him only one win against four losses.

He pitched during the 1960 Caribbean series with Cienfuegos, winning a game in relief, and was able to secure a 3-4 record during his two seasons with the Cuban Sugar Kings in 1959 and 1960. He pitched five innings in three games during the Little World Series, striking out five batters and walking one.

His career outside of Cuba began in 1954 with the Nogales Level C team where he won 15 games while losing 10. He ended his professional baseball career in 1961 in Mexico with the Monterrey team. His overall minor league record was 63 wins with 46 losses.

His 1960 travel record reflects he was born in Manacas, Las Villas on May 19, 1935 making him a year older in another publication. At this point, given his playing in Mexico following the 1960-61 season he is said to have returned to Cuba at the end of his playing career, as some of the other players had done.

Additional source: Iván Davis, telephone interview with author, January 31, 2018.

Year	Age	Tm	Lg	Lev
1954	19	Nogales Yaquis	Arizona-Texas League	C
1955	20	Duluth Dukes	Northern League	C
1955	20	Olean Oilers	Pennsylvania-Ontario-New York League	D
1956	21	Nuevo Laredo Tecolotes	Mexican League	AA
1956	21	Saltillo Saraperos	Central Mexican League	C
1957	22	Wenatchee Chiefs	Northwest League	B
1957	22	Clovis Redlegs	Southwestern League	B
1958	23	Albuquerque Dukes	Western League	A
1959	24	Havana Sugar Kings	International League	AAA
1960	25	Columbia Reds	South Atlantic League	A
1960	25	Havana Sugar Kings/ Jersey City Jerseys	International League	AAA
1960	25	San Antonio Missions	Texas League	AA
1960	25	Tulsa Oilers	Texas League	AA
1961	26	Monterrey Sultanes	Mexican League	AA

José Miguel (Mike) Fornieles Torres

A popular pitcher in Cuba and the U.S., Fornieles spent eight seasons playing professional baseball in the Cuban League, all with the Marianao Tigers. He was named the Rookie of the Year for the 1952-53 season, leading the league in earned run average, 2.33. Playing in 231 games, his 70-63 record and 2.93 ERA included 49 complete games

during that time. During his last season, he had 23 appearances, completing seven games with an 8 and 8 record and a low 2.36 ERA.

He played during the 1957 and 58 Caribbean Series, earning a 2-1 record and had 40 appearances with the Havana Cubans in 1952, winning 14 games while losing 12. His ERA during that season was 2.66.

In 1985 he was inducted into the Cuban Baseball Hall of Fame in Miami, Florida.

His playing career outside of Cuba began in 1951 at the age of 19 and ended in 1963. His overall record during his four seasons in the minors was 43 and 25. He played a total of twelve seasons in the majors, earning 63 wins with 64 losses and 3.96 ERA. He was named to the 1961 All Star team representing the Boston Red Sox, pitching 0.1 inning while giving up two hits.

He told a newspaper interviewer that “They didn’t want me to leave Cuba in 60. The only way I got out was to promise that I would come back. I told them, ‘Sure. I will’ but I knew at the time I wouldn’t.” He left with the five dollars we were allowed in those days but stashed $200 in the fingers of his baseball glove.

Unfortunately, his wife refused to come. “Her family had been communist, and I guess she became the same way.” He divorced his wife and remarried later on. Fornieles was very popular in the Boston area and had a successful auto sales business for a number of years.

José Miguel Fornieles died at 66 years old in St. Petersburgh Florida on February 11, 1998.

Additional source: Boston Globe February 14, 1998 by Tom Long.

Year	Age	Tm	Lg	Lev
1951	19	Big Spring Broncs	Longhorn League	C
1952	20	Havana Cubans	Florida International League	B
1952	20	Washington Senators	American League	MLB
1953	21	Chicago White Sox	American League	MLB
1954	22	Charleston Senators	American Association	AAA
1954	22	Chicago White Sox	American League	MLB
1955	23	Toronto Maple Leafs	International League	AAA
1955	23	Chicago White Sox	American League	MLB
1956	24	Chicago White Sox	American League	MLB
1956	24	Baltimore Orioles	American League	MLB
1957	25	Baltimore Orioles	American League	MLB
1957	25	Boston Red Sox	American League	MLB
1958	26	Boston Red Sox	American League	MLB
1959	27	Boston Red Sox	American League	MLB
1960	28	Boston Red Sox	American League	MLB
1961	29	Boston Red Sox	American League	MLB
1962	30	Boston Red Sox	American League	MLB
1963	31	Boston Red Sox	American League	MLB
1963	31	Minnesota Twins	American League	MLB

Lázaro (Habichuela) Gómez Calzadilla

Although his name appears as Lorenzo, his correct name is Lázaro, (see source cited below).

Gómez played one professional baseball season in Cuba, pitching in nine games and a total of 14.2 innings. During his career in the U.S. and Mexico, Gómez played a total of five seasons. In the minors at the age of 17, he won 14 games during the 1960 season, and would go on to win 49 games, losing 33 with a 3.60 ERA. He played in the U.S. minors until 1963 and in Mexico until 1965 only to return at the age of 30, in 1973, to play for the Triple A Mexico City Diablos Rojos.

He arrived on March 11, 1962 from Habana. Former teammate José Tartabull stated that *Habichuela* (String-bean) attested to that fact that they have seen each other during at least one of the old timers' game in Miami, Florida. In addition, his playing career indicates his stay in the U.S. following the end of the 1960-61 Cuban professional baseball season.

Additional source: José Tartabull, personal interview, January 27, 2017.

Year	Age	Tm	Lg	Lev
1960	17	Quincy Giants	Midwest League	D
1961	18	Eugene Emeralds	Northwest League	B
1962	19	El Paso Sun Kings	Texas League	AA
1963	20	El Paso Sun Kings	Texas League	AA
1964	21	Veracruz Aguilas	Mexican League	AA
1965	22	Puerto Mexico Portenos	Mexican Southeast League	A
1973	30	Mexico City Diablos Rojos	Mexican League	AAA

Manuel (Manny) Montejo Bofill

During his two seasons in Cuba, both with Marianao, Montejo had a 2.97 ERA in 76 appearances, and a 10 win, 9 loss record. His 2.97 ERA was a bit lower than his last season where his ERA was 3.86 with an 8-8 record in 36 games.

Montejo played for the Cuban Sugar Kings in 1957 and 58 in 21 games and had 3 losses with no wins and a 5.11 Earned Run Average.

In the seasons between 1957 and 1966, he played in the U.S. and Mexico. He appeared in 194 games in the minors with a 20-19 record and he played in eleven games in the Mexican League.

Following the end of the 1960-61 season in Cuba, he played in the majors in the second half of the 1961 season with the Detroit Tigers, appearing in twelve games, and had a 3.86 Earned Run Average. It is worthy of note that he appeared to have returned to Cuba after his one season in the major leagues. He, in fact, travelled from La Habana, Cuba to Miami on February of 1962 to join the Houston Sports Association with a visa secured in Windsor, Ontario, Canada. He would not play during that season, returning to baseball the following season with the Oklahoma City Triple A team affiliated with the Houston organization.

Ultimately Manuel Montejo returned to Cuba. He passed away of cancer in La Habana, Cuba on January 19, 2000 and is buried in the Christopher Columbus Cemetery of that city.

Year	Age	Tm	Lg	Lev
1957	21	Havana Sugar Kings	International League	AAA
1958	22	Havana Sugar Kings	International League	AAA
1958	22	Albuquerque Dukes	Western League	A
1959	23	Denver Bears	American Association	AAA
1959	23	San Antonio Missions	Texas League	AA
1960	24	Victoria Rosebuds	Texas League	AA
1961	25	Denver Bears	American Association	AAA

Year	Age	Tm	Lg	Lev
1961	25	Detroit Tigers	American League	MLB
1962	26	Oklahoma City 89ers	American Association	AAA
1963	27	Oklahoma City 89ers	Pacific Coast League	AAA
1965	29	Puebla Pericos	Mexican League	AA
1965	29	Tabasco Plataneros	Mexican Southeast League	A
1966	30	Salisbury Astros	Western Carolinas League	A

Antoliano Angel Oliva Acosta

For his last and fourth season in the Cuban League, Antoliano had a 2.60 Earned Run Average while winning four games and losing six in sixteen game appearances. Overall, his record in Cuba where he appeared in 90 games, shows he won fifteen games and lost nineteen with a combined 2.88 ERA.

Playing in the 1958 Caribbean Series with Marianao, Oliva participated in two games for a total of eight innings, with an outstanding 1.17 Earned Run Average.

A righty, he would play eight seasons in the minors, starting in 1954, at the age of 17, with the Roswell Rockets a Class C team in the Longhorn League. He had a total of 52 wins and 49 losses in the minors. He ended his career in Mexico in 1962 with Poza Rica.

Antoliano left Cuba after the 1960-61 season, arriving in Miami on March 24, 1961 via Mexico.

Year	Age	Tm	Lg	Lev
1954	17	Roswell Rockets	Longhorn League	C
1955	18	Roswell Rockets	Longhorn League	C
1955	18	Carlsbad Potashers	Longhorn League	C
1956	19	Carlsbad Potashers	Southwestern League	B

1956	19	Hobbs Sports	Southwestern League	B
1957	20	Charlotte Hornets	South Atlantic League	A
1958	21	Chattanooga Lookouts	Southern Association	AA
1959	22	Denver Bears	American Association	AAA
1959	22	Chattanooga Lookouts	Southern Association	AA
1960	23	Charleston Senators	American Association	AAA
1960	23	Chattanooga Lookouts	Southern Association	AA
1961	24	Charlotte Hornets	South Atlantic League	A
1961	24	Syracuse Chiefs	International League	AAA
1962	25	Poza Rica Petroleros	Mexican League	AA

Juan Andrés Piedra Torrens

Piedra played four seasons with Marianao for a total of 46 games, losing five games and winning none. One of his losses occurred during the last season, where he appeared in seven games and had a 4.00 ERA.

A lefty, he played in the U.S. minors for four seasons, winning 20 games and losing 24 with 3.68 ERA, and in the Mexican League during seven seasons, from 1956 through the 1964 season.

After the 1960-61 season, he played in Mexico following the end of that season and the subsequent three seasons while remaining in Cuba.

Additional source: Iván Davis, telephone interview with author, January 31, 2018.

Year	Age	Tm	Lg	Lev
1956	17	Fayetteville Highlanders	Carolina League	B
1957	18	Keokuk Kernels	Illinois-Indiana-Iowa League	B
1958	19	Nuevo Laredo Tecolotes	Mexican League	AA
1958	19	Yucatan Leones	Mexican League	AA

Year	Age	Tm	Lg	Lev
1959	20	Victoria Rosebuds	Texas League	AA
1959	20	Mexico City Tigres	Mexican League	AA
1960	21	Victoria Rosebuds	Texas League	AA
1960	21	Mexico City Diablos Rojos	Mexican League	AA
1961	22	Monterrey Sultanes	Mexican League	AA
1962	23	Monterrey Sultanes	Mexican League	AA
1963	24	Monterrey Sultanes	Mexican League	AA
1963	24	Reynosa Broncs	Mexican League	AA
1964	25	Yucatan Venados	Mexican Southeast League	A
1964	25	Reynosa Broncs	Mexican League	AA

Catchers

Alberto Alvarez Cortés

During his five seasons in Cuba, all with the Marianao team, he batted .258 in 240 appearances, a record consistent with his output in 1960-61 where he batted .254, but a higher batting average than his years with the Cuban Sugar Kings. In the 1958 and 59 seasons he had batted a low .188 in 96 times at the plate.

Outside of his professional seasons in Cuba, beginning in 1955, he played with the Fort Walton Beach Class D team affiliated with the Cincinnati Reds. He ended his career in 1962 playing for the Mexico City Tigers of the Mexican League at the age of 26. During his six-season minor league career, he had 1810 appearances at the plate in 558 games.

This catcher left Cuba via Mexico, arriving in Miami on March 21, 1961 on his way to Tampa to join the Cincinnati Reds. Nevertheless, he played for the Puebla team in Mexico during that season. He returned to Cuba only to leave again from La Habana, arriving in

Miami on April 4, 1962 on his way to join the Jacksonville ball club. He ended up playing in Mexico that season as well.

Both of the travel records kept during that time listed his birthday as May 14, 1936. But one showed Central Tinguaro as his birth place, the other Matanzas. Note: Central Tinguaro is located in the Matanzas Province which may lead to some confusion regarding his birthplace.

Year	Age	Tm	Lg	Lev
1955	19	Fort Walton Beach Jets	Alabama-Florida League	D
1955	19	Douglas Trojans	Georgia State League	D
1956	20	Douglas Reds	Georgia State League	D
1957	21	Wausau Lumberjacks	Northern League	C
1958	22	Havana Sugar Kings	International League	AAA
1958	22	Savannah Redlegs	South Atlantic League	A
1958	22	Albuquerque Dukes	Western League	A
1959	23	Topeka Hawks	Illinois-Indiana-Iowa League	B
1959	23	Havana Sugar Kings	International League	AAA
1960	24	Lincoln Chiefs	Illinois-Indiana-Iowa League	B
1961	25	Puebla Pericos	Mexican League	AA
1962	26	Mexico City Tigres	Mexican League	AA

Rene Friol González

Friol had his best batting average during his sixth and last season in Cuba, hitting .295 in 78 at bats. His career in the professional Cuban League included 545 times at bat, with a .239 batting average. He played in 1956 for the Cuban Sugar Kings and had ten times at bat with only one hit.

According to his travel record, he was born on May 28, 1933, making him almost a year and a half older than other publications.

Friol played outside of Cuba for 19 seasons, from 1954 with the Lakeland Pilots through 1970. He played eleven seasons in the minors where he batted .216 in 713 games, and eight in Mexico where he appeared in 555 games.

René Friol managed two seasons in the Mexican League with the Yucatán and Ciudad Madero Single A teams. He had a record of 139 wins with 103 losses.

Friol left Cuba from La Habana, arriving in Miami on his way to the Los Angeles Dodgers training Camp in Vero Beach Florida on March 26, 1962 having secured a visa from Toronto, Canada.

Year	Age	Tm	Lg	Lev
1954	21	Lakeland Pilots	Florida State League	D
1955	22	Grand Forks Chiefs	Northern League	C
1956	23	Yucatan Leones	Mexican League	AA
1956	23	Havana Sugar Kings	International League	AAA
1957	24	Mexico City Diablos Rojos	Mexican League	AA
1957	24	Fresnillo	Central Mexican League	C
1958	25	St. Paul Saints	American Association	AAA
1958	25	Montreal Royals	International League	AAA
1959	26	St. Paul Saints	American Association	AAA
1960	27	St. Paul Saints	American Association	AAA
1961	28	Spokane Indians	Pacific Coast League	AAA
1961	28	Omaha Dodgers	American Association	AAA
1962	29	Spokane Indians	Pacific Coast League	AAA
1963	30	Richmond Virginians	International League	AAA
1963	30	Augusta Yankees	South Atlantic League	AA
1964	31	Veracruz Aguilas	Mexican League	AA
1965	32	Veracruz Aguilas	Mexican League	AA

Year	Age	Tm	Lg	Lev
1966	33	Veracruz Aguilas	Mexican League	AA
1967	34	Yucatan Venados	Mexican Southeast League	A
1967	34	Veracruz Aguila	Mexican League	AAA
1968	35	Yucatan Venados	Mexican Southeast League	A
1969	36	Yucatan Stags	Mexican Southeast League	A
1970	37	Ciudad Madero Bravos	Mexican Center League	A

Infielders

Julio Bécquer Villegas

Bécquer played all ten of his seasons in the Cuban League with Marianao, and had a batting average of .266 in 2158 appearances at the plate in 573 games. During his last season he came to bat 262 times and his average dipped to .233 while leading the league in home runs with 15 and runs batted in with 50.

He played in the Caribbean Series on three different occasions, 1954, 57 and 58, coming to the plate 70 times and batting .200. In 1953 he played for the Havana Cubans where his batting average was a robust .296 leading the league in triples with eleven. The Cuban Sugar Kings had him in the lineup in 1954 during 133 games where he hit .268 in 430 plate appearances.

This first baseman played in the U.S. and Mexico from 1952 through 1964, including seven seasons in the minors in 689 games with a batting average of .270, and three seasons in the Mexican League. Becquer played in the major leagues for seven seasons in 488 games, batting .244.

Bécquer said, in the interview cited below that while away from his homeland in February of 1961, separated from his wife who had stayed in Cuba, "It was not a political decision, or anything like that, it was just like, I mean, what are we going to do if we go back to Cuba, there was no professional baseball, we are professional baseball players-what are we going to do?". Joe Cambria, the well-known scout, spent a month with Becquer's wife in Cuba and put her in the plane to the U.S.

Bécquer never saw his father. He died in early 1970s. After leaving Cuba, Becquer never returned. His wife Edith, who has passed away, and his daughter, Frances, returned twice. He regretted not having returned when his wife did. He has not seen family members in over 50 years (see source cited below).

Julio Bécquer was inducted into the Cuban Baseball Hall of Fame in 1997.

Additional Sources:

espn.com The Cuban Senators by Matt Welch March 3, 2002

Henninger Thom Tony Oliva University of Minnesota Press Minneapolis London 2015
page 196

Year	Age	Tm	Lg	Lev
1952	20	Drummondville Cubs	Provincial League	C
1953	21	Havana Cubans	Florida International League	B

Year	Age	Tm	Lg	Lev
1954	22	Havana Sugar Kings	International League	AAA
1955	23	San Diego Padres	Pacific Coast League	Opn
1955	23	Washington Senators	American League	MLB
1956	24	Louisville Colonels	American Association	AAA
1957	25	Washington Senators	American League	MLB
1958	26	Washington Senators	American League	MLB
1959	27	Washington Senators	American League	MLB
1960	28	Washington Senators	American League	MLB
1961	29	Buffalo Bisons	International League	AAA
1961	29	Los Angeles Angels	American League	MLB
1961	29	Minnesota Twins	American League	MLB
1962	30	Mexico City Diablos Rojos	Mexican League	AA
1962	30	Veracruz Aguilas	Mexican League	AA
1962	30	Vancouver Mounties	Pacific Coast League	AAA
1963	31	Veracruz Aguilas	Mexican League	AA
1963	31	Minnesota Twins	American League	MLB
1964	32	Veracruz Aguilas	Mexican League	AA

Lorenzo Mario (Chico) Fernández Mosquera

In three seasons for Marianao during his career in professional baseball in Cuba, Lorenzo Fernández had a total of 178 appearances at the plate, 160 of those during his last season where he had a batting average of .219.

His career outside of Cuba included eleven seasons in the minor leagues in the U.S., starting in 1958 at the age of 19, playing for the Class D Decatur Commodores in 111 games and hitting a strong .285. He went on to play through 1969. He played one season in the majors with the Baltimore Orioles in 24 games and had a .111 batting average.

His career began when he was signed out of Louisiana State University by Mel Didier. During the 1968 season, he suffered a fractured elbow after 24 games in the majors and was unable to play the rest of the season. Returning in 1969, he was pressed into action and sent to play when, at the age of 30, on July 23 of that year, he suffered a fractured skull when hit by a pitch by Larry Bearnarth of the Tidewater Tides. He was in a coma for ten days and spent two and a half months in the hospital. After he retired as an active player, he became for a time an infield instructor and coach in the minors for the Los Angeles Dodgers (see source cited below). He was reported to have said, "I feel pretty good, but my head still bothers me, swollen left side, can't write, trouble speaking…" (See source cited below).

Todd Hartman of El Nuevo Herald reported that Fernández was the father of Humberto (*Chico*) Fernández another former Cuban major leaguer, a confusion that was not unusual as both players were known as *"Chico"* Fernández. I had an opportunity to visit and get a tour of the museum to Cuban baseball by Fernández, the father, with my own father who knew him, given his connection to the Sports Complex of the Rosario Sugar Mill (Deportivo Rosario) in our hometown of Aguacate.

Lorenzo Fernández came to the U.S. via Mexico arriving in Miami on March 7, 1961 on his way to Tiger Town in Lakeland Florida to continue his career, after the end of the 1960-61 season.

He became a U.S. Citizen on March 4, 1969, with former major leaguer Leopoldo Posada serving as a witness in the Miami District Court.

Today, Fernández lives in Miami surrounded by family and friends and the admiration of baseball fans for all that he contributed to the sport.

Additional sources:

The Lethbridge Herald June 24, 1977.
Daytona Beach Morning Journal 8/19/69.
Clemente Amezaga, telephone interviews with author.

Year	Age	Tm	Lg	Lev
1958	19	Decatur Commodores	Midwest League	D
1959	20	Montgomery Rebels	Alabama-Florida League	D
1959	20	Durham Bulls	Carolina League	B
1960	21	Decatur Commodores	Midwest League	D
1960	21	Durham Bulls	Carolina League	B
1961	22	Durham Bulls	Carolina League	B
1962	23	Denver Bears	American Association	AAA
1962	23	Louisville Colonels	American Association	AAA
1963	24	Knoxville Smokies	South Atlantic League	AA
1963	24	Lynchburg White Sox	South Atlantic League	AA
1964	25	Lynchburg White Sox	Southern League	AA
1965	26	Lynchburg White Sox	Southern League	AA
1966	27	Evansville White Sox	Southern League	AA
1967	28	Indianapolis Indians	Pacific Coast League	AAA
1967	28	Evansville White Sox	Southern League	AA
1967	28	FIL White Sox	Florida Instructional League	WRk
1968	29	Baltimore Orioles	American League	MLB
1969	30	Rochester Red Wings	International League	AAA

Oscar Flores Apodaca

Flores played during two seasons in the Cuban League, both with Marianao, even though he only played in one game in his first season. He hit for a low .185 average in 42 games in the 1960-61 season at the young age of 18.

He played in the U.S. minor leagues from 1960 starting with the Class D Quincy Giants in the Midwest League and ending with the Class A Burlington Bees in the same league playing a total of 822 games while hitting .228.

His travel record to the U.S. in 1959 showed his full name and listed December 11, 1942 as his birthday in La Habana, Cuba. His playing record shows that he, in fact, came and stayed after the 1960-61 season through 1967, until the age of 25 when his baseball playing career ended.

Year	Age	Tm	Lg	Lev
1960	17	Quincy Giants	Midwest League	D
1960	17	Fresno Giants	California League	C
1961	18	Lincoln Chiefs	Illinois-Indiana-Iowa League	B
1961	18	Charleston White Sox	South Atlantic League	A
1962	19	Greensboro Yankees	Carolina League	B
1962	19	Savannah/Lynchburg White Sox	South Atlantic League	A
1962	19	Sarasota Sun Sox	Florida State League	D
1963	20	Lynchburg White Sox	South Atlantic League	AA
1963	20	Eugene Emeralds	Northwest League	A
1964	21	Lynchburg White Sox	Southern League	AA
1964	21	Tidewater Tides	Carolina League	A
1965	22	Burlington Bees	Midwest League	A
1966	23	Leesburg A's	Florida State League	A
1967	24	Burlington Bees	Midwest League	A

Martín Laza Rosell

Four seasons with Marianao, and 158 times at bat brought his average to .253, consistent with his last season where his batting average was .256 in 78 times at the plate.

This infielder played in the U.S. minors from 1955 with the Class C Hobbs Sports in the Longhorn League through 1962 with the Class D Tampa Tarpons in the Florida League. He played in no less than 825 games but his record is incomplete.

Following the end of the 1960-61 season, Martín Laza Rosell, as listed in his travel records, left La Habana and arrived in Miami on April 23, 1962, a few short days after his 24th birthday, listed as April 11, 1938, and born in Matanzas, Cuba. His travel destination was Tampa to join the ball club in the Al Lopez Field of the same city.

Year	Age	Tm	Lg	Lev
1955	20	Hobbs Sports	Longhorn League	C
1955	20	Yuma Sun Sox	Arizona-Mexico League	C
1955	20	Nogales Yaquis	Arizona-Mexico League	C
1956	21	Wausau Lumberjacks	Northern League	C
1957	22	Clovis Redlegs	Southwestern League	B
1957	22	Wenatchee Chiefs	Northwest League	B
1958	23	Albuquerque Dukes	Western League	A
1959	24	Topeka Hawks	Illinois-Indiana-Iowa League	B
1960	25	Topeka Reds	Illinois-Indiana-Iowa League	B
1961	26	Tampa Tarpons	Florida State League	D
1962	27	Tampa Tarpons	Florida State League	D

Ramón Luis Seara Caluino

His first name, Ramón, shown in baseball reference, was confirmed by both Omelis Hongamen and former player Iván Davis, even though he is listed as Ramón Seara and Luis Seara, depending on the publication.

He played but one game in Cuba in that last season and had one time at bat with no hits. According to Omelis Hongamen, his father was a "functionary of the baseball stadium in Habana".

He played from 1959 with the Class D Geneva team, through 1963 with the Class A Grandforks playing only one game hitting, .253 in 122 games, including one season with the Class D Palatka Redlegs in 1960. He ended his professional career at the age of 24.

Given his record in the U.S. from 1961 to 63, it suggests his having come and stayed, but research to date has not unveiled the actual travel record.

Additional sources:

Omalis Hongamen, telephone interview with author, October 5, 2016.
Iván Davis, telephone interview with author, October 24, 2016.

Year	Age	Tm	Lg	Lev
1959	20	Geneva Redlegs	New York-Pennsylvania League	D
1960	21	Palatka Redlegs	Florida State League	D
1961	22	Tampa Tarpons	Florida State League	D
1961	22	Jersey City Jerseys	International League	AAA
1962	23	Charleston Indians	Eastern League	A
1962	23	Jacksonville Suns	International League	AAA
1963	24	Grand Forks Chiefs	Northern League	A

José Valdivielso López

During his seven seasons in the Cuban professional baseball league, Valdivielso hit a low .222 in 1093 appearances at the plate while playing for Almendares and Marianao. His low average continued during that last season, hitting just .178 in 135 at bats.

He played in three Caribbean Series in 1955, 57 and 58, hitting .250 in 14 games and two plate appearances.

He started his U.S. minor league career playing for the Class C Lubbock Hubbers at the age of 19 and ended his professional career in 1964 with the Triple A Indianapolis Indians at the age of 30. During his ten seasons in the minors he played 745 games, hitting .264. He played in the majors for five seasons appearing in 41 games and hitting .219, including the 1961 season, playing his first game that season on April 27.

Born José Martínez Valdivielso López, he was born in the Isle of Pines in Cuba, according to his marriage certificate, to Wilda Watler, on September 19, 1960, in Arlington Virginia. The island is located off the southern coast of Cuba and known today as the *Island of Youth*, the site of a former major prison. It was reported that in 1966 his family came to the U.S., as their property had been confiscated by Castro regime. He has no family in Cuba, and no interest in returning. "I could not live under any circumstances like that." "He hopes for regime change in his life time. After retirement, he had a Broadcasting career with the Yankees and the Mets in the Telemundo and ESPN stations.

Additional source: Henninger Thom Tony Oliva University of Minnesota Press Minneapolis London 2015 page 195

Year	Age	Tm	Lg	Lev
1953	19	Lubbock Hubbers	West Texas-New Mexico League	C
1954	20	Rock Hill Chiefs	Tri-State League	B
1954	20	Charlotte Hornets	South Atlantic League	A
1954	20	Lubbock Hubbers	West Texas-New Mexico League	C

Year	Age	Tm	Lg	Lev
1955	21	Charlotte Hornets	South Atlantic League	A
1955	21	Washington Senators	American League	MLB
1956	22	Louisville Colonels	American Association	AAA
1956	22	Washington Senators	American League	MLB
1957	23	Indianapolis Indians	American Association	AAA
1958	24	Phoenix Giants	Pacific Coast League	AAA
1958	24	Minneapolis Millers	American Association	AAA
1959	25	Miami Marlins	International League	AAA
1959	25	Washington Senators	American League	MLB
1960	26	Washington Senators	American League	MLB
1961	27	Minnesota Twins	American League	MLB
1962	28	Vancouver Mounties	Pacific Coast League	AAA
1963	29	Indianapolis Indians	International League	AAA
1964	30	Indianapolis Indians	Pacific Coast League	AAA

Zoilo Casanova (Zorro) Versalles Rodríguez

Versalles, the slick fielder for Marianao, played a total of four seasons in the Cuban league hitting .223 in 323 times at bat. He had a low batting average of .214 during the last season in Cuba, in 1960-61. But he saved his best performances for when he played in the majors.

Zorro (Fox) began his minor league career in the U.S. in 1958 at the age of 18 years old with the Class D Elmira Pioneers of the New York-Penn League, and ended his professional career in 1974 with Poza Rica in the Mexican League. During that time, he played only four seasons in the minors hitting .283. He also played part of five seasons in the Mexican and Japanese leagues.

He played in the majors during twelve seasons starting in 1959 at 19 years old with the Washington Senators and played a total of 1400 games with a .242 batting average. This included seven games in the 1965 World Series, hitting.286, the year he was selected as the Most Valuable Player. Named to the All Star team on two occasions, 1963 and 1965, he came to bat twice with one hit.

It is not surprising to note that Versalles was elected to the Cuban Baseball Hall of Fame in Miami in 1983.

Following the end of the 1960-61 season in Cuba, Versalles came to the U.S. He was playing for the Minnesota Twins, in the majors on April 11 of that year, batting .280 when his career "took off". He had played for the Washington Senators during the 1960 season.

Newly married in 1961, his wife María was pregnant back in Cuba with the first of 6 daughters, but she was happily able to join him in 1962. Sadly, his mother died during those early years in Cuba but, ultimately, Versalles was able to reunite with his father and other members of his family years later (see source cited below).

Following his retirement from baseball, he did menial jobs and suffered from a bad back, dying at the young age of 55 on June 9, 1995 in Bloomington, Minnesota.

Additional sources:

Henninger Thom Tony Oliva University of Minnesota Press Minneapolis London 2015 Page 82

Henninger Thom Tony Oliva University of Minnesota Press Minneapolis London 2015 Page 85

Year	Age	Tm	Lg	Lev
1958	18	Elmira Pioneers	New York-Pennsylvania League	D
1959	19	Fox Cities Foxes	Illinois-Indiana-Iowa League	B
1959	19	Washington Senators	American League	MLB
1960	20	Charleston Senators	American Association	AAA
1960	20	Washington Senators	American League	MLB
1961	21	Minnesota Twins	American League	MLB
1962	22	Minnesota Twins	American League	MLB
1963	23	Minnesota Twins	American League	MLB
1964	24	Minnesota Twins	American League	MLB
1965	25	Minnesota Twins	American League	MLB
1966	26	Minnesota Twins	American League	MLB
1967	27	Minnesota Twins	American League	MLB
1968	28	Los Angeles Dodgers	National League	MLB
1969	29	Cleveland Indians	American League	MLB
1969	29	Washington Senators	American League	MLB
1970	30	Union Laguna Algodoneros	Mexican League	AAA
1971	31	Union Laguna Algodoneros	Mexican League	AAA
1971	31	Atlanta Braves	National League	MLB
1972	32	Union Laguna Algodoneros	Mexican League	AAA
1972	32	Hiroshima Toyo Carp	Japan Central League	Fgn
1972	32	Cordoba Cafeteros	Mexican League	AAA

Year	Age	Tm	Lg	Lev
1973	33	Jacksonville Suns	Southern League	AA
1973	33	Sabinas Piratas	Mexican League	AAA
1974	34	Poza Rica Petroleros	Mexican League	AAA

Outfielders

Juan (Cachano) Francisco Delís

Cachano played eight seasons in the Cuban baseball league, all with the Marianao Tigers and batted for an average of .269 in 1570 times at bat.

During the 1960-61 season, Delís kept a consistent batting average, hitting .266 in 203 times at the plate, and kept up this performance during two Caribbean series, in 1957 and in 1958, in 24 times, at bat hitting .250. He was named the Rookie of the Year for the 1953-54 season. He also played for the Havana Cubans in 1953, when his average was a solid .287 in 494 times at bat. A member of the Cuban Sugar Kings in 1954 and in 1956, Delís' average was .264 in 602 appearances at the plate for 221 games.

He played in the U.S. and Mexico from 1952, starting with the Class B Danville Leafs of the Carolina League, and went through 1966 (at the age of 38 years old) with the Single A Yucatan Venados in the Mexican League. His batting average in the minors, in 669 games was a strong .284. He became a member of the Washington Senators in the American League in 1955, playing in 54 games and hitting .189.

From all that is available, including interviews with former players, Juan Delís remained living in Cuba, while playing in the Mexican League after the 1960-61 season. He died in La Habana on July 23, 2003 and is buried in the *Cristóbal Colón* (Christopher Columbus) Cemetery in the same city.

Year	Age	Tm	Lg	Lev
1952	24	Danville Leafs	Carolina League	B
1953	25	Havana Cubans	Florida International League	B
1954	26	Havana Sugar Kings	International League	AAA
1955	27	Washington Senators	American League	MLB
1956	28	Havana Sugar Kings	International League	AAA
1957	29	Seattle Rainiers	Pacific Coast League	Opn
1958	30	Seattle Rainiers	Pacific Coast League	AAA
1959	31	Savannah Reds	South Atlantic League	A
1959	31	Monterrey Sultanes	Mexican League	AA
1960	32	Monterrey Sultanes	Mexican League	AA
1961	33	Monterrey Sultanes	Mexican League	AA
1962	34	Monterrey Sultanes	Mexican League	AA
1963	35	Monterrey Sultanes	Mexican League	AA
1964	36	Monterrey Sultanes	Mexican League	AA
1965	37	Monterrey Sultanes	Mexican League	AA
1965	37	Yucatan Venados	Mexican Southeast League	A
1966	38	Yucatan Venados	Mexican Southeast League	A

Orlando Leroux

Leroux played a total of six seasons, all with Marianao, hitting .248 in 266 times at bat. He moved his average up during the 1960-61 season to .273 in 44 appearances at the plate while backing up José Tartabull, Orestes Miñoso and Oscar Sardiñas.

Playing in the Caribbean Series in 1957 and in 1958, he came to bat six times, hitting .333 with a single and a double.

Leroux played only four seasons in the minors, starting with the Roanoke Rapids, a Class D team in the Coastal Plain League, and had a combined batting average of .312 in 389 games. Despite the high batting average he only played in teams in the B, C and D class in the Minors. He spent most of his professional career in Mexico, from 1956 through 1961, finishing with the Double A Poza Rica squad.

Following the 1960-61 season, Leroux stayed in Cuba and managed the Granjeros in 1964-1965 and the Henequeneros in 1967-1968 and 1968-1969. In the 1970s, he led the Agricultores to the Cuban Serie Nacional title in 1974-1975; it was their only national championship. He finished his career leading the La Habana squad during the 1979-1980, 1980-1981 and 1983-1984 seasons. INDER documentation reports him as managing eight seasons but the record is not conclusive as the 1966 Guia de Beisbol suggests one less season.

Additional sources:
Ecured.cu/Orlando Leroux
Rodríguez, Carlos. *Guía Oficial Beisbol.* La Habana, Cuba: Alejo Carpenter, 2002

Year	Age	Tm	Lg	Lev
1952	23	Roanoke Rapids Jays	Coastal Plain League	D
1953	24	Bluefield Blue-Grays	Appalachian League	D
1954	25	Hagerstown Packets	Piedmont League	B
1954	25	Kingsport Cherokees	Mountain States League	C
1955	26	Hagerstown Packets	Piedmont League	B
1956	27	Yucatan Leones	Mexican League	AA
1957	28	Yucatan Leones	Mexican League	AA
1958	29	Yucatan Leones	Mexican League	AA
1959	30	Veracruz Aguilas	Mexican League	AA
1960	31	Mexico City Diablos Rojos	Mexican League	AA
1961	32	Poza Rica Petroleros	Mexican League	AA

Saturnino Orestes Armas (Minnie) Arrieta Miñoso

The accomplishments of Orestes Miñoso can't be summarized adequately, but respect for all the other players who performed during the 1960-61 season makes it necessary to only highlight some of the contributions of this great player.

His date of birth has been the cause for lots of speculation. It is reported to be as early as November 23, 1923, as shown in his Cuban 1951 Drivers License and in his 1961 travel record from La Habana to Miami, as late as 1925. Hc played with a semipro factory team in Cuba (see source cited below) before he entered the professional league. His fourteen seasons in the Cuban professional league, all with Marianao, included 2992 times at the plate, hitting for average of .280. He was named the Rookie of the Year during the 1945-46 season for his contributions, including a .294 batting average. He was named the Most Valuable Player twice, in the 1952-53 and 1956-57 seasons. In his last season in Cuba he came to bat 128 times and had a batting average of .250 with the last place Marianao team.

He played two seasons in the Caribbean Series in 1957 and 1958, with a combined batting average of .356 in twelve games.

Miñoso played for the New York Cubans in 1946 through the 1948 season. During the 1948 season, he played for the Dayton Indians and, by 1949, he began his minor league career with San Diego, followed by the Cleveland Indians, thus becoming the first Cuban black to play in the majors. He also became the first black to play for the Chicago White Sox, in 1951.

He played a total of 32 seasons, three in the Negro, four in the minor, nine in the Mexican and seventeen in the major leagues. His minor league batting average was .318 and he had a .298 average in the majors. Following his regular playing through the 1973 season, he made brief appearances in 1976, in three games, in 1980, in two games and in 1993 and 2003, in one game each. During his appearance with the St Paul's Saints in 2003, Miñoso drew a walk, thus becoming the only player to appear professionally in seven different decades (see source cited below).

He was named to the All Star game from 1951-54, 1957, 1959 and 1960, being the first Cuban selected to the game. He played in eight games and coming to the plate 20 times he batted .300. The 1957 season marked the first one in which Gold Glove Awards were awarded, and Miñoso was chosen as the first honoree in left field. His average dropped to .280 during the 1961 season.

Called out of retirement in 1976, he became a first and third base coach for three seasons for the White Sox and he was a manager in the Mexican League from 1967 through the 1975 season with a record of 377 wins and 422 losses.

It is not surprising to note he was inducted into the Cuban Baseball Hall of Fame in Miami in 1983. Later on "Mr. White Sox" became a member of the Chicagoland Sports Hall of Fame in 1994, the Mexican Professional Baseball Hall of Fame in 1996, the Hispanic Heritage Baseball Museum Hall of Fame on August 11, 2002, and the Cuban Baseball Hall of Fame in 2014.

On September 19, 2004, Minnie Miñoso Day was celebrated at U.S. Cellular Field, and there was a pregame unveiling of a Minnie Miñoso statue at the field. Miñoso received the 2011 Jerome

Holtzman Award from the Chicago Baseball Museum (see source cited below). He has yet to be named to the Baseball Hall of Fame in Cooperstown, a recognition that it is long overdue.

During the 1960-61 season in Cuba, Miñoso had been the Player's Association President, as cited early on, and his travel record shows his leaving Cuba before the actual season ended, arriving in Miami, from La Habana, on January 14, 1961.

Miñoso was found dead in the driver's seat of a car near a gas station in Chicago at 1 am on March 1, 2015, after attending a friend's birthday party the previous day. He was cremated, and the location of the ashes were not disclosed.

Additional sources:
Bjarkman Peter C. The Cuban Comet Elysian Fields 2002, 22-37
Sarasota Herald Tribune July 17, 2003
chicagotribune.com 2011

Year	Age	Tm	Lg	Lev
1946	20	New York Cubans	Negro National League	NgM
1947	21	New York Cubans	Negro National League	NgM
1948	22	Dayton Indians	Central League	A
1948	22	New York Cubans	Negro National League	NgM
1949	23	San Diego Padres	Pacific Coast League	AAA
1949	23	Cleveland Indians	American League	MLB
1950	24	San Diego Padres	Pacific Coast League	AAA
1951	25	Cleveland Indians	American League	MLB
1951	25	Chicago White Sox	American League	MLB
1952	26	Chicago White Sox	American League	MLB
1953	27	Chicago White Sox	American League	MLB
1954	28	Chicago White Sox	American League	MLB
1955	29	Chicago White Sox	American League	MLB

Year	Age	Tm	Lg	Lev
1956	30	Chicago White Sox	American League	MLB
1957	31	Chicago White Sox	American League	MLB
1958	32	Cleveland Indians	American League	MLB
1959	33	Cleveland Indians	American League	MLB
1960	34	Chicago White Sox	American League	MLB
1961	35	Chicago White Sox	American League	MLB
1962	36	St. Louis Cardinals	National League	MLB
1963	37	Washington Senators	American League	MLB
1964	38	Indianapolis Indians	Pacific Coast League	AAA
1964	38	Chicago White Sox	American League	MLB
1965	39	Jalisco Charros	Mexican League	AA
1966	40	Jalisco Charros	Mexican League	AA
1967	41	Orizaba Charros	Mexican Southeast League	A
1967	41	Jalisco Charros	Mexican League	AAA
1968	42	Jalisco Charros	Mexican League	AAA
1968	42	Puerto Mexico Portenos	Mexican Southeast League	A
1969	43	Jalisco Charros	Mexican League	AAA
1969	43	Puerto Penasco	Mexican Northern League	A
1970	44	Union Laguna Algodoneros	Mexican League	AAA
1971	45	Union Laguna Algodoneros	Mexican League	AAA
1972	46	Union Laguna Algodoneros	Mexican League	AAA
1973	47	Union Laguna Algodoneros	Mexican League	AAA
1976	50	Chicago White Sox	American League	MLB
1980	54	Chicago White Sox	American League	MLB

Year	Age	Tm	Lg	Lev
1993	67	St. Paul Saints	Northern League	Ind
2003	--	St. Paul Saints	Northern League	Ind

Oscar Sardiñas

Sardiñas played for ten seasons in the Cuban League, for the Habana and Cienfuegos teams, before finishing his two seasons with Marianao. His combined batting average of .275 came in 1039 appearances at the plate, raising his batting average to .287 in 129 times at the plate during his last season. He played during three Caribbean Series in 1953, 54 and 55, coming to bat only six times while hitting a low .167.

He began his minor league career in the U.S. in 1952 playing for the Class D Sheboygan Indians of the Wisconsin State League where he hit .310. He ended his professional career playing for the Veracruz Aguilas after four seasons in the Mexican League. During his time in the minors, he played in 436 games and had a batting average of .338.

Sardiñas travelled to the U.S. in 1960 in September and December. Following the end of the 1960-61 season records reflect that on March 31, 1962 he arrived in Miami on his way to Jacksonville Florida having boarded a flight in Maiquetía located in the outskirts of the capital city of Caracas, Venezuela where his permanent address is recorded. His date of birth can be a source of speculation, showing a July 18, 1930 and 1937 in two publications, but his travel papers in 1960 and 1962 show a September 27, 1930 date. His place of birth is listed in four different sources, including a baseball card when playing for the Habana Lions showing Manguito and Colón both in the province of Matanzas, La Habana and Perico which is also located in the Matanzas Province north of the town of Colón. It is the latter, Perico, that is listed in those same travel records in 1962.

Additional sources:

Figueredo, Jorge S. *Who's Who in Cuban Baseball 1878-1961*. Jefferson, North Carolina and London: McFarland and Company, 2003 page 194
CubaCollectibles.com Oscar Sardinas Baseball card #50

Year	Age	Tm	Lg	Lev
1952	21	Sheboygan Indians	Wisconsin State League	D
1952	21	Lancaster Red Roses	Interstate League	B
1953	22	Great Falls Electrics	Pioneer League	C
1954	23	Elmira Pioneers	Eastern League	A
1955	24	Monterrey Sultanes	Mexican League	AA
1956	25	Montreal Royals	International League	AAA
1957	26	Monterrey Sultanes	Mexican League	AA
1958	27	Nuevo Laredo Tecolotes	Mexican League	AA
1958	27	Monterrey Sultanes	Mexican League	AA
1960	29	Veracruz Aguilas	Mexican League	AA

José Milages Tartabull Guzmán

José Tartabull ended his last and third season in the Cuban professional Baseball League hitting .264 leading the league with 265 times at bat. This is a higher percentage than his average during those three seasons which was .246, coming to bat a total of 407 times.

His career in the U.S. began in 1958 playing for the Class D Hastings Giants of the Nebraska State League. He was signed by Giants scout Alex Pompez and playing through the 1972 season, at the age of 33, with the Yucatan team of the Mexican League. During his ten seasons in the minors he played a total of 819 games hitting a strong .296, but he would be challenged and troubled by the lack of the English language and the racist behavior he encountered especially in restaurants and on buses (see source cited below).

This sure-gloved outfielder was soon promoted to the major leagues with the Kansas City Athletics where he established himself with a .277 batting average during the 1962 season. Following his career as a player, Tartabull was a manager for the Braves minor league squad team during the 2011 and 12 seasons and secured a 70-64 record.

He was elected to the Cuban Baseball Hall of Fame in Miami in 1997.

Leaving Cuba after the end of the 1960-61 season Tartabull, said, "I had to make a decision in 1961-play ball or stay in Cuba. I was a ballplayer, that's what I had done all my life, so I really had no choice. Our children can't relate to the way we feel about Cuba because they didn't have to leave family and home behind. When I see what Danny has done for the Tartabull name (referring to his son former major leaguer Danny Tartabull), I realize that the decision I made in 1961 was the right one." But, as he commented in an interview for the SABR Bio Project, "Who would have ever thought in 1961 that I still never been back or seen our families." Following that interview and, after not seeing his family for 43 years, Tartabull has returned and travelled back to Cuba regularly.

Looking back at the opportunity to play professionally enabled him to help his family. His father's message was, "This is your career, this is Communism, this is the end, and you can't pursue your career here." (Cuba). Everybody deserves respect, was the message and a significant influence in his decision.

At that time, everybody knew that players were leaving from Cuba to the U.S. via Mexico where he had a contract to play professional baseball. He played in 1961, in the Texas League, for the Rio Grande/ Victoria Giants, Tartabull went back to Cuba and left again on February 22, 1962. He arrived in Miami, having boarded in La Habana, on his way to the Municipal Stadium in Kansas. His date of birth on the travel papers shows his birthday to be in 1937, the year prior to that listed in other publications.

At the present time, Tartabull continues to share his knowledge of the sport. He worked with Paulino Casanova, who passed away in 2017. They both worked at the Casanova baseball academy along with former major league players Cholly Naranjo and Jackie Hernández.

Additional sources:

José Tartabull, personal interview with author, February 2016.
Boston Globe Peter Gammons Feb 21, 1992 Page 47
Hulbert Joanne SABR BioProject "José Tartabull" (http://sabr.org/bioproj/person)
José Tartabull, telephone interview with author, August 2017.

Year	Age	Tm	Lg	Lev
1958	19	Hastings Giants	Nebraska State League	D-
1958	19	Michigan City White Caps	Midwest League	D
1959	20	Michigan City White Caps	Midwest League	D
1960	21	Eugene Emeralds	Northwest League	B
1961	22	Rio Grande Valley/Victoria Giants	Texas League	AA
1962	23	Kansas City Athletics	American League	MLB
1963	24	Portland Beavers	Pacific Coast League	AAA

Year	Age	Tm	Lg	Lev
1963	24	Kansas City Athletics	American League	MLB
1964	25	Kansas City Athletics	American League	MLB
1965	26	Vancouver Mounties	Pacific Coast League	AAA
1965	26	Kansas City Athletics	American League	MLB
1966	27	Kansas City Athletics	American League	MLB
1966	27	Boston Red Sox	American League	MLB
1967	28	Pittsfield Red Sox	Eastern League	AA
1967	28	Boston Red Sox	American League	MLB
1968	29	Boston Red Sox	American League	MLB
1969	30	Iowa Oaks	American Association	AAA
1969	30	Louisville Colonels	International League	AAA
1969	30	Oakland Athletics	American League	MLB
1970	31	Iowa Oaks	American Association	AAA
1970	31	Oakland Athletics	American League	MLB
1971	32	Iowa Oaks	American Association	AAA
1972	33	Yucatan Leones	Mexican League	AAA

Chapter 9

THE ENDURING EXODUS AND THE MINOR LEAGUERS

The end of the Cuban Professional Baseball League in February of 1961 did not reflect the full and complete exodus of baseball players who wished to pursue their dreams of playing professional baseball and, sadly, felt compelled to leave their families, their friends and their home country.

In fact, some baseball players who had played in the U.S. Negro Leagues, or in the U.S. minor league system, not including players in the Cuban Sugar Kings previously addressed, during 1960 and 1961, also left or stayed in the U.S. after their baseball season ended. This included others who had not played during that last season in the Cuban League. In addition to the players, one manager was also among those included.

This chapter also shows those players that may not have been on the active roster of the Cuban Professional League but were, in effect, part of the "practice" squad. The one constant between this group of players and those that were on the active roster is that they also experienced the difficult decision needed to be made. They faced the same challenge about what to do with their career aspirations along with the inherent personal consequences. Therefore, their career and life experience during that time is worthy of inclusion here because they too would need to endure the same heart-wrenching decision. Some are virtually unknown and never reached the majors, but some did and had outstanding careers, including induction into the Baseball Hall of Fame in Cooperstown.

The 1960 and 1961 period has been selected because it was during that very time that players needed to make their personal decision since professional baseball was abolished by the Castro government. My research led to the identification of the 145 affiliates of the sixteen major league Franchises in 1960 and the 151 corresponding affiliates of the eighteen Franchises in 1961. The identification of Cuban born players has been a challenge since resources available do not always include country of birth. Therefore, the players and manager included here are the best that the research was able to produce. I would welcome any information that would lead to the identification of any other Cuban born player during that period but not included here.

A similar baseball history, including a summary or some of the highlights of the baseball players' careers in and outside of Cuba (if applicable), their playing teams' history and travel record from Cuba, or if they chose to stay or returned at some point, is shared here, and is based on immigration records or, along with some personal stories, is provided through personal interviews and references cited below. To the degree possible, I have included an image of the corresponding player with the credit to the organization which gave the permission to use these images. The acknowledgement page features these organizations.

A note about references and sources. You will find included here baseball records, outside of Cuba, for most of these players at the end of each of their historical summary. This is to provide some context for the story of the players as they left Cuba or chose to stay; courtesy of baseball-reference.com. However, I have avoided writing or including the entire set of baseball accomplishments and records for each of these players since that information is readily available in many other and more complete sources such as the Figueredo, Jorge S. *Cuban Baseball A Statistical History 1878-1961.* Jefferson, North Carolina and London: McFarland and Company, 2003 Figueredo, Jorge S. *Who's Who in Cuban Baseball 1878-1961.* Jefferson, North Carolina and London: McFarland and Company, 2003, González, Echevarría, Roberto. *The Pride of Havana A History of Cuban Baseball.* New

York Oxford: Oxford University Press, 1999 and baseball-reference.com which I used as the primary reference sources for this effort. Immigration, travel records and pertinent information was secured via ancestry.com. As previously indicated, I have relied on the immigration record when facing inconsistencies with information previously published. My reason behind this, is that I presume that players did not wish to jeopardize their travel especially to the U.S. or U.S. citi-zenship application by inserting incorrect information. Other sources were used which I have endeavored to reference throughout the text.

A look at the players:

Aurelio Ala Hechavarría

Ala listed his birthdate as August 2, 1928 on the official travel documents from Cuba rather than the listed date of August 3, 1930 elsewhere. His birthplace of Santiago de Cuba could not be verified in the same travel documents due to the poor quality of the image available. He reportedly travelled to the U.S. on March 26, 1960 from La Habana to Miami with a destination to join the Visalia Athletics baseball club in California. This was a Class C team affiliated with Kansas City who apparently demonstrated sufficient talent to play for the Sioux City Soos, Class B that season.

He also travelled leaving Cuba in 1961, following the end of the last professional baseball season, and arrived in New Orleans, Louisiana on March 20 with a visa provided in Mexico on the 17th with a destination of Pensacola, Florida.

Ala played in the U.S. minors at third base from 1952 through 1961, appearing in a total of 907 games and was 3353 times at the plate. Unfortunately, statistics for one short period prevents the ability to secure the batting average actual number. However, a look at his hitting performance from the 1954 through the 1961 season–at the age of 30 years old–Ala came to the plate 4177 times and had 1336 with a very strong .319 batting average.

His baseball career ended with the 1961 season in the U.S., which came about after the end of the 60-61 professional baseball season in

Cuba, its last. Obviously, he clearly had made the decision to stay at least during that time.

Year	Age	Tm	Lg	Lev	Aff
1952	21	Drummondville Cubs	Provincial League	C	WSH
1953	22	Thetford Mines Miners	Provincial League	C	SLB
1954	23	York White Roses	Piedmont League	B	BAL
1954	23	Thetford Mines Miners	Provincial League	C	BAL
1955	24	Burlington A's	Provincial League	C	KCA
1956	25	Pocatello Bannocks	Pioneer League	C	KCA
1956	25	Abilene Blue Sox	Big State League	B	KCA
1957	26	Pocatello A's	Pioneer League	C	KCA
1958	27	Pocatello A's	Pioneer League	C	KCA
1959	28	Pocatello A's	Pioneer League	C	KCA
1960	29	Sioux City Soos	Illinois-Indiana-Iowa League	B	KCA
1961	30	Pocatello Bannocks	Pioneer League	C	KCA-SFG

Inael Alarcon

This young outfielder played only two seasons in the U.S. minors, appearing in 46 games. He landed in the U.S. on April 5, 1960 on his way to play for the Palatka Redlegs, a Cincinnati affiliate, playing in the city by the St. John River in Florida, for 29 games and hitting a low .159. Returning to Cuba he traveled back to the U.S. on November 5, 1960.

At the end of the Cuban League in 1961, he obtained a visa through the Mexican Embassy on April 12, 1961 and arrived in Miami, from Mexico, on April 16, 1961 on his way to Fernandina Beach outside of Jacksonville, Florida. The travel record of that time shows his having been born in Bayamo–although the name is not conclusive given the poor physical condition of the travel record–on January 24, 1939, one year older than published elsewhere.

Alarcon played for the Class D Fort Walton Beach Jets in only seventeen games with a .206 batting average, the season that began following the end of professional baseball in Cuba. At the very least, he had decided to stay in the U.S. consistent with his travel in April of 1961.

Year	Age	Tm	Lg	Lev
1960		Palatka Redlegs	Florida State League	D
1961	21	Fort Walton Beach Jets	Alabama-Florida League	D

Dagoberto (Bert) Blanco Campaneris

Campaneris was a cousin to former player José Cardenal. He was on tour at the age of 19 years old with a Cuban team in Costa Rica, with fellow player Tito Fuentes, in April 1961 but returned to Cuba according to his travel records.

Ultimately, he secured an exit permit and a visa "waiver" allowing to leave Cuba from the La Habana airport. He arrived in the U.S., in Miami, on April 4, 1962 on his way to join the Lewiston ball club in Daytona Beach, Florida. The date of birth listed on his travel papers shows a March 9, 1942 date which is a different date than that shown on his application for U.S. Citizenship on March 9, 1944. His U.S. Naturalization Application was transferred while living in Alameda, California to the U.S. District in Kansas City, Missouri on December 2, 1971. During that process he requested his name be changed from Campanería to Campaneris.

His career in the U.S. began in 1962 with the Daytona Beach squad, an affiliate of the Kansas City Athletics. He played in the minors for four seasons hitting a robust .310 in 258 games. By 1964 he was in the majors where he played a total of 19 seasons in 2328 games while hitting .259.

Towards the end of his career, in 1982, he also played one season in the Mexican League with the Veracruz and Poza Rica Triple AAA teams. He finished his career with the New York Yankees in 1983 at the age of 41, with a .322 batting average in 60 games. Campaneris, not surprisingly, is a member of the Cuban Baseball of Fame in Miami, Florida.

Year	Age	Tm	Lg	Lev
1962	20	Binghamton Triplets	Eastern League	A
1962	20	Daytona Beach Islanders	Florida State League	D
1963	21	Lewiston Broncs	Northwest League	A
1963	21	Binghamton Triplets	Eastern League	AA
1964	22	Birmingham Barons	Southern League	AA
1964	22	Kansas City Athletics	American League	MLB
1965	23	Kansas City Athletics	American League	MLB
1966	24	Kansas City Athletics	American League	MLB
1967	25	AIL Athletics	Arizona Instructional League	WRk

Year	Age	Tm	Lg	Lev
1967	25	Kansas City Athletics	American League	MLB
1968	26	Oakland Athletics	American League	MLB
1969	27	Oakland Athletics	American League	MLB
1970	28	Oakland Athletics	American League	MLB
1971	29	Oakland Athletics	American League	MLB
1972	30	Oakland Athletics	American League	MLB
1973	31	Oakland Athletics	American League	MLB
1974	32	Oakland Athletics	American League	MLB
1975	33	Oakland Athletics	American League	MLB
1976	34	Oakland Athletics	American League	MLB
1977	35	Texas Rangers	American League	MLB
1978	36	Texas Rangers	American League	MLB
1979	37	Texas Rangers	American League	MLB
1979	37	California Angels	American League	MLB
1980	38	California Angels	American League	MLB
1981	39	California Angels	American League	MLB
1982	40	Veracruz Aguila	Mexican League	AAA
1982	40	Poza Rica Petroleros	Mexican League	AAA
1983	41	Columbus Clippers	International League	AAA
1983	41	New York Yankees	American League	MLB

José Rosario Domec Cardenal

Born on October 7, 1943 in Matanzas, Cardenal was signed by the San Francisco Giants as an amateur free agent in 1960. A cousin to major leaguer Bert Campaneris, Cardenal had a long career spent mostly in the major leagues.

He began in 1961 in the Sophomore League at the age of 17, playing for the Class D El Paso Sun Kings where he hit .355 in 128 games. He also played for the Class B Eugene Emeralds of the Northwest

League for a brief nine games, hitting .280 and reaching the majors by the 1963 season, played for the San Francisco Giants.

In 1973, as a right fielder for the Cubs, Cardenal led the team with a .303 batting average, including 33 doubles and 19 stolen bases. He was named Cubs Player of the Year by the Chicago baseball writers. Famously temperamental, in 1974, Cardenal was at odds with the Cubs management and notoriously refused to play the season opener, claiming that he was injured because the eyelids of one eye were stuck open (see source cited below).

During his four-season minor league career, Cardenal played a total of 515 games with a batting average of .298. In an 18-season career in the majors, Cardenal was a .275 hitter with 138 home runs and 775 RBI in 2017 games played. In addition, he collected 1913 hits, 936 runs, 46 triples and 329 stolen bases. He finished his playing career in 1980 playing for the Kansas City Royals at the age of 36 playing 25 games and hitting .340 in 53 appearances at the plate.

José Cardenal was the first base coach for the Yankees World Championships in 1996, 1998, and 1999. He resigned from his position with the Yankees prior to the 2000 season over a contract dispute (see source cited below).

In 2005, Cardenal became the senior advisor to the Washington Nationals General Manager. On September 14, he announced that he wanted to help the victims of Hurricane Katrina, and was seeking to auction the World Series ring he won with the New York Yankees in 1998. Cardenal was relieved of his position with the Nationals following the 2009 season. Following the end with the Nationals, Cardenal indicated that his interests going forward was to help Cuban players in Cuba come to the U.S., legally, to play professional baseball.

His extensive baseball career after 1961 led to his induction into the Cuban Baseball of Fame in Miami, Florida and reflects his stay in the U.S.

Additional sources:

Justonebadcentury.com/chicago_cubs_tales9_27_asp
Bill Madden 2/23/2000 To José Cardenal First things First Daily News New York
Tyler Kepron 1/1/2000 Baseball Mazzilli is back in New York and wearing Stripes The New York Times.
Bill Ladson 14 September 2005 Cardenal wants to help MLB .com
Bill Ladson MLB.com 10/8 2009 Nationals cut ties with Cardenal.

Year	Age	Tm	Lg	Lev
1961	17	El Paso Sun Kings	Sophomore League	D
1961	17	Eugene Emeralds	Northwest League	B
1962	18	Tacoma Giants	Pacific Coast League	AAA
1963	19	El Paso Sun Kings	Texas League	AA
1963	19	San Francisco Giants	National League	MLB
1964	20	Tacoma Giants	Pacific Coast League	AAA
1964	20	San Francisco Giants	National League	MLB
1965	21	California Angels	American League	MLB

Year	Age	Tm	Lg	Lev
1966	22	California Angels	American League	MLB
1967	23	California Angels	American League	MLB
1968	24	Cleveland Indians	American League	MLB
1969	25	Cleveland Indians	American League	MLB
1970	26	St. Louis Cardinals	National League	MLB
1971	27	St. Louis Cardinals	National League	MLB
1971	27	Milwaukee Brewers	American League	MLB
1972	28	Chicago Cubs	National League	MLB
1973	29	Chicago Cubs	National League	MLB
1974	30	Chicago Cubs	National League	MLB
1975	31	Chicago Cubs	National League	MLB
1976	32	Chicago Cubs	National League	MLB
1977	33	Chicago Cubs	National League	MLB
1978	34	Philadelphia Phillies	National League	MLB
1979	35	Philadelphia Phillies	National League	MLB
1979	35	New York Mets	National League	MLB
1980	36	New York Mets	National League	MLB
1980	36	Kansas City Royals	American League	MLB

Paulino Casanova Ortíz

Casanova played ten games in 1960 for the Class D Minot Mallards, a team in the Northern League, affiliated with the Cleveland organization. But his playing days at that level did not last. He was signed to play in the Cuban League but, unfortunately, was never able to join the playing roster during the 1960-61 season. When the last out of the 1960-61 season was registered, Casanova was kneeling in the on-deck circle getting ready to hit and fulfill his dream to play in the league. This last out in the last season ended by the Castro regime denied him the opportunity to secure an active record in the books

since he would have been clearly able to play had another season had taken place.

Casanova left Cuba, heeding his mother's message that playing professional baseball was his job, and that he could better help his family from the U.S. while admonishing not to go back to Cuba. He remembers that all he wanted was to help his family, to play ball and pursue his career. He made his way to the Mexican Embassy in Cuba and secured a visa like others had done previously and were doing at the time. He left Cuba with other players via Mexico Cuba arriving in Miami on March 9, 1961 on his way to Daytona Beach to join the Cleveland Indians organization.

He was released by the Cleveland team in April of that same year and went on to play for the Indianapolis Clowns a barnstorming club in the Negro Leagues during which time he became a teammate of Hank Aaron. He remembers getting a hit off the great Satchel Paige.

Living in the U.S. without a family and unable to speak English he suffered the experience of many others who played in the U.S. at a time when some of the support system and bilingual coaches that are in place today simply did not exist. Relying on other teammates, these players were able to cope with these difficulties until they became more adept with the new language and culture.

Following his time with the Clowns, Casanova played in only two games in 1962 with the Double A San Antonio team. The following year he was able to enter in 94 games batting .261. At that point, his seven-season career in the minors took off where he had a combined .261 batting average. He also played a number of years in the Venezuelan League, starting in the 1965-66 season. At the end of the 1965 season, Paulino Casanova made it to the major leagues for five games and would stay there during all the following seasons through 1974 when he retired from professional baseball at the age of 32.

During his ten seasons in the majors, he batted .225 and was a member of the All Star team in 1967, but his contributions were much more as a receiver given his outstanding arm and knowledge of the game. He was inducted into the Cuban Baseball of Fame in Miami, Florida. His many baseball contributions can be found in a more complete fashion in his biography found in the SABR Biography which served in part as a source for this story (see source cited below).

He founded a baseball Academy which continued to thrive for many years under his personal leadership. He and fellow former players like José Tartabull, Cholly Naranjo and Jackie Hernández worked with local youngsters, baseball prospects and some more established players that came by to hone their skills and seek some pointers to help their game from this cadre of knowledgeable baseball players. JD (Julio Daniel) Martínez, now of the Boston Red Sox, was said to be among those who benefited from Casanova's academy efforts and it was well remembered with some pride in his voice, when *el flaco*, referring to Martínez, hit his first home run in the majors.

Casanova returned to Cuba after a 40 year absence. During some of my personal visits to the academy to secure information, interview players and simply enjoy watching how young players were nurtured, I listened Casanova lament over what he felt was the lack of recognition of many of his fellow players who had contributed so much to the sport in Cuba and the U.S. This would lead to a discussion about the *"Olvidados"*, the forgotten ones, which would ultimately, influence my direction to write this book, to acknowledge these players and managers of that era, and show the sacrifices they and their families made over the years in pursuit of their dream to continue to play professional baseball. This also led to my decision to dedicate this book to him and their memories.

Following a series of medical setbacks over the years, Paulino Casanova passed away on August 12, 2017 surrounded by family members. Jackie Hernández summarized it best by reflecting on how Casanova, to the end was a good and well-respected person by all who knew him. Similarly, the great Luis Tiant, who learned of Casanova's passing through the also great Tony Oliva, was sadden by the news of his longtime friend with whom he had played in Cuba and Venezuela.

Additional sources:

Costello, Rory and Ramírez, José "*Paul Casanova*" SABR Bio Project (http://sabr.org/bioproj/person)
Paulino Casanova, personal interview with author, February 2016.
Jackie Hernández, telephone interview with author, August 13, 2017.
Luis Tiant Jr., telephone interview with author, August 13, 2017.

Year	Age	Tm	Lg	Lev
1960	18	Minot Mallards	Northern League	C
1961	19	Indianapolis Clowns		
1962	20	San Antonio Missions	Texas League	AA
1963	21	Geneva Senators	New York-Pennsylvania League	A
1964	22	Geneva Senators	New York-Pennsylvania League	A
1964	22	FIL Senators	Florida Instructional League	WRk
1965	23	Burlington Senators	Carolina League	A
1965	23	FIL Senators	Florida Instructional League	WRk
1965	23	Washington Senators	American League	MLB
1966	24	York White Roses	Eastern League	AA

Year	Age	Tm	Lg	Lev
1966	24	Washington Senators	American League	MLB
1967	25	Washington Senators	American League	MLB
1968	26	Buffalo Bisons	International League	AAA
1968	26	Washington Senators	American League	MLB
1969	27	Washington Senators	American League	MLB
1970	28	Washington Senators	American League	MLB
1971	29	Washington Senators	American League	MLB
1972	30	Atlanta Braves	National League	MLB
1973	31	Atlanta Braves	National League	MLB
1974	32	Atlanta Braves	National League	MLB

Oscar Feliz Chinique Ortega

Pitching six seasons in the U.S. minors, Chinique appeared in 192 games and secured a record of 30 wins and 35 losses in 736 innings while striking out 268 and walking 314 batters. He also played one season in Mexico for Yucatán. He also played in the Cuban professional baseball league in the 1957-58 and the 1959-60 seasons, pitching for the Habana and Almendares squads respectively, for a total of five games and seven innings, striking out one player and walking two.

His birthplace is listed as Regla, in 1936, but his petition for U.S. citizenship in 1974, and travel papers from Cuba show a birthday of August 23, 1934 in Guanabacoa, Cuba, which is located adjacent to Regla and the capital city of La Habana.

His arrival in the U.S. via Mexico with a visa issued on March 22, 1961 followed the end of the Cuban professional Baseball League in Miami Florida on March 24, 1961.

His residence during the 1990s in the state of Tennessee began much earlier. His petition for Naturalization was approved on July 12, 1974 while he was living in Goodlettsville, Tennessee. Joyce Chinique served as one of his witnesses.

From everything shown here, it can be said with certainty that Chinique stayed in the U.S. after obviously concluding he could no longer pursue his professional baseball career in his home country.

Year	Age	Tm	Lg	Lev	Aff
1956	19	Louisville Colonels	American Association	AAA	WSH
1956	19	Hobbs Sports	Southwestern League	B	WSH
1957	20	Kinston Eagles/ Wilson Tobs	Carolina League	B	WSH
1957	20	Charlotte Hornets	South Atlantic League	A	WSH
1958	21	Yucatan Leones	Mexican League	AA	
1960	23	Charlotte Hornets	South Atlantic League	A	WSH
1961	24	Nashville Volunteers	Southern Association	AA	MIN
1962	25	Charlotte Hornets	South Atlantic League	A	MIN
1963	26	Statesville Owls	Western Carolinas League	A	

Sandalio (Sandy) Simeón Consuegra Castellón

The well-known player Consuegra's birthplace is listed as either Santa Clara or Potrerillos in the Las Villas Province, depending on the source. However, when completing his travel plans to come to the U.S., the more specific site of San Juan de Los Yeras, located in the Villas Province near Potrerillo is listed. Given his arrival to Miami, Florida from La Habana on August 18, 1961 and the political situation at the time, one could gather that much care was taken to ensure accuracy of official documentation. Consuegra was born on September 3rd, 1920. His mother and father were Luisa Castellón and Sotero.

His baseball career spanned from 1945 in Cuba through 1961 in the U.S., including eight seasons in the Cuban professional League, three in Mexico, eight in the U.S. major leagues, and six in the minor leagues.

In Cuba, he appeared in 206 games, pitching in 832 innings and had a 52-55 record with a 3.64 ERA, while pitching in the 1956 Caribbean Series for the Cienfuegos squad. His overall record in Cuba included 270 strikeouts and 280 walks. He did not play in several seasons, including the 1954 season, when he was not allowed to play by Major League Baseball rules, like other Cubans such Orestes Miñoso and Camilo Pascual. During his eight seasons in the majors, Consuegra had a 51 and 32 record in 248 games in 809.1 innings and a 3.37 ERA while pitching in the 1954 All Star game for the Chicago White Sox. Playing in the minors during six seasons, his record of 24 wins and 12 losses came about as he appeared in 84 games and pitched in 311.1 innings.

It is worthy of mention that Consuegra would begin his career in the rich Cuban Amateur League, playing in Cumanayagua and pitching for the Deportivo Matanzas in the early 1940s. Echevarría's book provides a rich account of the "Amateur League" in this time period. See source cited below.

Ultimately, Consuegra's contributions to baseball led to his induction into the Hall of Fame in Miami in 1983. He passed away on November 16, 2005 in Miami where his remains were cremated. A more complete and quality essay about Consuegra can be found in the SABR Biography by Rory Costello. See source cited in the "Resources Consulted" section. His playing career and life history indicates he remained in the U.S.

Additional source: González, Echevarría, Roberto. *The Pride of Havana A History of Cuban Baseball.* New York Oxford: Oxford University Press, 1999.

Year	Age	Tm	Lg	Lev	Aff
1946	25	Puebla Angeles	Mexican League	Ind	
1947	26	Puebla Angeles	Mexican League	Ind	
1948	27	Puebla Angeles	Mexican League	Ind	
1949	28	Havana Cubans	Florida International League	B	WSH
1950	29	Havana Cubans	Florida International League	B	WSH
1950	29	Washington Senators	American League	MLB	WSH
1951	30	Washington Senators	American League	MLB	WSH
1952	31	Washington Senators	American League	MLB	WSH
1953	32	Washington Senators	American League	MLB	WSH
1953	32	Chicago White Sox	American League	MLB	CHW
1954	33	Chicago White Sox	American League	MLB	CHW
1955	34	Chicago White Sox	American League	MLB	CHW
1956	35	Havana Sugar Kings	International League	AAA	CIN
1956	35	Chicago White Sox	American League	MLB	CHW
1956	35	Baltimore Orioles	American League	MLB	BAL
1957	36	Vancouver Mounties	Pacific Coast League	Opn	BAL
1957	36	Baltimore Orioles	American League	MLB	BAL
1957	36	New York Giants	National League	MLB	NYG
1958	37	Monterrey Sultanes	Mexican League	AA	
1958	37	Havana Sugar Kings	International League	AAA	CIN
1961	40	Charlotte Hornets	South Atlantic League	A	MIN

Mario Germán Caballero (Chico) Díaz

The young second baseman Díaz was born on May 2, 1941 in Isabela de Sagua, according to his travel papers to the U.S., even though the date May 12 is listed elsewhere. He played six seasons in the U.S. minors, appearing in 517 games in 1996 at bats while hitting a solid .285.

Following the end of the Cuban professional baseball league, Diaz played for the Boise Braves during the 1961 season, but apparently returned to Cuba only to come back to the U.S., arriving in Miami on March 12, 1962 on a flight from La Habana. At the time of this flight in the Pan American Airlines, he listed his U.S. address to be Waycross, Georgia. His playing career indicates he stayed in the U.S. following the end of professional baseball in Cuba.

Year	Age	Tm	Lg	Lev	Aff
1959	18	Wellsville Braves	New York-Pennsylvania League	D	MLN
1960	19	Eau Claire Braves	Northern League	C	MLN
1961	20	Boise Braves	Pioneer League	C	MLN
1962	21	Cedar Rapids Braves	Midwest League	D	MLN
1963	22	Boise Braves	Pioneer League	A	MLN
1964	23	Tulsa Oilers	Texas League	AA	STL
1964	23	Raleigh Cardinals	Carolina League	A	STL

José Ramón Padilla Dieguez

Padilla, an infielder who also pitched during his seven seasons in the minors, began in 1955 at the age of 20 with the Ocean Oilers a Class D team with the Penn/Ontario League, playing in 91 games, and had a .240 batting average. That same season he played for the Duluth Dukes, a Class C team with the Northern League for 29 games and hitting .134.

During his seven seasons, 1955-1962, he played in 741 games and had a low .209 batting average, but also pitched in 34 games and had a 4-3 record.

His travel record from 1959 on his way to Palatka, Florida, shows his date of birth as August 28, 1935, which was also found in his 1962 record. It was during that latter trip from La Habana that the length of his stay in the U.S. was marked "indefinitely".

He played during the 1961 season for the Erie Sailors and finished his career in 1962 with the Sarasota Sun Sox playing in 89 games and hitting .253 at the age of 27.

In the midst of his playing career, Padilla obtained a degree in Civil Engineering from Northeastern University in Boston Massachusetts, Class of 1956. His name appears as José Ramón Dieguez and his address as Ciudad Trujillo Santo Domingo in the Dominican Republic. It also shows a Co-op work record at the Barnes Engineering Company in Stanford, Connecticutt.

His playing career indicates he remained in the U.S. after the 1960-61 season in Cuba.

Additional source: .ebooksread.com/authors-eng/mass-northeastern-university-boston/cauldron-volume-1956-tro/page-4-cauldron-volume-1956-tro.shtm

Year	Age	Tm	Lg	Lev
1955	20	Duluth Dukes	Northern League	C
1955	20	Olean Oilers	Pennsylvania-Ontario-New York League	D
1956	21	West Palm Beach Sun Chiefs	Florida State League	D
1957	22	Clovis Redlegs	Southwestern League	B
1957	22	Wenatchee Chiefs	Northwest League	B
1958	23	San Antonio Missions	Texas League	AA
1958	23	Nashville Volunteers	Southern Association	AA

Year	Age	Tm	Lg	Lev
1959	24	Palatka Redlegs	Florida State League	D
1959	24	Topeka Hawks	Illinois-Indiana-Iowa League	B
1961	26	Jacksonville Jets	South Atlantic League	A
1961	26	Erie Sailors	New York-Pennsylvania League	D
1962	27	Sarasota Sun Sox	Florida State League	D

Martín Francisco Dihigo Reyna

The son of baseball great Martín Dihigo had a brief minor league career in the U.S., playing the outfield for teams affiliated to the Cincinnati Reds. His birth date of September 17, 1942 in Cruces, Las Villas is documented in his travel papers in 1959. Dihigo started at age 16 with the Palatka Redlegs of the Florida State League. That same season played for the Geneva Redlegs of the New York Penn League in 1959. His last year came in 1962, also as a member of the Geneva team.

He appeared in a total 316 games and had a combined .241 batting average. At the end of professional baseball in Cuba, Dihigo came to the U.S. to play for the Topeka Reds in 1961, arriving in Miami to report to the Cincinnati organization on March 25, 1961, via Mexico with a visa issued the previous day. Although he played in 1962, travel papers between the previous season and this last were not found, leaving open to question whether he returned to Cuba during that time.

However, following his playing days in 1962 Dihigo, returned to Cuba to stay.

Additional source: Bjarkman, Peter C. *A History of Cuban Baseball 1864-2006*. Jefferson, NC, and London: McFarland, 2007.

Year	Age	Tm	Lg	Lev	Aff
1959	16	Palatka Redlegs	Florida State League	D	CIN
1959	16	Geneva Redlegs	New York-Pennsylvania League	D	CIN

Year	Age	Tm	Lg	Lev	Aff
1960	17	Geneva Redlegs	New York-Pennsylvania League	D	CIN
1961	18	Topeka Reds	Illinois-Indiana-Iowa League	B	CIN
1962	19	Macon Peaches	South Atlantic League	A	CIN
1962	19	Geneva Redlegs	New York-Pennsylvania League	D	CIN

Pedro Fernández Arbas

A lesser known player of that time, Fernández was a young outfielder at the age of 18, born on May 4, 1941 in La Habana. He played in 1959 for the Class D Morristown Cubs of the Appalachian League and the Palatka Red Legs for a total of 29 games with fifteen hits in 57 times at bat. He played in 1960 and 61, the latter year with the Fort Walton Beach Jets of the Alabama Florida League.

He must have returned to Cuba after the season ended, which was the best in his short career, batting .293. He subsequently left Cuba, arriving in Miami, from La Habana, on March 15, 1962 with the intention of joining the Houston Colts organization in Arizona. He played his last season in 1962 for the Fort Walton and the Modesto Colts, a Houston affiliate, for only 16 games, and hitting but .146.

During his four season-minor league career he played in 231 games and had a .265 batting average**.** Given his playing days in 1961 and 1962, he remained in the U.S. following the end of professional baseball in Cuba.

Year	Age	Tm	Lg	Lev
1959	18	Morristown Cubs	Appalachian League	D-
1959	18	Palatka Redlegs	Florida State League	D
1960	19	Tampa Tarpons	Florida State League	D
1961	20	Fort Walton Beach Jets	Alabama-Florida League	D

Year	Age	Tm	Lg	Lev
1962	21	Modesto Colts	California League	C
1962	21	Fort Walton Beach Jets	Alabama-Florida League	D

Rigoberto (Tito) Fuentes Peat

Tito Fuentes was on tour with a Cuban team in Costa Rica in April of 1961, with fellow player Bert Campaneris, but returned to Cuba. He ultimately secured an exit permit with a visa "waiver", leaving La Habana and arriving in the U.S., in Miami, on May 27, 1962 on his way to join the Lakeland Baseball Club, according to his travel record. His birthday was listed as 1942 according to his travel record to the U.S. from Cuba but was shown as 1944 elsewhere, which it is not an unusual discrepancy.

His playing days in the U.S. began in 1962 with the Salem Rebels and the Lakeland Giants, teams affiliated with the San Francisco Giants. He played a total of seven seasons and 484 games in the minors, hitting .295. In August of 1965, Fuentes reached the major leagues with the San Francisco Giants and played a total of 1499 games while hitting. 268 in thirteen seasons in the "bigs." He retired from professional baseball in 1979. Fuentes became a radio announcer in 1981, the Giant's first year of Spanish language radio broadcasts, serving in this role until 1992. Tito Fuentes was inducted into the Hispanic Heritage Baseball Museum Hall of Fame on February 23, 2002 in San Francisco, California and to the Cuban Baseball Hall of Fame in Miami, Florida in 1997. In 2004, Fuentes was brought back as an analyst. He remains with the team in this role as these lines were written.

Additional source: mlb.com "The San Francisco Giants partner with Lazer Broadcasting on a three-year deal" (Press release). San Francisco Giants. March 24, 2017

Year	Age	Tm	Lg	Lev
1962	18	Lakeland Giants	Florida State League	D
1962	18	Salem Rebels	Appalachian League	D-
1963	19	El Paso Sun Kings	Texas League	AA
1963	19	Decatur Commodores	Midwest League	A
1964	20	El Paso Sun Kings	Texas League	AA
1964	20	Tacoma Giants	Pacific Coast League	AAA
1965	21	Tacoma Giants	Pacific Coast League	AAA
1965	21	San Francisco Giants	National League	MLB
1966	22	San Francisco Giants	National League	MLB
1967	23	San Francisco Giants	National League	MLB
1968	24	Phoenix Giants	Pacific Coast League	AAA
1969	25	Phoenix Giants	Pacific Coast League	AAA
1969	25	San Francisco Giants	National League	MLB
1970	26	San Francisco Giants	National League	MLB
1971	27	San Francisco Giants	National League	MLB
1972	28	San Francisco Giants	National League	MLB
1973	29	San Francisco Giants	National League	MLB

Year	Age	Tm	Lg	Lev
1974	30	San Francisco Giants	National League	MLB
1975	31	San Diego Padres	National League	MLB
1976	32	San Diego Padres	National League	MLB
1977	33	Detroit Tigers	American League	MLB
1978	34	Oakland Athletics	American League	MLB
1979	35	Santo Domingo Azucareros	Inter-American League	AAA

Reinold García Alfaro

This native of Arroyo Arena El Cano, which is located on the fringes of the capital city of La Habana was born on November 12, 1944.

His three years in the minors began at age 16 in 1961. It appears he returned to Cuba only to come back to the U.S. after securing a visa in Toronto, Canada in September 1961. Later on he arrived in Miami on March 31, 1962 on his way to Linsboro, Florida to join the Philadelphia baseball camp. He played a total 214 games at second base, maintaining a .201 batting average.

On May 14, 1990 Reinold applied for U.S. citizenship with the Southern District Court in Miami only to sadly pass away soon after on December 4, 1995. His baseball career and personal history indicates he remained in the U.S.

Year	Age	Tm	Lg	Lev	Aff
1961	16	Williamsport Grays	Eastern League	A	PHI
1961	16	Elmira Pioneers	New York-Pennsylvania League	D	PHI
1962	17	Miami Marlins	Florida State League	D	PHI
1963	18	Miami Marlins	Florida State League	A	PHI

Pedro (Preston) Gómez Martínez

Best known by his nickname "Preston," the name of the Sugar Mill where he was born on April 20, 1922, according to his U.S. Citizenship application while living in Los Angeles California. The Sugar Mill was located near the city of Holguín in the Oriente Province, known today as Holguín.

Gómez was most famous as a manager, but he did have a career as a player, however. Starting as a player in the Cuban Sugar Mill League and the Cuban Amateur league for the Fortuna squad in 1942, he jumped to the Cuban professional baseball league in 1944 playing for the Cienfuegos *Elefantes* and then to the *Tigres* of Marianao through the 1947-48 season. During his three seasons in the league, he played the infield with 79 times at bat and a .101 batting average with eight hits. In 1944, he started his career in the U.S. with the Minneapolis Millers. The same year he was promoted to the majors with the Washington Senators, playing from May through August, appearing in eight games, batting a robust .286. Returning to the minors, he played a total of nine seasons in 559 games and batting .245.

His U.S. playing career is summarized below:

Year	Age	Tm	Lg	Lev	Aff
1944	21	Minneapolis Millers	American Association	AA	
1944	21	Washington Senators	American League	MLB	WSH
1945	22	Buffalo Bisons	International League	AA	DET
1946	23	Vicksburg Billies	Southeastern League	B	
1947	24	New London Raiders	Colonial League	B	
1947	24	Vicksburg Billies	Southeastern League	B	
1948	25	Florence Steelers	Tri-State League	B	
1949	26	Saginaw Bears	Central League	A	
1950	27	Voluntarily Retired			
1951	28	Trois-Rivieres Royals	Provincial League	C	
1952	29	Toledo Mud Hens/ Charleston Senators	American Association	AAA	CHW
1952	29	Havana Cubans	Florida International League	B	WSH
1953	30	Out of Baseball			
1954	31	Yakima Bears	Western International League	A	

Soon after his playing career, he began to manage, in 1957, in the Mexican League where his team had a 66-54 record. He would manage from 1957 through 1980. During that period, he led teams in Mexico, the U.S. minors, and the major leagues for fifteen seasons and 2038 games with a combined record of 906 wins and 1123 losses. His record as a major league manager with San Diego, the first manager during its inaugural season in 1969, Houston and Chicago for seven seasons in 875 games with a 346-529 record. He would remain involved with the team including serving as the Assistant to the General Manager, for a period of time.

A crowning achievement came as the manager of the 1959 Cuban Sugar Kings when the team had a 92-78 record and won the Little World Series against Minneapolis as the final game was played in La Habana. His managerial career is below. His many achievements led to his well-deserved induction in the Cuban Baseball Hall of Fame in Miami in 1984.

Gómez applied for U.S. citizen at the Los Angeles District Court where he established his permanent U.S. resident status as of February 20, 1960. He changed his first name formally to Preston.

Preston Gómez passed away on January 13, 2009 in Fullerton, California. His death was the result of head injuries when struck by a vehicle in 2008 from which he never fully recovered.

His baseball career and personal life shows that he remained in the U.S. following the end of the last professional baseball season in Cuba.

Additional source: obits.ocregister.com

Year	Age	Tm	Lg	Lev	Aff	G	W	L
1957	34	Mexico City Reds	MEX	AA		124	66	54
1958	35	Mexico City Reds	MEX	AA		121	65	55
1959	36	Havana	IL	AAA	CIN	154	80	73
1960	37	Spokane	PCL	AAA	LAD	154	92	61
1961	38	Spokane	PCL	AAA	LAD	155	68	86
1962	39	Spokane	PCL	AAA	LAD	154	58	96
1963	40	Richmond	IL	AAA	NYY	147	66	81
1964	41	Richmond	IL	AAA	NYY	154	65	88
1969	46	San Diego	NL	MLB	SDP	162	52	110
1970	47	San Diego	NL	MLB	SDP	162	63	99
1971	48	San Diego	NL	MLB	SDP	161	61	100
1972	49	San Diego	NL	MLB	SDP	11	4	7
1974	51	Houston	NL	MLB	HOU	162	81	81

Year	Age	Tm	Lg	Lev	Aff	G	W	L
1975	52	Houston	NL	MLB	HOU	127	47	80
1980	57	Chicago	NL	MLB	CHC	90	38	52

Jacinto (Jackie) Hernández Zulueta

Hernández was among those players who were signed to play with Almendares in the Cuban League but never got to do so because of the high level talent in that team playing behind Enrique Izquierdo and Jesús McFarlane, both of whom would play later in the major leagues.

He came from a poor family and had a dream of playing professional baseball while seeking economic improvement. With his mother's blessing, Jackie left after the end of the 1960-61 season. Monchy de Arcos, the Almendares General Manager and scout for the Cleveland Indians, signed and secured a visa for young Jacinto who promptly went to the Mexican Embassy in Habana and travelled to Miami via Mexico. He did not return to Cuba until 29 years later, and then only for five days, in 1990 when his mother passed away.

During his early period in the U.S., the Cleveland organization paid for housing and got him some money, but the language barrier, and racist-like experiences, especially in restaurants made the 20-year-old think that maybe he should return home to Cuba. He reached out to his mother by phone, but she advised him not to return. "If you come back (to Cuba) you may not be able to return (to the US.) Things are getting worse," he remembered her saying years later during our interview for his SABR biography. Deciding to stay in the U.S. was a decision he would not change as he looked back on his life (see source cited below).

His career began with the Class D Dubuque Packers of the Midwest League where his average was .274 in the 108 games he played. During his eight seasons in the minors, he played 904 games and had a batting average of .244. He also played in the Mexican League during his last two years, with Villa Hermosa and Nuevo Laredo in 1975 and 76, respectively. In between, he played nine seasons, from 1965 through 1973, in 618 games at the major league level hitting .208, but his fielding ability was never questioned. His experience in the World Series with the Pittsburgh Pirates is best described in his SABR biography. After his playing days, Jackie managed for one season, in 2007, the Charlotte County team, of the South Coast League, who ended with a 24 and 65 record.

In recent years he continued to tutor young players in the Pirates Training Camp, and spending time at the Casanova Baseball Academy in Miami, Florida. He has also participated in speaking panels of former Cuban players, sharing his experiences in the field of play to the delight of his fans, especially those from Pittsburgh who remembered him well for his contributions during the World Series as the short stop for the 1971 Champions.

Additional sources:

Costello, Rory and Ramírez, José *"Jackie Hernández"* SABR Bio Project (http://sabr.org/bioproj/person)

Jackie Hernández, personal interviews with author, January-May 2016.

Year	Age	Tm	Lg	Lev
1961	20	Dubuque Packers	Midwest League	D
1962	21	Burlington Indians	Carolina League	B
1963	22	Charleston Indians	Eastern League	AA
1964	23	Charleston Indians	Eastern League	AA
1965	24	Portland Beavers	Pacific Coast League	AAA
1965	24	Seattle Angels	Pacific Coast League	AAA
1965	24	California Angels	American League	MLB
1966	25	California Angels	American League	MLB
1967	26	Denver Bears	Pacific Coast League	AAA
1967	26	Minnesota Twins	American League	MLB
1968	27	Denver Bears	Pacific Coast League	AAA
1968	27	Minnesota Twins	American League	MLB
1969	28	Kansas City Royals	American League	MLB
1970	29	Kansas City Royals	American League	MLB
1971	30	Pittsburgh Pirates	National League	MLB
1972	31	Pittsburgh Pirates	National League	MLB
1973	32	Pittsburgh Pirates	National League	MLB
1974	33	Charleston Charlies	International League	AAA
1975	34	Villahermosa Cardenales	Mexican League	AAA
1976	35	Nuevo Laredo Tecolotes	Mexican League	AAA

Juan Antonio Iglesias

Another lesser known player that left Cuba, Iglesias, whose date of birth is listed on his travel records from 1959 and 1961 as July 26, 1939, a year older than was published elsewhere. He was born in Guanajay, Pinar del Río, in Cuba.

On that first trip, he traveled from La Habana to Miami on his way to Morristown, Tennessee to join the local Class D affiliate of the Chicago Cubs. There he played 66 games and had a .278 batting average.

That same season, he played for the Palatka Redlegs in 1959, for the Cincinnati organization where, as a young short stop, he appeared in 54 games with a low .211 batting average.

He played for five teams the following year, 1960, but was good enough to secure a contract in the Cincinnati organization. This led to his getting a visa from the Mexican Embassy, enabling him to leave Cuba via Mexico, arriving in Miami on March 28, 1961 on his way to Tampa to join the Reds organization. During the 1961 season, his last in the minors, he played for the Columbia Reds in the South Atlantic League, in only five games and five times at bat with no hits.

His overall minor league record included fifty-five games in 211 times at bat and a .209 batting average.

At the very least, one may conclude that he remained in the U.S. following the end of professional baseball, since he played for the Columbia Reds during the 1961 season.

Year	Age	Tm	Lg	Lev
1959	19	Morristown Cubs	Appalachian League	D-
1959	19	Palatka Redlegs	Florida State League	D
1960	20	Burlington Indians	Carolina League	B
1960	20	Palatka Redlegs	Florida State League	D
1960	20	Topeka Reds	Illinois-Indiana-Iowa League	B
1960	20	Indianapolis Indians	American Association	AAA
1960	20	Asheville Tourists	South Atlantic League	A
1961	21	Columbia Reds	South Atlantic League	A

Ricardo Alberto Izquierdo Pelaez

Known as "Lefty," Izquierdo arrived in Miami on March 28, 1961 on his way to Hollywood to join the Chicago White Sox organization via Mexico. His travel papers showed his birth date as May 1, 1938, a year older that published elsewhere, and his birth place as La Habana.

During that first season, in 61, this young catcher played for the Idaho Falls Russets, a Class C team, affiliated with the White Sox, in 94 games and batted .289. It appears that he went back to Cuba at the end of the season, because, on March 12 of 1962 he travelled from La Habana to Miami on his way to Indianapolis.

He played a total of four seasons, through 1964, stayed in the U.S. and ended his career with the Double A, Lynchburg White Sox in the Southern League. He played a total of 265 games and had .272 batting average.

Year	Age	Tm	Lg	Lev
1961	21	Idaho Falls Russets	Pioneer League	C
1962	22	Visalia White Sox	California League	C
1962	22	Savannah/Lynchburg White Sox	South Atlantic League	A
1963	23	Clinton C-Sox	Midwest League	A
1963	23	Eugene Emeralds	Northwest League	A
1964	24	Lynchburg White Sox	Southern League	AA

David Hernández Jimenez

He was born in Camajuani, in the Las Villas Province, in Cuba. The town is located an equal distance between Remedios and the city of Santa Clara. His birthplace was found in four travel documents readily available from 1959 and 1960. Jimenez listed his birthdate as December 30, 1930, a date that does not correspond with previously published information. In 1959, he came to the U.S. on three different occasions, reporting either to the Pittsburgh training camp in Jacksonville, Florida, or to Columbus. The last record available shows his traveling on March 19, 1960, from Nicaragua to Miami, on his way to report to the Pittsburgh organization.

His playing career extended from 1953 through the 1972 season in the Mexican League. During his six seasons in the U.S. minors, he appeared in 163 games, pitching in 803 innings, and ending with a record of 50 wins and 42 losses. His foreign baseball record is not complete, but it appears he pitched 80 games during that time. David Jimenez played for the Almendares and Habana Lions for three seasons in the Cuban professional Baseball League, in 54-55, 55-56 and 59-60. This corresponds with his playing career and travel. Jimenez appeared in 36 games and had a 2-5 record in 66 innings pitched with a 4.16 ERA.

Given his extensive career beyond 1961, one may assume he did not return to Cuba during that period, especially following the end of the Cuban professional Baseball League in February of 1961, since he played for the Padres and the New Jersey teams after that date.

Year	Age	Tm	Lg	Lev	Aff
1953	19	Batavia Clippers	Pennsylvania-Ontario-New York League	D	PIT
1954	20	Clinton Pirates	Mississippi-Ohio Valley League	D	PIT
1955	21	Mexico City Tigres	Mexican League	AA	
1958	24	Mexico City Tigres	Mexican League	AA	
1958	24	Salt Lake City Bees	Pacific Coast League	AAA	PIT
1959	25	Columbus Jets	International League	AAA	PIT
1959	25	Columbus/ Gastonia Pirates	South Atlantic League	A	PIT
1960	26	Salt Lake City Bees	Pacific Coast League	AAA	PIT
1961	27	San Diego Padres	Pacific Coast League	AAA	CHW
1961	27	Jersey City Jerseys	International League	AAA	CIN
1962	28	Mexico City Diablos Rojos	Mexican League	AA	
1965	31	Puerto Mexico Portenos	Mexican Southeast League	A	

Year	Age	Tm	Lg	Lev	Aff
1965	31	Campeche Pirates	Mexican Southeast League	A	
1965	31	Yucatan Venados	Mexican Southeast League	A	
1967	33	Tabasco Cattleman	Mexican Southeast League	A	
1967	33	Ciudad Del Carmen Cameroneros	Mexican Southeast League	A	
1968	34	Veracruz Aguila	Mexican League	AAA	
1968	34	Tabasco Cattleman	Mexican Southeast League	A	
1971	37	Monterrey Sultanes	Mexican League	AAA	
1971	37	Reynosa Broncs	Mexican League	AAA	
1972	38	Veracruz Aguila	Mexican League	AAA	

Orlando Martínez Oliva

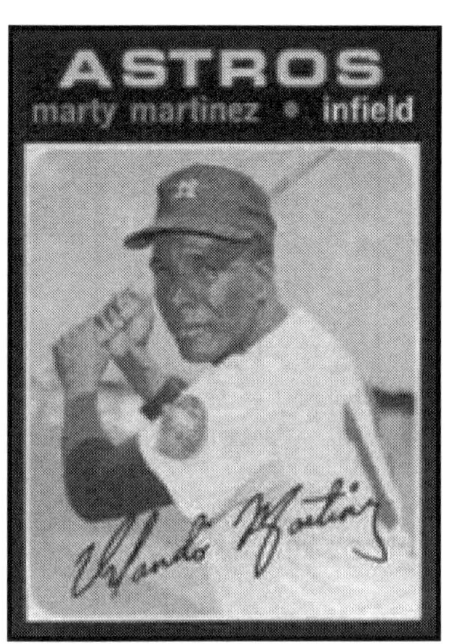

He was born on August 23, 1941 in La Habana according to official travel records. He listed Batabanó, a city located on the southern coast of Cuba directly down from the capital city of La Habana, as his place of birth when he travelled to the U.S. in 1961.

Martínez was signed by the Washington Senators as an amateur free agent in 1960 and went on on to a long professional career, both as a player and a manager.

His first recorded entry into the U.S. was on August 25, 1959 on his way to Charlotte, North Carolina. He returned the following March, arriving in Fernandina Beach on March 29, on his way to join the Erie Sailors, a Class D team in the New York/Penn League where, as a young man, he hit .222 in his first professional season.

Martínez secured a visa like other players under contract to a major league team through the Mexican Embassy in La Habana, arriving in Miami on March 4, 1961 on his way to Orlando.

During his second season, his average went up to .265 with the Wilson Tobs, a Class B team in the Appalachian League. The versatile Martínez played all infield positions during his 20-season career, 1970-1980, including pitcher and catcher. In his thirteen seasons in the minors, he played a total 797 games with a .243 batting average which he would match during his seven seasons in the majors, starting in 1962, at age 20, with the Minnesota Twins.

Orlando Martínez managed a total of nine seasons, including one in the majors with the Seattle Pilots, with a record of 67 wins and 95 losses. His overall record as a manager was 476 wins and 606 losses.

On March 8, 2007 Martínez passed away in Santo Domingo, in the Dominican Republic and is buried in the Green Acres Memorial Gardens Cemetery in Sperry Oklahoma along with his wife Jessie Faye.

Year	Age	Tm	Lg	Lev
1960	18	Erie Sailors	New York-Pennsylvania League	D
1961	19	Wilson Tobs	Carolina League	B
1962	20	Minnesota Twins	American League	MLB

Year	Age	Tm	Lg	Lev
1963	21	Charlotte Hornets	South Atlantic League	AA
1963	21	Dallas-Fort Worth Rangers	Pacific Coast League	AAA
1964	22	Atlanta Crackers	International League	AAA
1965	23	Denver Bears	Pacific Coast League	AAA
1966	24	Denver Bears	Pacific Coast League	AAA
1966	24	FIL Twins	Florida Instructional League	WRk
1967	25	Atlanta Braves	National League	MLB
1968	26	Atlanta Braves	National League	MLB
1969	27	Houston Astros	National League	MLB
1970	28	Houston Astros	National League	MLB
1971	29	Houston Astros	National League	MLB
1972	30	St. Louis Cardinals	National League	MLB
1972	30	Oakland Athletics	American League	MLB
1972	30	Texas Rangers	American League	MLB
1973	31	Spokane Indians	Pacific Coast League	AAA
1974	32	Spokane Indians	Pacific Coast League	AAA
1975	33	Pittsfield Rangers	Eastern League	AA
1976	34	San Antonio Brewers	Texas League	AA
1977	35	Tulsa Drillers	Texas League	AA
1978	36	Tulsa Drillers	Texas League	AA
1980	38	Wausau Timbers	Midwest League	A

Pedro Rafael Martínez Santa María

Another young player of that era, Martínez began his nine U.S. minor league season career in 1960 playing for the Palatka Redlegs, a Cincinnati affiliate in the Florida League.

He continued his career in 1961 with the Tampa Tarpons, another Class D team, with his average moving up to the .240 level.

Pedro Martínez played a total of 803 games and had a batting average of .209, finishing his career in 1968 with the Ashville Tourists of the Southern League in North Carolina at the age of 28, playing in 63 games, with a .170 batting average. Given his playing career it can be presumed correctly, that he remained in the U.S. following the end of the 1960-61 season. This was confirmed by a fellow player.

Additional source: Iván Davis, telephone interview with author, January 31, 2018.

Year	Age	Tm	Lg	Lev
1960	20	Palatka Redlegs	Florida State League	D
1961	21	Tampa Tarpons	Florida State League	D
1962	22	Rocky Mount Leafs	Carolina League	B
1962	22	Tampa Tarpons	Florida State League	D
1963	23	Cedar Rapids Red Raiders	Midwest League	A
1964	24	Tampa Tarpons	Florida State League	A
1965	25	Elmira Pioneers	Eastern League	AA
1966	26	Peninsula Grays	Carolina League	A
1966	26	Knoxville Smokies	Southern League	AA
1966	26	Rochester Red Wings	International League	AAA
1967	27	Tampa Tarpons	Florida State League	A
1967	27	FIL Reds	Florida Instructional League	WRk
1968	28	Asheville Tourists	Southern League	AA

Rodolfo Hector Santos Martínez

Born May 11, 1939 in Las Villas, Santos Martínez arrived in the U.S. in 1957 via Cuban Airlines on June 22nd. On the record, his last name is spelled "Martones," not Martínez, the year he was signed by the Milwaukee Braves.

That first year he would play for the McCook Braves, a Class D team in the Nebraska State League. He came to bat only five times and did not have a hit. The following year playing for the Batavia Indians in the New York/Penn League, he played in 116 games, hitting .240 now with the Cleveland organization.

He played during the 1960 season for the Albuquerque Dukes. His travel record when he arrived on March 31, 1960 showed his last name spelled as "Martínez." He played in the U.S. the subsequent seasons through 1967. His minor league record during his nine seasons included 851 games with a .283 batting average. He played during two seasons in the majors for a total of seven games and had 4 hits in 15 times at the plate.

Although he played through the 1967 thus staying in the U.S., he ultimately died in Cuba on December, 14, 1999.

Year	Age	Tm	Lg	Lev
1957	18	McCook Braves	Nebraska State League	D-
1958	19	Batavia Indians	New York-Pennsylvania League	D
1960	21	Albuquerque Dukes	Sophomore League	D
1961	22	Lewiston Broncs	Northwest League	B
1962	23	Albuquerque Dukes	Texas League	AA
1962	23	Kansas City Athletics	American League	MLB
1963	24	Portland Beavers	Pacific Coast League	AAA
1963	24	Kansas City Athletics	American League	MLB
1964	25	Dallas Rangers	Pacific Coast League	AAA
1966	27	Vancouver Mounties	Pacific Coast League	AAA
1967	28	Peninsula Grays	Carolina League	A

Vladimir Mirabal y Díaz

Born on August 27 1939, this young second baseman played only two seasons in the minors at levels D and B for the Palatka Redlegs and the Topeka Red and Salem Senators respectively. Playing for a total of 148 games, he came to bat 491 times, with a final average of .259

Mirabal became the player who tried to rescue Elio Ribet who drowned tragically at Silver Lake in Florida. See Elio Ribet Jr.'s write-up.

Mirabal's traveled to the U.S. from 1958 through his last documented arrival in Miami on March 30, 1960 from La Habana, Cuba, with his destination being Tampa Florida. His travel documents maintain a consistent birthdate and birthplace in the capital city of La Habana. Following the end of the 1960 season, it was reported that Mirabal Díaz returned to Cuba to stay.

Additional source: Iván Davis, telephone interview with the author, May 23, 2018.

Year	Age	Tm	Lg	Lev	Aff
1959	20	Palatka Redlegs	Florida State League	D	CIN
1960	21	Palatka Redlegs	Florida State League	D	CIN
1960	21	Topeka Reds	Illinois-Indiana-Iowa League	B	CIN
1960	21	Salem Senators	Northwest League	B	

Guillermo (Willy) Miranda Pérez

One of the better-known defense specialist at short in Cuba is "Willy" Miranda, born on May 24, 1926 in Velasco, located in the Oriente Province, known today as the Holguín Province on the eastern side of Cuba near the city of the same name. His parents were Teodoro and Isolina Pérez according to his marriage certificate to Agnes Margie Castillo Caruso. It was their second marriage, and it took place in Alexandria, Virginia on August 14, 1972, while he lived in Baltimore, Maryland.

Miranda played in the U.S. from 1948 through 1961 spending nine seasons in the majors, five of which with the Baltimore Orioles of the American League. Playing in 824 games in the "bigs," his batting average was a weak .221 and, during his six seasons in the U.S. minors, he appeared in 751 games batting .243. But it was his defense skills and knowledge of the game that kept him playing with a fielding percentage of .961 over those fifteen seasons.

In addition to his U.S. playing days, Miranda played amateur baseball in Cuba for the Teléfonos team from 1942-47. He was considered among the best in his position in the Cuban baseball league where played for twelve seasons, starting in 1948 and named the season's Rookie of the Year. He played with a minor exception with the Almendares team and came to bat 2214 times hitting .236. He also played five Caribbean Series, all with Almendares, in 16 games and batted .250. He did not play in the last professional baseball season in 1960-61.

Despite of his busy playing career, he attended the Maristas High School in la Víbora, La Habana and also graduated from College.

Following the end of his playing days, Miranda managed two seasons, one in Mexico in 1968 where his team, Monterrey Sultanes, gathered a 58-82 record, and another in Panama with the Banqueros in 1979 when the Panama team had a 15-36 record.

His contributions to the game earned him a well-deserved spot in the Hall of Fame in Miami, Florida in 1983.

Guillermo Miranda passed away on September 7, 1996 in Baltimore, Maryland and is buried at the Gardens of Faith Memorial Cemetery Rosedale Baltimore County Maryland. His overall life history indicates he did not return to Cuba except during the Mariel boatlift in 1980 to help family and friends to obtain the freedom that many sought.

Additional source: Costello, Rory. *"Willy Miranda"* SABR Bio Project (http://sabr.org/bioproj/person)

Year	Age	Tm	Lg	Lev	Aff
1948	22	Sherman-Denison Twins	Big State League	B	WSH
1949	23	Chattanooga Lookouts	Southern Association	AA	WSH
1950	24	Chattanooga Lookouts	Southern Association	AA	WSH
1951	25	Chattanooga Lookouts	Southern Association	AA	WSH
1951	25	Washington Senators	American League	MLB	WSH
1952	26	Chicago White Sox	American League	MLB	CHW
1952	26	St. Louis Browns	American League	MLB	SLB
1952	26	Chicago White Sox	American League	MLB	CHW
1953	27	St. Louis Browns	American League	MLB	SLB
1953	27	New York Yankees	American League	MLB	NYY
1954	28	New York Yankees	American League	MLB	NYY
1955	29	Baltimore Orioles	American League	MLB	BAL
1956	30	Baltimore Orioles	American League	MLB	BAL
1957	31	Baltimore Orioles	American League	MLB	BAL
1958	32	Baltimore Orioles	American League	MLB	BAL
1959	33	Baltimore Orioles	American League	MLB	BAL
1960	34	St. Paul Saints	American Association	AAA	LAD
1961	35	Syracuse Chiefs	International League	AAA	MIN

Aurelio Faustino Monteagudo Cintra

The son of former major league player René Monteagudo had a long career that included 14 seasons in the minors, 8 in the Mexican League and 7 in the majors.

He began his career during the 1961 season at the age of 18 with the Albuquerque Dukes, a Class D team for the Kansas City Athletics. He appeared to have returned to Cuba, then entered the United States again directly from La Habana to Miami on March 6, 1962. Here his birth date is shown as November 28, rather than November 29, shown in his burial record.

His debut in the majors came early, on September 1, 1963, at the age of 19 with the Kansas City Athletics. He appeared in four games without a win/loss record.

His minor league career included 102 wins and 73 losses with a 3.50 ERA. During his time in the majors, he won three games and loss seven with a 5.05 ERA.

In addition to his playing career, he managed four seasons in the Single A Midwest League and three at the Triple A level in the

Mexican League. His record as a manager consisted of 214 wins and 316 losses.

Aurelio Monteagudo died on November 10, 1990 in Arizpe, Coahuila de Zaragoza, Mexico and is buried in the Sacramento Municipal Cemetery in Coahuila, Mexico.

Year	Age	Tm	Lg	Lev
1961	17	Albuquerque Dukes	Sophomore League	D
1962	18	Albuquerque Dukes	Texas League	AA
1962	18	Lewiston Broncs	Northwest League	B
1962	18	Binghamton Triplets	Eastern League	A
1963	19	Portland Beavers	Pacific Coast League	AAA
1963	19	Kansas City Athletics	American League	MLB
1964	20	Dallas Rangers	Pacific Coast League	AAA
1964	20	Kansas City Athletics	American League	MLB
1965	21	Vancouver Mounties	Pacific Coast League	AAA
1965	21	Kansas City Athletics	American League	MLB
1966	22	Oklahoma City 89ers	Pacific Coast League	AAA
1966	22	Kansas City Athletics	American League	MLB
1966	22	Houston Astros	National League	MLB
1967	23	Indianapolis Indians	Pacific Coast League	AAA
1967	23	Chicago White Sox	American League	MLB
1968	24	Asheville Tourists	Southern League	AA
1968	24	Hawaii Islanders	Pacific Coast League	AAA
1968	24	Indianapolis Indians	Pacific Coast League	AAA
1969	25	Indianapolis Indians	American Association	AAA
1969	25	Tulsa Oilers	American Association	AAA
1970	26	Omaha Royals	American Association	AAA
1970	26	Kansas City Royals	American League	MLB

Year	Age	Tm	Lg	Lev
1971	27	Omaha Royals	American Association	AAA
1972	28	Hawaii Islanders	Pacific Coast League	AAA
1973	29	Hawaii Islanders	Pacific Coast League	AAA
1973	29	Salt Lake City Angels	Pacific Coast League	AAA
1973	29	California Angels	American League	MLB
1974	30	Puebla Pericos	Mexican League	AAA
1975	31	Puebla Pericos	Mexican League	AAA
1976	32	Puebla Angeles	Mexican League	AAA
1977	33	Coahuila Mineros	Mexican League	AAA
1977	33	Jalisco	Mexican Center League	A
1977	33	Mexico		
1978	34	Coahuila Mineros	Mexican League	AAA
1979	35	Coahuila Mineros	Mexican League	AAA
1980	36	Monclova Acereros	Mexican League	AAA
1980	36	Toluca Osos Negros	Mexican League	AAA
1981	37	Nuevo Laredo Tecolotes	Mexican League	AAA
1981	37	Veracruz Aguila	Mexican League	AAA
1983	39	Edmonton Trappers	Pacific Coast League	AAA

Pedro Moret Pedraga

Pedro Moré, without the "t" at the end, is reported to have played for the Marianao squad during the 1959-60 season. Little has been found at this time of the 24-year-old Moret who, in 1959, traveled from La Habana to Miami on his way to Chicago. The spelling of his last name, Moret, is shown on his travel document and his marriage documentation. He was born on March 11, 1936. This Santa Clara native married a Marie White on January 12, 1957. He played for the Palatka team in 1960, appearing in nine games with 30 at bats and 10 hits for a .333 batting average. He is said to have remained in Cuba thereafter.

Additional source: Iván Davis, telephone interview with author, January 31, 2018.

Edilio Oliva Acosta

This young pitcher played in the minors from the 1958 through the 1962 season, appearing in 149 games for teams affiliated with the Washington Senators and Minnesota franchises. During that period, he pitched in 523.2 innings striking out 449 and walking 269 batters. His record of 30 wins and 33 losses led to a 4.02 ERA.

While his birthdate is recorded as June 3, 1939 in Central Portugalete in Cuba, according to his travel records from Cuba, he was born on June 10, 1939 in the town of San José de las Lajas where the Portugalete sugar mill was located. Today, the town is the capital of the Mayabeque Province, situated less than an hour from this author's hometown.

Oliva arrived in Miami on March 4, 1961, soon after the end of the Cuban Baseball League, via Mexico on his way to Orlando Florida. His visa in Mexico was issued only one day earlier. He appeared to have returned to Cuba because he travelled back to Miami on April 3, 1962 on his way to Fernandina Beach near Jacksonville Florida. Playing in the U.S. for two seasons after the end of the Cuban professional baseball league shows his stay in the U.S.

Year	Age	Tm	Lg	Lev	Aff
1958	19	Superior Senators	Nebraska State League	D-	WSH
1959	20	Sanford Greyhounds	Florida State League	D	WSH
1960	21	Erie Sailors	New York-Pennsylvania League	D	WSH
1961	22	Charlotte Hornets	South Atlantic League	A	MIN
1961	22	Fort Walton Beach Jets	Alabama-Florida League	D	MIN
1961	22	Wilson Tobs	Carolina League	B	MIN

Year	Age	Tm	Lg	Lev	Aff
1962	23	Wilson Tobs	Carolina League	B	MIN
1962	23	Bismarck-Mandan Pards	Northern League	C	MIN

Pedro (Tony) Oliva López

The story of "Tony" Oliva captured by Thom Henninger (see source cited below) describes in some detail the many challenges that baseball players experienced during those early years.

In Oliva's case, after his parents agreed to have him sign a professional contract, they learned that without a birth certificate, he was unable to get a passport. So, they substituted his brother

Antonio's passport, so that the contract and the needed travel could take place.

He along other Cuban players, secured a visa to travel to Mexico and went on to the U.S., arriving in April of 1961, and heading for Fernandina Beach outside of Jacksonville, Florida to join the Minnesota

Twins organization. Oliva had hoped to play in the U.S. and return to Cuba for the remainder of the year like many players had done before him over the years. But that did not come to pass. Following the Bay of Pigs invasion, he knew that going home would not be possible given the political instability and lack of diplomatic relations between Cuba and the United States.

Like many before and after him, he learned to compartmentalize his feelings to combat isolation and stay focused on his playing career while coping with being cut off from loved ones and everything familiar. Facing racism in restaurants, dealing with the language barrier, unfamiliar food and limited as to what he could do between games made for a difficult existence in the early days.

Upon arrival in the U.S., Oliva was initially assigned to the Class D Wytheville Twins of the Appalachian League but, by the end of the 1962 season, he played nine games in the majors with the Minnesota Twins followed by seven more games in 1963. He broke full time into the major leagues to stay in 1964 playing 161 games and by 1965, he was selected to the All Star squad with fellow Cubans Cookie/Cuqui Rojas, Leo Cárdenas and Zoilo Versalles. He played three seasons in the minor leagues batting .342 and fifteen seasons in the majors with a solid batting average of .304 in 1676 games He was selected to eight All Star games. A record that many believe should have earned him a spot in the Baseball Hall of Fame in Cooperstown. He is a member of the Cuban Baseball Hall of Fame in Miami, Florida.

He was able to reunite with his mother and sister in both 1970 and in 1972. His mother and father met with him in Mexico. His father said in 1972, "If I knew in 61 what I know now, I'd still want Tony to leave his home. It was a great opportunity for him to do what he loved."

He travels to Cuba every year to see family, travel that began in 1973, and in 1981 he attended his mother's funeral.

Looking back Oliva said, "If I had to do it all over again, I would do it in a minute, this difficult decision. I have nothing to regret. I love that I had the opportunity so that I was able to help my family and help some other people close to my family. I wish I could help more, but you only can help so much."

Additional source: Henninger, Thom Tony Oliva "The Life and Times of a Minnesota Twins Legend" University of Minnesota Press Minneapolis London 2015.

Year	Age	Tm	Lg	Lev
1961	22	Wytheville Twins	Appalachian League	D-
1962	23	Charlotte Hornets	South Atlantic League	A
1962	23	Minnesota Twins	American League	MLB
1963	24	Dallas-Fort Worth Rangers	Pacific Coast League	AAA
1963	24	Minnesota Twins	American League	MLB
1964	25	Minnesota Twins	American League	MLB
1965	26	Minnesota Twins	American League	MLB
1966	27	Minnesota Twins	American League	MLB
1967	28	Minnesota Twins	American League	MLB
1968	29	Minnesota Twins	American League	MLB
1969	30	Minnesota Twins	American League	MLB
1970	31	Minnesota Twins	American League	MLB
1971	32	Minnesota Twins	American League	MLB
1972	33	Minnesota Twins	American League	MLB
1973	34	Minnesota Twins	American League	MLB
1974	35	Minnesota Twins	American League	MLB
1975	36	Minnesota Twins	American League	MLB
1976	37	Minnesota Twins	American League	MLB

Carlos González Paz

Born on November 7, 1942 in Regla, the versatile Paz played the infield and was also a pitcher. He played only three seasons in the minors, appearing in 148 games and had a batting average of .171

followed by a long 22-year career as a manager in the Mexican League where his teams won 1390 games losing 1546. He ended his managing career in 2006 as the manager for the Triple A Córdoba team in Mexico. His residence, according to official records, is shown as Miami, Florida and his playing days in 1972 and 1975 indicates his having stayed in the U.S.

Year	Age	Tm	Lg	Lev
1960	18	Daytona Beach Islanders	Florida State League	D
1972	30	Key West Conchs	Florida State League	A
1973	31	Yucatan Leones	Mexican League	AAA
1974	32	Yucatan Leones	Mexican League	AAA
1974	32	Tampico Alijadores	Mexican League	AAA
1974	32	Reynosa Bravos	Mexican League	AAA
1975	33	Fort Lauderdale Yankees	Florida State League	A
1975	33	Villahermosa Cardenales	Mexican League	AAA
1977	35	Nuevo Laredo Tecolotes	Mexican League	AAA

Gerardo (Jerry) E. Pedroso

This young outfielder was born on September 24, 1940 in La Habana, Cuba.

He played only three seasons for a total of 253 games and had a batting average of .221. He died on May 24, 2016 in Decatur, Macon County, Illinois where he had played for the Decatur Commodores. He is known to have lived there in 1993 and is buried at the Greenwood Cemetery of the same city. His playing record shows his staying in the U.S. following the end of the last professional baseball season in Cuba.

Year	Age	Tm	Lg	Lev	Aff
1961	20	El Paso Sun Kings	Sophomore League	D	SFG
1962	21	Decatur Commodores	Midwest League	D	SFG

Year	Age	Tm	Lg	Lev	Aff
1962	21	Fresno Giants	California League	C	SFG
1963	22	Decatur Commodores	Midwest League	A	SFG

Atanasio (Tony) Pérez Rigal

Hall of Famer "Tony" Pérez did not play in the Cuban professional Baseball League even though he had played in the Sugar Mill teams in Cuba (see source cited below). Perhaps he was thought to be "too green" and was not yet an "established ball player" (see source cited below). He was signed by the Cincinnati Reds in 1960 and assigned to the Instructional team of the Cuban Sugar Kings. He played for the Class D Geneva Redlegs at the age of 18, arriving from Cuba on April 3, 1960 on his way to Tampa to join the Reds organization. His travel papers show May 14, 1942 as his birth date in Camagüey and him living in the Central Violeta. His first professional season, he played his first of five seasons, he played in the minors in 104 games and had a .279 batting average. He recalled during the filming of "Major League Cuban" (see source cited below) how he traveled and lived with other black players, was not able to enter restaurants with his teammates, and waited in the bus for them to bring him back his food. In 1961, he went back to the Geneva team, playing in 121 games and his batting average zoomed to .348. Overall, he played 526 games in the minors and had a very strong .310 batting average.

Between the 1964-65 and the 1982-83 seasons he played in the Puerto Rico Winter League (see source cited below).

He played in the major leagues for a total of 23 seasons in 2777 games, had a .279 batting average with 1652 runs batted in. Not surprisingly, he was named to the All Star Game a total of seven times. He ended his playing career in 1986 at the age of 44.

In 1993, he became a manager for the Cincinnati Reds which had a 73-89 record, and went back in 2001 with the Florida team that had a 76-86 win and loss record.

In November 1972, Tony Pérez was granted a 20-day visa to return to Cuba for the first time since a 1963 trip. However, the visa did not permit his wife and children to go (see source cited below). Tony and his wife became U.S. Citizens during this time.

Tony's father, José Manuel, died in 1979 at age 84, though some sources list his year of death as 1977. Tony has stated that, during his playing career, his family in Cuba would listen to the Voice of America, which would give daily updates on Cubans playing in the majors. Tony's mother, Teodora, "Tita", was 88 when Tony was elected to the Hall of Fame and he made a return visit to Cuba in 2002. His mother died in 2008.

His great career led him, deservedly, to inductions in the Hall of Fame in Cooperstown, the Cincinnati Reds, Cuban Sports, the Hispanic Heritage Baseball Museum, Caribbean and Latino Baseball, and the Cuban Baseball of Fame in Miami, Florida.

Additional sources:

The Miami News Google News 2014

Omelis Hongamen, telephone interview with author, 2016.

Cardona, Joe and González Ralf "Major League Cuban" a co-production of South Florida PBS and Royal Palms Films 2017.
Van Hyning, T.E. (2004). Puerto Rico's Winter League: A History of Major League Baseball's Launching Pad. McFarland & Company. p. 19.
Freedman, Lew "Latino Baseball Legends: An Encyclopedia"
"Perez: From Cuba to Hall". Reds.enquirer.com. 2000-01-13
"Araton, Harvey (2009-03-17). "Tony Pérez on Cuba and Its Team – NYTimes.com"

Year	Age	Tm	Lg	Lev
1960	18	Geneva Redlegs	New York-Pennsylvania League	D
1961	19	Geneva Redlegs	New York-Pennsylvania League	D
1962	20	Rocky Mount Leafs	Carolina League	B
1963	21	Macon Peaches	South Atlantic League	AA
1963	21	San Diego Padres	Pacific Coast League	AAA
1964	22	San Diego Padres	Pacific Coast League	AAA
1964	22	Cincinnati Reds	National League	MLB
1965	23	Cincinnati Reds	National League	MLB
1966	24	Cincinnati Reds	National League	MLB
1967	25	Cincinnati Reds	National League	MLB
1968	26	Cincinnati Reds	National League	MLB
1969	27	Cincinnati Reds	National League	MLB
1970	28	Cincinnati Reds	National League	MLB
1971	29	Cincinnati Reds	National League	MLB
1972	30	Cincinnati Reds	National League	MLB
1973	31	Cincinnati Reds	National League	MLB
1974	32	Cincinnati Reds	National League	MLB
1975	33	Cincinnati Reds	National League	MLB
1976	34	Cincinnati Reds	National League	MLB

Year	Age	Tm	Lg	Lev
1977	35	Montreal Expos	National League	MLB
1978	36	Montreal Expos	National League	MLB
1979	37	Montreal Expos	National League	MLB
1980	38	Boston Red Sox	American League	MLB
1981	39	Boston Red Sox	American League	MLB
1982	40	Boston Red Sox	American League	MLB
1983	41	Philadelphia Phillies	National League	MLB
1984	42	Cincinnati Reds	National League	MLB
1985	43	Cincinnati Reds	National League	MLB
1986	44	Cincinnati Reds	National League	MLB

Elio Ribet Jr.

This right-handed pitcher, born on September 4, 1941 in Habana had a short career. He died in a drowning accident on July 27, 1960.

When he came to play for the Palatka Redlegs in 1959, his residence in Cuba was listed as Avenue 85, No 12, 808 Marino, though it is very likely "Marianao," located in the capital city near the Palmar Park. He came to the Cincinnati Baseball Training Camp on April 1, 1959 with his full name listed as Elio Moises Ribet Sambat. Ribet traveled along with four others on PAA Flight 416 from Havana; Ramon Seara Y Calvino; born on May 9, 1939 in Havana, Martin Francisco Dihigo Reyna; born on September 17, 1942 in Cruces Las Villas,; Mario Esteban Zambrano Montes de Oca, born on March 4, 1938 in San Luis Oriente; and Erwin Regis Sipson, born on March 22, 1936 in Victoria de la Tunas. Publications have the latter's name listed as "Regis Simpson," presenting a challenge for researchers.

Ribet returned to Cuba on March 30, 1960, with his residence listed as the Hotel Hillsboro in Tampa, Florida. He had a record of 4 wins and 5 losses while appearing in 20 games.

Sadly, Ribet drowned on July 27, 1960 at the young age of eighteen while swimming in Silver Lake in Florida, apparently, and suffering from cramps. His body was recovered after ten minutes under water, and he could not be revived by his teammate and fellow Cuban, Vladimir Mirabal. Mirabal tried to rescue Ribet, but the 6ft. 2in. or 6ft. 3in., 200-pound youth was thrashing around so much he couldn't pull him to safety, according to sources listed below.

The Palatka Redlegs were playing at St. Petersburg and Ribet had remained behind because he was hurt. Upon returning to Palatka after a loss, team players were notified by the manager of the drowning. Ribet's tragic death does not make it possible to come to a responsible conclusion of whether he would have stayed in the U.S. or returned to Cuba.

His remains were sent to Cuba, as his parents had expressed concern over whether their young son might have been a victim of some foul play. They wished to confirm that he had not been the victim of a shooting or stabbing.

It is interesting to note that, despite this tragic accident involving a young man from the local team who would go on to become the Florida State League Champions, news was published in the Pensacola and Palm Beach newspapers, but despite further research and communications with the staff, it has not uncovered any mention in the Palatka Daily News.

Additional sources:
Iván Davis, telephone interviews with author, October 24, 2016, January 31, February 2 and 28, 2018.
Pensacola News July 28, 1960 page 5.
Palm Beach Post July 28, 1960
Michael Phelps, telephone interviews with author, February 2018.
Darrell D Kathman SGES Jacksonville Research Assistant March 9 2018.
Andy Hall Sports Editor Palatka Daily News, telephone interview, February 2018.

Year	Age	Tm	Lg	Lev	Aff
1959	18	Palatka Redlegs	Florida State League	D	CIN
1960	19	Palatka Redlegs	Florida State League	D	CIN

Hilario (Larry) Cándido Rojas Molina

Rojas arrived in Miami via Habana with a visa provided in Windsor, Ontario in Canada on February 21, 1962, a full year after the end of the Cuban professional Baseball league. He listed his birth date as February 2, 1943, and birthplace as Güines located near the capital city of La Habana. At the time of his arrival, he listed his residence as Detroit, Michigan. He had joined the Decatur team, an affiliate of the Detroit franchise.

His career spanned from 1961 through the 1971 season, playing mostly at second and third base. He maintained a .957 and a .951 fielding percentage. Playing in the U.S. minors in 1027 games, Rojas came to bat 3451 times hitting .257. He also played 190 games in the Rookie League, coming to bat 618 times.

Beyond his playing days, Hilario Rojas managed during two different seasons. At the A level, in 1974, his team, the Auburn Phillies of the New York-Penn League, had a 34-32 record. And in 1978, at the Rookie league level, leading his team, Helena Phillies in the Pioneer League, to 30 wins and 38 losses. Both teams were affiliated with the Philadelphia franchise.

A 22-year heart transplant recipient, Hilario Rojas passed away on October 27, 2007 in Clearwater Florida. A complete obituary can be read and its source are cited below.

His career and personal history both clearly show he remained in the U.S. after he left Cuba.

Additional source: www.legacy.com

Year	Age	Tm	Lg	Lev	Aff
1961	19	Decatur Commodores	Midwest League	D	DET
1962	20	Jamestown Tigers	New York-Pennsylvania League	D	DET
1963	21	Lakeland Tigers	Florida State League	A	DET
1963	21	Knoxville Smokies	South Atlantic League	AA	DET
1963	21	Jamestown Tigers	New York-Pennsylvania League	A	DET
1964	22	Knoxville Smokies	Southern League	AA	DET
1964	22	FIL Tigers	Florida Instructional League	WRk	DET
1965	23	Syracuse Chiefs	International League	AAA	DET
1965	23	Montgomery Rebels	Southern League	AA	DET
1965	23	FIL Tigers	Florida Instructional League	WRk	DET
1966	24	Montgomery Rebels	Southern League	AA	DET
1966	24	Syracuse Chiefs	International League	AAA	DET
1966	24	Rochester Red Wings	International League	AAA	BAL
1966	24	FIL Tigers	Florida Instructional League	WRk	DET
1967	25	Montgomery Rebels	Southern League	AA	DET
1967	25	FIL Tigers	Florida Instructional League	WRk	DET
1968	26	Montgomery Rebels	Southern League	AA	DET
1968	26	FIL Tigers	Florida Instructional League	WRk	DET
1969	27	Hawaii Islanders	Pacific Coast League	AAA	CAL
1970	28	Reading Phillies	Eastern League	AA	PHI
1971	29	Eugene Emeralds	Pacific Coast League	AAA	PHI

Roberto Guillermo Sánchez

He was born on January 31, 1935, in Camagüey, Cuba. His father and mother were Felice Sánchez and Hilda Serrano, respectively. Sánchez passed away of a Cardiopulmonary Arrest on November 15 1981 in Beaumont County, in Jefferson, Texas and had been suffering from health problems for the previous two years. He was buried at the Live Oak Cemetery. He was married at the time of his death to Earline Malbrough and was only 46 years old.

A Roberto Sánchez played for the Almendares squad in the infield from 1954 through 1959 but his stats are incomplete since the first-year numbers are not available. However, the infielder, mostly a short stop, played for twelve seasons in the minors, from 1953, at 19 years of age, through the 1965 season, at age 31. He appeared in 1476 games and had a very respectful .273 batting average. At the end of his career he became a machinist.

He arrived in the U.S. via Mexico to Miami, Florida on April 14, 1961 on his way to Jacksonville to join the Pittsburgh organization. His visa from Mexico was issued only four days earlier, given the arrangements between U.S. Baseball and Mexican authorities. Given his playing history, Roberto G. Sánchez chose to stay in the U.S. and pursue his professional baseball career.

Year	Age	Tm	Lg	Lev	Aff
1953	19	Batavia Clippers	Pennsylvania-Ontario-New York League	D	PIT
1954	20	Waco Pirates	Big State League	B	PIT
1955	21	Hollywood Stars	Pacific Coast League	Opn	PIT
1955	21	Waco Pirates	Big State League	B	PIT
1956	22	Mexico City Tigres	Mexican League	AA	
1957	23	Beaumont Pirates	Big State League	B	PIT
1957	23	Lincoln Chiefs	Western League	A	PIT
1958	24	Grand Forks Chiefs	Northern League	C	PIT

Year	Age	Tm	Lg	Lev	Aff
1959	25	Idaho Falls Russets	Pioneer League	C	PIT
1960	26	Burlington Bees	Illinois-Indiana-Iowa League	B	PIT
1961	27	Batavia Pirates	New York-Pennsylvania League	D	PIT
1962	28	Grand Forks Chiefs	Northern League	C	PIT
1962	28	Columbus Jets	International League	AAA	PIT
1963	29	Kinston Eagles	Carolina League	A	PIT
1964	30	Kinston Eagles	Carolina League	A	PIT
1965	31	Asheville Tourists	Southern League	AA	PIT

Pedro Pastor Sierra Quintana

The record shows Sierra's being born in La Habana on July 26, 1938 and his travel records clarify this information further. Sierra's travel records from 1959 points out his birthday as July 26, 1935, or three years older. This is not unusual since many players are known to have made themselves seem younger. And the likelihood that Sierra would not jeopardize his ability to travel to the U.S. to play professional baseball suggests clearly that his birth year was indeed 1935. The same record indicates his birthplace as Arroyo-Naranjo one of the fifteen municipalities on the outskirts of the capital city of La Habana, found about six miles to the south. His travel record arriving in Miami, Florida on May 11, 1959, on his way to join the Sanford Ball club, is consistent with his having played for the Sanford Greyhounds that year.

Here again, his playing career indicates that this right-handed pitcher began his career outside of Cuba, in 1957, at the Central Mexican League, for the Durango-Laguna team. In 1959, he jumped to the U.S. minors at the Appalachian and Florida State League. He remained in the minors through the 1971 season. Following that period he returned to play in Mexico at the Triple A level, from 1972 through 1975, finishing his career with Aguascalientes at the age of 36. During his eight seasons in the U.S., he had a 52-57 record, striking out 528 batters while giving up 325 walks in 819 innings pitched.

However, his career was much richer than indicated. In 1954 Sierra signed with the Indianapolis Clowns of the Negro League and the following year he played for the Detroit Stars and was subsequently selected to the East-West All Star game for four straight years. Soon after he began his career in the U.S. minors. However, an interesting gap in his playing career shown in the table below, following the 1959 season is due to the fact that he was drafted into the U.S. Army and served for two and half years. A second gap in the table from 1967 through 1969, is explained by his playing at the Provinciale League in Quebec, Canada where he was selected to the All Star game for three consecutive years.

At the end of his playing career, Sierra attended College in Washington DC and pursued a career in community service. This included assisting fellow Cubans arriving during the 1980 Cuban Refugee Crisis known as the Mariel program. He retired in 2010.

His playing career, his military service and a visit with the author many years later, shows that he stayed in the U.S. following the end of the 1960-61 baseball season in Cuba.

Additional sources:
baseballinlivingcolor.com
NLBM Legacy 2000 Players' Reunion Alumni Book, Kansas City Missouri: Negro Leagues Baseball Museum, Inc., 2000. cnlbr.org

Year	Age	Tm	Lg	Lev	Aff
1957	18	Durango-Laguna	Central Mexican League	C	
1959	20	Lynchburg Senators	Appalachian League	D-	WSH
1959	20	Sanford Greyhounds	Florida State League	D	WSH
1962	23	Erie Sailors	New York-Pennsylvania League	D	MIN
1963	24	Bismarck-Mandan Pards	Northern League	A	MIN
1964	25	Wisconsin Rapids Twins	Midwest League	A	MIN
1965	26	Thomasville Hi-Toms	Western Carolinas League	A	MIN
1966	27	Thomasville Hi-Toms	Western Carolinas League	A	MIN
1970	31	Pittsfield Senators	Eastern League	AA	WSA
1971	32	Burlington Senators	Carolina League	A	WSA
1971	32	Pittsfield Senators	Eastern League	AA	WSA
1972	33	Puebla Pericos	Mexican League	AAA	
1973	34	Puebla Pericos	Mexican League	AAA	
1973	34	Mexico City Diablos Rojos	Mexican League	AAA	
1973	34	Tampico Alijadores	Mexican League	AAA	
1973	34	Chihuahua Dorados	Mexican League	AAA	
1974	35	Chihuahua Dorados	Mexican League	AAA	

Year	Age	Tm	Lg	Lev	Aff
1974	35	Veracruz Aguila	Mexican League	AAA	
1975	36	Aguascalientes Rieleros	Mexican League	AAA	

Emiliano Urbina Tellería

Tellería played mostly short stop and in the outfield for a total of five seasons on teams affiliated with the Pittsburgh Pirates. He batted a robust .301 in 2116 times at bat. He stole 114 bases during his short career. He was born on May 25, 1936 in Puerta de Golpe, located in the western Province of Pinar del Río near its capital city, Pinar del Río.

Tellería's travel record shows his arrival on March 22, 1960 in Miami and his destination to report to the Pittsburgh Training Camp in Jacksonville Florida. His date of birth on the official travel document shows 1936 as his birth year. Given his playing for the Tri-City Braves, one can conclude correctly he remained in the United States following the end of his brief career.

Year	Age	Tm	Lg	Lev	Aff
1958	20	Salem Rebels	Appalachian League	D-	PIT
1958	20	Clinton Pirates	Midwest League	D	PIT
1959	21	San Angelo/ Roswell Pirates	Sophomore League	D	PIT
1960	22	Burlington Bees	Illinois-Indiana-Iowa League	B	PIT
1961	23	Grand Forks Chiefs	Northern League	C	PIT
1962	24	Tri-City Braves	Northwest League	B	

Jesus Torres Elosegui

According to his travel records coming to the U.S., Torres was born in 1936, not 1939, on July 30, in Reglas, located across the bay from the city of La Habana.

He played in the minors from 1958 through 1962 mostly at third and short stop, appearing in 581 games and had a .253 batting average. His last recorded entry into the U.S., at Miami, Florida, was on April 7, 1960 on his way to Fernandina Beach. His brief baseball career ended in 1962 thus demonstrating that he stayed in the U.S. after the end of the 1960-61 professional baseball season in Cuba.

Year	Age	Tm	Lg	Lev	Aff
1958	18	Daytona Beach Islanders	Florida State League	D	STL
1958	18	Keokuk Cardinals	Midwest League	D	STL
1959	19	Daytona Beach Islanders	Florida State League	D	STL
1960	20	Wilson Tobs	Carolina League	B	WSH
1961	21	Wilson Tobs	Carolina League	B	MIN
1962	22	Charlotte Hornets	South Atlantic League	A	MIN
1962	22	Wilson Tobs	Carolina League	B	MIN

Nestor Velázquez Herrera

Velázquez was playing as early as 1958 with the Class C St. Cloud Rox in the Northern League for four short games. He also played that season in Mexico for the Double A Yucatán Leones.

He went on to play a total of thirteen seasons, all in the minors. He played in 1303 games and had a .265 batting average finishing, with the Lynchburg Twins in 1970 at the age of 30.

It is worthy of note to indicate his birthday was listed as March 16, not 6, in his travel record from La Habana, Cuba to Miami on his way to St. Petersburg Florida in 1960.

Nestor Velázquez passed away on July 31, 2014 in Charlotte, North Carolina.

Year	Age	Tm	Lg	Lev
1958	18	St. Cloud Rox	Northern League	C
1958	18	Yucatan Leones	Mexican League	AA
1959	19	Artesia Giants	Sophomore League	D
1959	19	Michigan City White Caps	Midwest League	D
1960	20	Erie Sailors	New York-Pennsylvania League	D
1961	21	Charlotte Hornets	South Atlantic League	A
1962	22	Charlotte Hornets	South Atlantic League	A
1963	23	Wilson Tobs	Carolina League	A
1964	24	Wilson Tobs	Carolina League	A
1965	25	Wilson Tobs	Carolina League	A
1965	25	Charlotte Hornets	Southern League	AA
1966	26	Wilson Tobs	Carolina League	A
1967	27	Charlotte Hornets	Southern League	AA
1968	28	Charlotte Hornets	Southern League	AA
1969	29	Charlotte Hornets	Southern League	AA
1970	30	Lynchburg Twins	Carolina League	A

Through the years Cuban born players of the previous eras distinguished themselves in a variety of ways. The following were selected to play at the All Star game.

Player	# of Selections
Azcue, José Joaquin	1
Campaneris, Dagoberto (Bert)	6
Cárdenas, Leonardo (Leo)	5
Casanova, Paulino	1
Cuellar, Miguel	4

Fornieles, Miguel	1
Miñoso, Orestes (Minnie)	9
Oliva, Pedro (Tony)	8
Pascual, Camilo	7
Pérez, Atanasio (Tony)	7
Ramos, Pedro	1
Rojas, Octavio (Cookie-Cuqui)	5
Taylor, Antonio (Tony)	2
Tiant, Luis	3
Versalles, Zoilo	2

All-Star game

- MVP Award (since 1962) – Tony Pérez in 1967
- Starting Pitcher – Luis Tiant Jr. in 1968

PART III

"The Transition Period" 1962–1989

Chapter 1

HISTORY

This period of time, of my own creation, reflects a period when many Cubans came to the U.S. for personal as well as professional reasons. A question may be asked why the players I have included here, who were born in Cuba but came here as young children would be part of this narrative. It is a fair question.

My basic response, and reason, for their inclusion is that these players along with their parents are, in fact, as much a part of the Cuban baseball and political story of those that found themselves in a position to leave or stay as those more established players of the past. In fact, some of these players came to the U.S. before the end of the end of the final professional baseball season in Cuba. Had they or their family stayed, Cuban baseball presence in the U.S. would have been affected. And possibly, the history of baseball in Cuba past 1961 would have been different than that which existed, given the talent these players possessed. Maybe it is best to underscore, at this point, just how the political reality in Cuba affected baseball since the decision to end professional baseball went beyond the end of the 1960-61 season.

Following the end of professional baseball in Cuba, as the Castro Revolution and the new government became more entrenched in the Cuban society, people on the island became aware of what living in a socialist/communist regime truly meant. The absence of human rights, and the high level governmental control on all aspects of people's lives, including education, travel, the economy, and religion, among other things, like food rationing that began in 1962, prompted many to flee their country.

Camarioca

A well-documented exodus, which became known as the Camarioca boatlift, began, in effect, on September 29, 1965 at what was re-named the Plaza de La Revolución in La Habana. Fidel Castro made the surprising announcement, that beginning October 10 of that year, the port of Camarioca would be opened so that any Cubans desiring to leave for "the Yankee paradise" could do so. Also, any boats of Cuban exiles that wished to return to Cuba to evacuate relatives would be permitted into Camarioca, located on the north coast near the city of Matanzas.

Camarioca remained "opened" until November 15, 1965, and a total of 2,979 Cubans took advantage of Castro's offer through that period. Those migrants who were still at the port, numbering in the thousands, were ultimately taken by officially chartered passenger vessels to Florida.[51]

Vuelos de la libertad-Freedom Flights

Another better-known exodus, known as "Freedom Flights," *Vuelos de la Libertad,* during which 300,000 people left Cuba, went on from 1965 through 1973, starting during Lyndon Johnson's presidency. Once again, Fidel Castro and his government made an agreement with the U.S. that allowed Cubans to leave the country providing they met certain criteria. These included the presence of aging family members in Cuba, or minors in the U.S. It also facilitated the exit by family members if they lived in the same home among others. It was during this particular exodus that this author's family left after a separation of many years. The flights originating from the Varadero beach area in the Matanzas province brought Cubans to the U.S.

Mariel

Later on in 1980 the Mariel exodus, during the Carter presidency, took place as 125,000 left their country. Mariel is a port located west of the capital city of La Habana where Cubans, mostly from the Miami area, landed to seek out their family members and brought them to the U.S. A family member of this author was among those that rushed to Cuba and brought back his father and his second wife. Parenthetically, the Castro regime took advantage of this effort by releasing people from their jails or removing people they considered undesirables. They forced them on the owners of the boats that were in Cuba to take their family out.[52]

The "Transition" Continued

In the wake of this exodus activity, one interesting example of this period related to baseball is the story of Rogelio Alvarez who played in the majors in 1960, as previously cited but worthy of repetition. Alvarez had returned to his homeland but found himself unable to leave the island by the (Cuban) government in 1963, but the Cuban government would not let him leave the island. Ultimately, he did leave through the assistance of the Mexican government but was never able to return to the majors.

Since many families left, it was not surprising to learn that many of the children were raised and educated in the U.S. and pursue a job or career of their choice rather than what the government would approve of. This was the reality of life under the Castro regime.

More research would unveil other names. To support the point in question, one can look at the history of the families of the Canseco brothers, José and Ozzie, who came in 1965, and Emilio Antonio (Tony) Fossas whose family left in 1966. Others, like Nelson Santovenia, who came at the age of 5, or Rafael Palmeiro, Leo Sutherland, Roberto (Bobby) Ramos, and Orestes Destrade can be included as well. The parents of Fredi González, Miami Marlins former manager, came with their two other children.[53]

There were some who had stayed in Cuba but following a number of years living there, decided that leaving was a choice they had to make. A prominent name is that of Antonio (Tony) Castaño who, as stated earlier, resigned his manager's position in protest when the

Sugar Kings were moved out of Cuba. He finally left in 1962. He died on October 13, 1989 in Miami, Florida.

The presence of Cuban players in the U.S. majors during this period shifted significantly. From 1962 to 1969, a total of twenty-six Cubans were in the majors. Many had played in earlier years or had been in the minor league system in the U.S. Nevertheless, from 1970 through 1989 only twelve Cuban born players would be in the "bigs."

Meanwhile baseball in Cuba had taken a downturn due to the exit by many of their stars. It began to improve during the 1970s and 80s. But Cubans in the island were, in effect, prohibited from watching, reading about or enjoying the accomplishments of fellow Cubans playing baseball in the U.S. This included such stellar performances as those by Tany Pérez and Luis Tiant Jr. during the 1975 World Series.[54]

The following players' information was obtained from baseball-reference.com and ancestry.com in addition to other sources documented. As previously indicated, when face with inconsistent information in prior publications, I would rely on the information found in the immigration or official records. My reason for this, was that I presumed that players did not wish to jeopardized travel or U.S. citizenship applications as two examples, by inserting incorrect information. Excerpts associated with each of these players who came with their parents or on their own follow. To the degree possible, I have included an image of the corresponding player with the credit to the organization which gave the permission to use these images. The acknowledgement page features these organizations.

Chapter 2

THE PLAYERS

José Raimundo Arcia Orta

El Flaco, the "skinny one", as he was known, was a pitcher in Cuba as a teenager, with the amateur team "Rayonitro." He came to the U.S. with a Visa Waiver on November 4, 1961 via La Habana during the Pedro Pan Program era. It was said that he, in fact, did not participate in the program, and research has not shown his name as one of the children that came to the U.S. through that program. Given the secrecy associated with the program, especially during the early days when parents and program administrators alike feared for the safety of the young children, the lack of available documentation and the difficulties of the time, makes it impossible to say with certainty that he was or was not part of the program.

Born August 22, 1943 in La Habana, Arcia was signed as an amateur free agent by the Houston Colt 45s in 1962, but did not make his major league debut for six years. Known as a utility player, Arcia made the most of his talent as he performed at every position except for catcher.

He started his playing career in 1962 at the age of 18, having arrived from Cuba the year prior. His 12 seasons in the minors including 1017 games, hitting .239, with a pitching record of 21 wins and 18 losses.

Arcia played in the majors for three seasons. He opened the 1968 season as a member of the Cubs and remained with the club the whole season, batting .190 in 58 games as a rookie, hitting his only major league home run, and playing six positions in the field. Arcia saw considerable playing time over the next two seasons with San Diego, serving as a rather versatile utility player. He played a total of 293 games and hit a low .215 but his versatility was his strength.

He finished his active playing career in 1976 at the age of 32 years old playing for the Double A Columbus Astros, a team affiliated with the Houston Astros.

In 1982, José Arcia managed the Single A Miami Marlins whose record for that season was 53 wins and 84 losses.

He died on July 30, 2016 in Miami, Florida.

Additional source: José (Chamby) Campos, personal interview with author, January 26, 2018.

Year	Age	Tm	Lg	Lev
1962	18	Modesto Colts	California League	C
1962	18	Moultrie Colt .22s	Georgia-Florida League	D
1962	18	Thomasville Tigers	Georgia-Florida League	D

Year	Age	Tm	Lg	Lev
1963	19	Dubuque Packers	Midwest League	A
1963	19	Grand Forks Chiefs	Northern League	A
1964	20	Rock Hill Cardinals	Western Carolinas League	A
1964	20	Burlington Indians	Carolina League	A
1964	20	FEIL Cardinals	Florida East Coast Instructional League	WRk
1965	21	Raleigh Cardinals	Carolina League	A
1965	21	FIL Cardinals	Florida Instructional League	WRk
1966	22	Cedar Rapids Cardinals	Midwest League	A
1966	22	FIL Cardinals	Florida Instructional League	WRk
1967	23	Arkansas Travelers	Texas League	AA
1967	23	FIL Cardinals	Florida Instructional League	WRk
1968	24	Chicago Cubs	National League	MLB
1969	25	San Diego Padres	National League	MLB
1970	26	San Diego Padres	National League	MLB
1971	27	Hawaii Islanders	Pacific Coast League	AAA
1971	27	Salt Lake City Angels	Pacific Coast League	AAA
1972	28	Tacoma Twins	Pacific Coast League	AAA
1973	29	Omaha Royals	American Association	AAA
1974	30	Omaha Royals	American Association	AAA
1975	31	Jacksonville Suns	Southern League	AA
1976	32	Columbus Astros	Southern League	AA

José Canseco Capas Jr.

The better-known Canseco brother and player José was born on July 2, 1964. He is the brother of Ozzie and the son of José Sr. and Bárbara Canseco. He came to the U.S. on 1965 as part of the Freedom Flights

Program. His father, who had lost everything in Cuba, and his family settled in the Miami area where the younger twin José played baseball at Miami Coral Park High School but failed to make the varsity team until his senior year. He was named The Most Valuable Player of the junior varsity team in his junior year, and was a member of the varsity team the following year. He graduated in 1982 and was drafted by the Oakland Athletics.

During a long 17 season career in the major leagues he played in 1887 games with a .266 batting average. He was known for his power at the plate and named the Rookie of the Year, the American League Most Valuable Player, and was selected six times to the All Star team. He played eight seasons in the minors, appearing in 392 games and had a .277 batting average. He also played in eight different seasons at the Independent league level, ending his playing career in 2016 at the age of 51. Canseco managed one season for the Yuma Independent League team, ending with a 35-52 record. Unfortunately, Canseco is also well known for his personal activities off the field of play, which has detracted from his accomplishments as a player and his relationship with the baseball establishment and many fans.

Year	Age	Tm	Lg	Lev
1982	17	Miami Marlins	Florida State League	A
1982	17	Idaho Falls A's	Pioneer League	Rk
1983	18	Madison Muskies	Midwest League	A
1983	18	Medford A's	Northwest League	A-
1984	19	Modesto A's	California League	A
1985	20	Huntsville Stars	Southern League	AA
1985	20	Tacoma Tigers	Pacific Coast League	AAA
1985	20	Oakland Athletics	American League	MLB
1986	21	Oakland Athletics	American League	MLB
1987	22	Oakland Athletics	American League	MLB
1988	23	Oakland Athletics	American League	MLB
1989	24	Huntsville Stars	Southern League	AA
1989	24	Oakland Athletics	American League	MLB
1990	25	Oakland Athletics	American League	MLB
1991	26	Oakland Athletics	American League	MLB
1992	27	Oakland Athletics	American League	MLB
1992	27	Texas Rangers	American League	MLB
1993	28	Texas Rangers	American League	MLB
1994	29	Texas Rangers	American League	MLB
1995	30	Pawtucket Red Sox	International League	AAA
1995	30	Boston Red Sox	American League	MLB
1996	31	Pawtucket Red Sox	International League	AAA
1996	31	Boston Red Sox	American League	MLB
1997	32	Oakland Athletics	American League	MLB
1998	33	Toronto Blue Jays	American League	MLB
1999	34	Tampa Bay Devil Rays	American League	MLB
2000	35	Tampa Bay Devil Rays	American League	MLB

Year	Age	Tm	Lg	Lev
2000	35	New York Yankees	American League	MLB
2001	36	Newark Bears	Atlantic League	Ind
2001	36	Chicago White Sox	American League	MLB
2002	37	Charlotte Knights	International League	AAA
2006	41	San Diego Surf Dawgs	Golden Baseball League	Ind
2006	41	Long Beach Armada	Golden Baseball League	Ind
2010	45	Laredo Broncos	United League Baseball	Ind
2011	46	Yuma Scorpions	North American League	Ind
2012	47	Worcester Tornadoes	Canadian-American Association	Ind
2013	48	Fort Worth Cats	United League Baseball	Ind
2015	50	Sonoma Stompers	Pacific Association	Ind
2015	50	Pittsburg Mettle	Pacific Association	Ind
2016	51	Pittsburg Mettle	Pacific Association	Ind

Ozzie Canseco Capas

Canseco was born in La Habana, Cuba on July 2, 1964, the son of José Sr. and Bárbara Canseco and brother to José. He came to the U.S. as part of the Freedom Flights Program in 1965. His father was a territory manager for the Esson Oil and Gasoline Corporation, as well as a part-time English teacher, but like many before and after him lost his job and eventually his home. The family settled in the Miami area, where José Sr. became a territory manager for another oil and gasoline concern, Amoco, and a part-time security guard.

Ozzie went to school at Miami-Dade College, Kendall Campus in Miami, Florida and was drafted by the New York Yankees in the 2nd round of the 1983 MLB January Draft.

His career spanned from 1983 in Greensboro at the age of 18, through 2014 at the age of 49. The last few years he played one or two games per season at the Independent League level. During his eleven seasons in the minors, he played a total of 794 games with a .241 batting average. Canseco played during three brief seasons in the majors in 24 games and a .200 batting average and also played in Mexico for one season.

Year	Age	Tm	Lg	Lev
1983	18	Greensboro Hornets	South Atlantic League	A
1984	19	Greensboro Hornets	South Atlantic League	A
1984	19	Oneonta Yankees	New York-Pennsylvania League	A-
1985	20	Fort Lauderdale Yankees	Florida State League	A
1985	20	GCL Yankees	Gulf Coast League	Rk
1986	21	GCL Yankees	Gulf Coast League	Rk
1986	21	Madison Muskies	Midwest League	A
1987	22	Madison Muskies	Midwest League	A
1988	23	Huntsville Stars	Southern League	AA
1988	23	Madison Muskies	Midwest League	A

Year	Age	Tm	Lg	Lev
1989	24	Huntsville Stars	Southern League	AA
1990	25	Huntsville Stars	Southern League	AA
1990	25	Oakland Athletics	American League	MLB
1992	27	Louisville Redbirds	American Association	AAA
1992	27	St. Louis Cardinals	National League	MLB
1993	28	Louisville Redbirds	American Association	AAA
1993	28	St. Louis Cardinals	National League	MLB
1994	29	New Orleans Zephyrs	American Association	AAA
1998	33	Duluth-Superior Dukes	Northern League	Ind
1998	33	Fargo-Moorhead Redhawks	Northern League	Ind
1999	34	Tabasco Ganaderos	Mexican League	AAA
1999	34	Monterrey Sultanes	Mexican League	AAA
2000	35	Newark Bears	Atlantic League	Ind
2001	36	Newark Bears	Atlantic League	Ind
2010	45	Laredo Broncos	United League Baseball	Ind
2011	46	Yuma Scorpions	North American League	Ind
2013	48	Edinburg Roadrunners	United League Baseball	Ind
2014	49	Brownsville Charros	United League Baseball	Ind

Orestes Destrade Cuevas

Destrade was born in Santiago de Cuba, on May 8, 1962. He came to the U.S. with his family at the age of six in 1968 via the Freedom Flights program. (See source cited below.) He was drafted by the California Angels in the 23rd round of the 1980 MLB June Amateur Draft from Christopher Columbus High School in Miami, Florida. Destrade began his playing career in 1981 at the age of 19 years old ending in 1995. During that time, he applied for U.S. Citizenship in 1989 at the Miami District Court.

He played during 9 seasons in the minors in 906 games with a .256 batting average. A first baseman, he played four seasons in the major leagues and had a .241 batting average in 237 games. He became a hitting sensation early on during his five years in the Japanese League where he appeared in 517 games and had a .262 batting average.

Following his retirement, Destrade began a successful broadcasting career and is currently with the Tampa franchise.

Additional source: José (Chamby) Campos, personal interview with author, January 26, 2018.

Year	Age	Tm	Lg	Lev
1981	19	Paintsville Yankees	Appalachian League	Rk
1982	20	Oneonta Yankees	New York-Pennsylvania League	A-
1982	20	Greensboro Hornets	South Atlantic League	A
1983	21	Fort Lauderdale Yankees	Florida State League	A
1984	22	Fort Lauderdale Yankees	Florida State League	A
1984	22	Nashville Sounds	Southern League	AA

Year	Age	Tm	Lg	Lev
1985	23	Albany-Colonie Yankees	Eastern League	AA
1986	24	Columbus Clippers	International League	AAA
1987	25	Columbus Clippers	International League	AAA
1987	25	New York Yankees	American League	MLB
1988	26	Buffalo Bisons	American Association	AAA
1988	26	Pittsburgh Pirates	National League	MLB
1989	27	Seibu Lions	Japan Pacific League	Fgn
1989	27	Buffalo Bisons	American Association	AAA
1990	28	Seibu Lions	Japan Pacific League	Fgn
1991	29	Seibu Lions	Japan Pacific League	Fgn
1992	30	Seibu Lions	Japan Pacific League	Fgn
1993	31	Florida Marlins	National League	MLB
1994	32	Florida Marlins	National League	MLB
1995	33	Seibu Lions	Japan Pacific League	Fgn

Emilio Antonio (Tony) Fossas Morejon

Tony Fossas is, in my opinion, one of the most effective pitching specialists I have witnessed. He would be brought in to handle left-handed batters, something he did well, as some baseball Hall of Fame batters can attest to.

Born on September 23, 1957 in La Habana, Fossas arrived to the U.S. in Miami Florida on May 21, 1968 with his brother Mikail and his parents Emilio and Nelida via the Freedom Flights program. (See source cited below). He went to high school in Boston where he later played at some point in his major league career. Drafted by the Minnesota Twins in 1978, he did not sign in order to continue college studies the following year. But the Rangers were able to sign the young prospect.

Starting his professional career in 1979, Fossas went on to play for a total of 15 seasons in the minors where he won 78 games and lost 67 with a 3.88 ERA. He played twelve seasons in the major leagues and had a record of 17-24 with a 3.90 ERA. This did not accurately reflect his value as a pitcher against left-handed batters. As a Red Sox fan, I would relax as he came to the mound to handle only one batter to put out a potential rally by "our" opponents.

He finished his career in 1999 at 41 years of age, having arrived to the "bigs" at the age of 30.

Additional sources:

José (Chamby) Campos, personal interview with author, January 26, 2018.
Peter Gammons Boston Globe April 26, 1991

Year	Age	Tm	Lg	Lev
1979	21	Tulsa Drillers	Texas League	AA
1979	21	GCL Rangers	Gulf Coast League	Rk
1980	22	Asheville Tourists	South Atlantic League	A
1981	23	Tulsa Drillers	Texas League	AA
1982	24	Tabasco Plataneros	Mexican League	AAA

Year	Age	Tm	Lg	Lev
1982	24	Burlington Rangers	Midwest League	A
1983	25	Tulsa Drillers	Texas League	AA
1983	25	Oklahoma City 89ers	American Association	AAA
1984	26	Oklahoma City 89ers	American Association	AAA
1984	26	Tulsa Drillers	Texas League	AA
1985	27	Oklahoma City 89ers	American Association	AAA
1986	28	Edmonton Trappers	Pacific Coast League	AAA
1987	29	Edmonton Trappers	Pacific Coast League	AAA
1988	30	Oklahoma City 89ers	American Association	AAA
1988	30	Texas Rangers	American League	MLB
1989	31	Denver Zephyrs	American Association	AAA
1989	31	Milwaukee Brewers	American League	MLB
1990	32	Denver Zephyrs	American Association	AAA
1990	32	Milwaukee Brewers	American League	MLB
1991	33	Boston Red Sox	American League	MLB
1992	34	Boston Red Sox	American League	MLB
1993	35	Boston Red Sox	American League	MLB
1994	36	Pawtucket Red Sox	International League	AAA
1994	36	Boston Red Sox	American League	MLB
1995	37	St. Louis Cardinals	National League	MLB
1996	38	St. Louis Cardinals	National League	MLB
1997	39	St. Louis Cardinals	National League	MLB
1998	40	Iowa Cubs	Pacific Coast League	AAA
1998	40	Oklahoma RedHawks	Pacific Coast League	AAA
1998	40	Seattle Mariners	American League	MLB
1998	40	Chicago Cubs	National League	MLB
1998	40	Texas Rangers	American League	MLB

Year	Age	Tm	Lg	Lev
1999	41	Columbus Clippers	International League	AAA
1999	41	New York Yankees	American League	MLB

Bárbaro Garbey

A less clear story involves that of Bárbaro Garbey who came via the Mariel exodus without his wife and two children. At the time he had been banned from playing by the Cuban government and accused of fixing games. There are those that consider him the earliest "defector". But others do not. I have chosen to place him during the "Transition Years" since he came like many others at the time under a Cuban government approved exodus rather than leaving like those who left after 1990 as will be shown later in Part IV.

A well-publicized incident involving Garbey was his swinging a bat at a fan who had taunted him yelling, "Your wife and kids must be really starving for you to miss that one Garbey." The Detroit Tigers provided medical care to help Garbey deal with depression and other difficulties during that time. Signed soon after his arrival by Detroit's scout, Orlando Peña, he played through 1994 but over the years has been able to find some work in the minors. He played from 1980 through the 1994 season in the U.S. and in Mexico at first and third base in the infield as well as in the outfield. In 7 seasons in the minors, he played in 493 games, with a .302 batting average and connected 45 homers. In three seasons in the major leagues, he played with Detroit and the Texas Rangers with a .267 batting average and 11 home runs. He finished his career playing for the Minatitlan Petroleros in the Mexican League.

Additional source: A Cuban with Clout New York Times May 7, 1984 by Joe Lapointe

Year	Age	Tm	Lg	Lev	Aff
1980	23	Lakeland Tigers	Florida State League	A	DET
1981	24	Birmingham Barons	Southern League	AA	DET
1981	24	Evansville Triplets	American Association	AAA	DET
1982	25	Birmingham Barons	Southern League	AA	DET
1983	26	Evansville Triplets	American Association	AAA	DET
1984	27	Detroit Tigers	American League	MLB	DET
1985	28	Detroit Tigers	American League	MLB	DET
1986	29	Dos Laredos Tecolotes	Mexican League	AAA	
1987	30	Campeche Alacranes	Mexican League	AAA	
1988	31	Oklahoma City 89ers	American Association	AAA	TEX
1988	31	Texas Rangers	American League	MLB	TEX
1989	32	Jacksonville Expos	Southern League	AA	MON
1990	33	Albuquerque Dukes	Pacific Coast League	AAA	LAD
1990	33	Mexico City Tigres	Mexican League	AAA	

Year	Age	Tm	Lg	Lev	Aff
1991	34	Mexico City Tigres	Mexican League	AAA	
1992	35	Mexico City Tigres	Mexican League	AAA	
1993	36	Mexico City Tigres	Mexican League	AAA	
1994	37	Yucatan Leones	Mexican League	AAA	
1994	37	Minatitlan Petroleros	Mexican League	AAA	

Orlando Eugenio González y Behar

Orlando González arrived from La Habana with a Visa Waiver on November 8, 1961 as one of the 14,048 Pedro Pan unaccompanied children at the age of 9 years old and sent to 253 NW 46St. Miami. The Pedro Pan Program began helping children leave the island in December of 1960 and lasted through October of 1962.

Born on November 15, 1951 in La Habana, he went on to play for the University of Miami Hurricanes, making the difference in that team in 1975, on the way to Omaha, hitting .400 with 62 stolen bases. In 1974, he was awarded the Lefty Gomez Plate as the outstanding amateur baseball player in the U.S. He was drafted by the San Francisco Giants in 1972, and by the Cleveland Indians in 1974 out of the University of Miami. The previous year he was granted U.S. Citizenship in the District Court of Miami. In 1974 at the age of 22, he went on to play in San Antonio for the AA Brewers, affiliated with the Indians. He played a total of seven seasons in the minors, appearing in 729 games and hitting a robust .312 average. As an outfielder and a first baseman, he played during three seasons in the major leagues in 79 games and had a .238 batting average. He finished his career at the age of 28 in 1980, playing for the American League Oakland Athletics.

Additional sources:

http://grfx.cstv.com/photos/schools/mifl/sports/m-basebl/auto_pdf/1011-basebl-mg3.
José (Chamby) Campos, personal interview with author, January 26, 2018.
Ramírez, José I. *Defining Moments A Cuban Exile's Story about Discovery and the Search for a Better Future.* North Charleston, South Carolina: CreateSpace, 2013.

Year	Age	Tm	Lg	Lev
1974	22	San Antonio Brewers	Texas League	AA
1975	23	Oklahoma City 89ers	American Association	AAA
1975	23	San Antonio Brewers	Texas League	AA
1976	24	Toledo Mud Hens	International League	AAA
1976	24	Cleveland Indians	American League	MLB
1977	25	Toledo Mud Hens	International League	AAA
1978	26	Oklahoma City 89ers	American Association	AAA
1978	26	Philadelphia Phillies	National League	MLB
1979	27	Oklahoma City 89ers	American Association	AAA
1980	28	Oklahoma City 89ers	American Association	AAA
1980	28	Oakland Athletics	American League	MLB

George Albert Lauzerique

An early arrival to the U.S. he secured a Resident Status in 1956. Jorge Alberto Lauzerique became George Albert by changing his name during his Petition for Naturalization in 1973 in the Miami District Court. Born on July 22, 1947 in La Habana, Lauzerique went to high school in New York and was drafted from high school at age 18 by the Kansas City Athletics in the 10th round in 1965.

Research did not unveil his return to Cuba after leaving at the age of nine years old.

The young pitcher began his playing career in 1965 with the St. Cloud Rox, affiliated with the Minnesota Twins and the Leesburg A's of the Kansas City Athletics. During his nine seasons in the minors, he had a record of 69-56 with a 3.33 ERA. In 1972, he played in the Mexican League. Lauzerique was promoted to the majors on four different occasions and had a 4-8 record with a 5.00 ERA. He finished his career in 1976 playing for the Dubuque Packers at the age of 28. Two years later, he married Jacqueline Rosergarten according to California records.

Year	Age	Tm	Lg	Lev
1965	17	Leesburg A's	Florida State League	A
1965	17	St. Cloud Rox	Northern League	A
1966	18	Leesburg A's	Florida State League	A
1966	18	AIL Athletics	Arizona Instructional League	WRk
1967	19	Birmingham A's	Southern League	AA
1967	19	AIL Athletics	Arizona Instructional League	WRk
1967	19	Kansas City Athletics	American League	MLB
1968	20	Vancouver Mounties	Pacific Coast League	AAA
1968	20	Oakland Athletics	American League	MLB
1969	21	Iowa Oaks	American Association	AAA
1969	21	Oakland Athletics	American League	MLB
1970	22	Portland Beavers	Pacific Coast League	AAA
1970	22	Milwaukee Brewers	American League	MLB
1971	23	Tulsa Oilers	American Association	AAA
1971	23	Portland Beavers	Pacific Coast League	AAA
1972	24	Mexico City Diablos Rojos	Mexican League	AAA
1975	27	Dubuque Packers	Midwest League	A
1975	27	Columbus Astros	Southern League	AA
1976	28	Dubuque Packers	Midwest League	A

Antonio Gustavo Menéndez Remon

Born on February 20, 1965 in La Habana, Menéndez came to the U.S. via the Freedom Flights Program. (See source cited below). He was drafted by the Chicago White Sox in the 1st round of the 1984 MLB June Amateur Draft from American High School in Miami, Florida.

At the age of 19, the young pitcher played for the White Sox in the Gulf Coast Rookie League. He spent twelve seasons in the minors, winning 75 games and losing 72. with a 3.97 ERA. He went on to play in the majors briefly, for three seasons, winning three games, and losing one, and a 4.97 ERA. He played one season for the Mexico City Diablos Rojos, where he finished his career in 1996 at the age of 31.

He became a U.S. citizen in 1988 applying on September 29. He requested his name be changed to "Tony Menendez" and was issued a certificate on December 19.

Additional source: José (Chamby) Campos, personal interview with the author, January 26, 2018.

Year	Age	Tm	Lg	Lev
1984	19	GCL White Sox	Gulf Coast League	Rk
1985	20	Buffalo Bisons	American Association	AAA
1985	20	Appleton Foxes	Midwest League	A
1986	21	Peninsula White Sox	Carolina League	A
1986	21	Birmingham Barons	Southern League	AA

Year	Age	Tm	Lg	Lev
1987	22	Birmingham Barons	Southern League	AA
1988	23	Birmingham Barons	Southern League	AA
1989	24	Birmingham Barons	Southern League	AA
1990	25	Vancouver Canadians	Pacific Coast League	AAA
1991	26	Oklahoma City 89ers	American Association	AAA
1991	26	Tulsa Drillers	Texas League	AA
1992	27	Nashville Sounds	American Association	AAA
1992	27	Cincinnati Reds	National League	MLB
1993	28	Buffalo Bisons	American Association	AAA
1993	28	Pittsburgh Pirates	National League	MLB
1994	29	Phoenix Firebirds	Pacific Coast League	AAA
1994	29	San Francisco Giants	National League	MLB
1995	30	Phoenix Firebirds	Pacific Coast League	AAA
1996	31	Mexico City Diablos Rojos	Mexican League	AAA

Adrián Nieto

He was born on November 12, 1989 in La Habana, and went on to the American Heritage High School. From there where he was drafted by the Washington Nationals in the 5th round of the 2008 MLB June Amateur Draft.

However, the story about Nieto the player pales in comparison to his personal story coming to the U.S. This story is worth telling. Excerpts of the story are cited here:

"…left Cuba at 4 1/2 years of age with his parents and 18 other people in the middle of the night on a 20-foot wooden boat in search of the American dream."

"We were worried about dying," Nieto told MLB.com of his family's departure from Cuba during a rare down moment in his first week of camp.

"I didn't know how to swim. My mom didn't know at all. It was just a journey that you hope for the best and just go out there and you hit land somewhere that's not Cuba. It's a risk definitely, but it was worth it."

Nieto recounted how his family left Cuba around midnight and was out on the water for 13 hours, guided north only by a compass that they didn't know was right or wrong. They were rescued by the U.S. Coast Guard and taken to Guantanamo Bay, where they remained for six months and six days before coming to the United States.

"This is a great opportunity here. I can play baseball and do whatever I want. Back home, I wouldn't be able to do whatever I wanted. It's a blessing. This country has given me more than I ever thought would give me."

Following the baseball draft, he was assigned to the Nationals team in the Gulf Coast League at 18 and began an eight-season career in the minors, playing in 475 games and hitting .242. Sadly, this young catcher was suspended for 50 games in 2011 after testing positive for steroids, but that did not prevent him from reaching the majors in 2014 with the Chicago White Sox. He appeared in 48 games and had a .236 batting average. He ended his career in 2016 at the age of 26, playing for the New Orleans Zephyrs at the Triple A Level.

Additional Source: Scott Merkin / MLB.com Feb 21, 2014

Year	Age	Tm	Lg	Lev
2008	18	GCL Nationals	Gulf Coast League	Rk
2009	19	GCL Nationals	Gulf Coast League	Rk
2010	20	Hagerstown Suns	South Atlantic League	A
2011	21	Auburn Doubledays	New York-Pennsylvania League	A-
2011	21	Potomac Nationals	Carolina League	A+
2011	21	Hagerstown Suns	South Atlantic League	A
2012	22	Hagerstown Suns	South Atlantic League	A
2012	22	GCL Nationals	Gulf Coast League	Rk
2013	23	Potomac Nationals	Carolina League	A+
2013	23	Mesa Solar Sox	Arizona Fall League	Fal
2014	24	Chicago White Sox	American League	MLB
2014	24	Gigantes del Cibao	Dominican Winter League	FgW
2015	25	Birmingham Barons	Southern League	AA
2016	26	New Orleans Zephyrs	Pacific Coast League	AAA

Rafael Palmeiro Corrales

Palmeiro was born in September of 1964. In 1971, at the age of 6, he left Cuba with his parents, and his parents José and María, and a brother, Ricardo. They had lived in the Lawton neighborhood in La Habana and left as part of the Freedom Flights Program. As he tells it, "We left that country because my parents were against that regime and came to this country in search of freedom. I don't think I would have played baseball." Another son, José, remained in Cuba but rejoined the family in 1992.

Palmeiro went to High School in Miami and attended Mississippi State University where he was drafted by the Chicago Cubs.

He started his playing career at the age of 20 and played through 2005, including 20 seasons in the majors where he was named to the All Star team four times. He had 3020 hits with a .288 batting average. During his eight seasons in the minors, he played in 269 games and had a .302 batting average. At the age of 50, he played one game at the Independent League level and went 2 for 4. Despite his great baseball career, his steroid related history prevented him from a realistic consideration for the Hall of Fame in Cooperstown. Asked how he would like to be remembered, Palmeiro said, "As somebody who played the game the right way, who respected the game, respected the history of the game and the players who came before me."

His application for U.S. Citizenship in the Chicago District Court was recorded on October 12, 1988.

Additional source: NY Times 7/17/05 by Bob Sherwin "Palmeiro Born In Cuba, Raised in Miami and Third Hispanic to Hit 3000".

Year	Age	Tm	Lg	Lev
1985	20	Peoria Chiefs	Midwest League	A
1986	21	Pittsfield Cubs	Eastern League	AA
1986	21	Chicago Cubs	National League	MLB
1987	22	Iowa Cubs	American Association	AAA
1987	22	Chicago Cubs	National League	MLB
1988	23	Chicago Cubs	National League	MLB
1989	24	Texas Rangers	American League	MLB
1990	25	Texas Rangers	American League	MLB
1991	26	Texas Rangers	American League	MLB
1992	27	Texas Rangers	American League	MLB
1993	28	Texas Rangers	American League	MLB
1994	29	Baltimore Orioles	American League	MLB
1995	30	Baltimore Orioles	American League	MLB
1996	31	Baltimore Orioles	American League	MLB
1997	32	Baltimore Orioles	American League	MLB
1998	33	Baltimore Orioles	American League	MLB
1999	34	Texas Rangers	American League	MLB
2000	35	Texas Rangers	American League	MLB
2001	36	Texas Rangers	American League	MLB
2002	37	Texas Rangers	American League	MLB
2003	38	Texas Rangers	American League	MLB
2004	39	Baltimore Orioles	American League	MLB
2005	40	Baltimore Orioles	American League	MLB
2015	50	Sugar Land Skeeters	Atlantic League	Ind

Roberto (Bobby) Ramos

Another arrival on the Freedom Flights Program was Ramos, born on November 5, 1955, in Calabazar de Sagua in Cuba. (See source cited

below.) He was drafted by the Montreal Expos in the 7th round of the 1974 MLB June Amateur Draft from Jackson High School in Miami, Florida.

During his 12 seasons in the minors, he played in 929 games and had a .256 batting average. This talented catcher played during six seasons in the majors for a total of 103 games and a .190 batting average. Following his retirement as an active player, he became a manager in the minor league system for Houston and Tampa, with a combined record of 241 wins and 264 losses in seven seasons. He also acted as a bullpen coach for the Angels and Tampa clubs and was named the Latin American Player Development Coordinator for the Miami Marlins.

Additional source: José (Chamby) Campos, personal interview with the author, January 26, 2018.

Year	Age	Tm	Lg	Lev
1974	18	GCL Expos	Gulf Coast League	Rk
1975	19	West Palm Beach Expos	Florida State League	A
1976	20	West Palm Beach Expos	Florida State League	A
1977	21	West Palm Beach Expos	Florida State League	A
1978	22	Denver Bears	American Association	AAA

Year	Age	Tm	Lg	Lev
1978	22	Memphis Chicks	Southern League	AA
1978	22	Montreal Expos	National League	MLB
1979	23	Salt Lake City Gulls	Pacific Coast League	AAA
1979	23	Denver Bears	American Association	AAA
1980	24	Denver Bears	American Association	AAA
1980	24	Montreal Expos	National League	MLB
1981	25	Montreal Expos	National League	MLB
1982	26	Columbus Clippers	International League	AAA
1982	26	New York Yankees	American League	MLB
1983	27	Montreal Expos	National League	MLB
1984	28	Montreal Expos	National League	MLB
1985	29	Edmonton Trappers	Pacific Coast League	AAA
1986	30	Iowa Cubs	American Association	AAA
1987	31	Omaha Royals	American Association	AAA
1988	32	Phoenix Firebirds	Pacific Coast League	AAA

Israel Sánchez Matos

Sánchez was born on August 20, 1963 in Falcon Lasvias, Cuba, a town approximately 170 miles from the capital city of La Habana, and centrally located travelling East to West. He came to the U.S. at the age of 6 according to some records. However, during our interview he indicated he had come to the U.S. at the age of 4 ½, which would indicate his date of arrival as being in 1967 or 1968. He came with his mother Elsa via the Freedom Flights Program. His father, Israel, was unable to come with the family due to concerns raised by the Cuban government. But he was able to join his family eleven months later. It is worthy of note that his grandfather Francisco Matos was a member of the military during the Cuba Administration that was in place prior to Fidel Castro. His mother's sister lived in Illinois at the time and, after spending eleven months in Miami, Florida, the family moved to Illinois.

Sánchez was drafted by the Kansas City Royals in the 9th round of the 1982 MLB June Amateur Draft from Von Steuben High School in Chicago, Illinois. The family lived in Skokie, Illinois. His father, who had been a catcher in Falcon Cuba, has since passed away, but his mother still lived in Illinois at the time of our interview. At one period, his parents returned to Cuba on two different occasions, but Israel did not travel there since at the time, he was going through the U.S. citizenship application process and did not wish to jeopardize that process.

This young pitcher began his minor league career at the age of 18 in the Gulf Coast League, playing for the Royals, affiliated with the Kansas City team. He played a total of eleven seasons, earning a 58-49 record and a 3.44 ERA. He played at the end of two seasons, 1988 and 1990, in the majors with the Kansas City Royals winning three games and losing two with a 5.36 ERA. He completed his career in 1992 at the age of 28 playing with the Rochester Red Wings in the International League, affiliated with the Baltimore organization. At different times he played with fellow Freedom Flights arrivals, the Canseco brothers.

His daughter Brittany a centerfielder for Niles North High School in Skokie, Illinois, was reported to have an arm which was a genetic gift from her dad, Israel Sanchez, who was also a lefty. While Israel has a working position with a Local Union, he has been a High School baseball coach for nine years and is currently the pitching coach for the Niles North High School baseball team. During our interview he was considering whether he would return for the next season.

His daughter Brittany has said, "He doesn't get to see a lot of my games in the spring, but he makes a lot of my games in the summer" He does help me during the season. He is the only person who taught me how to bat. When I'm not doing well he will take me out to hit to get my confidence back." Israel and his wife Angela have two other children, Natalie and Anthony.

Additional sources:

Israel Sánchez, telephone interview with author, September 5, 2017.
High school softball spotlight's on Niles North's Brittany Sanchez: Like major league father, like daughter May 01, 2010|By Bill Harrison | Special to the Tribune

Year	Age	Tm	Lg	Lev
1982	18	GCL Royals	Gulf Coast League	Rk
1983	19	Charleston Royals	South Atlantic League	A
1984	20	Fort Myers Royals	Florida State League	A
1985	21	Fort Myers Royals	Florida State League	A
1986	22	Memphis Chicks	Southern League	AA
1986	22	Omaha Royals	American Association	AAA
1987	23	Omaha Royals	American Association	AAA
1988	24	Omaha Royals	American Association	AAA
1988	24	Kansas City Royals	American League	MLB
1989	25	Baseball City Royals	Florida State League	A
1990	26	Memphis Chicks	Southern League	AA
1990	26	Baseball City Royals	Florida State League	A+

Year	Age	Tm	Lg	Lev
1990	26	Kansas City Royals	American League	MLB
1991	27	Rochester Red Wings	International League	AAA
1992	28	Rochester Red Wings	International League	AAA

Nelson Gil Santovenia Mayol

Santovenia was born on July 27, 1961 in Pinar del Rio, Pinar del Rio, a few short months after the end of the 1960-61 Cuban Baseball League. He moved at age 5, in 1966, to the U.S. with his mother Caridad, father, Antonio, sisters, Mirta and Alyeda, and brother, Luis, via the Freedom Flights program. (See source cited below). Later, the family would spend time in the Boston area before moving to Miami Florida.

Graduating from Miami Southridge Sr. High School in Miami, Florida in 1979, he was drafted by the Philadelphia Phillies in the 29th round of the 1979 MLB June Amateur Draft, but chose to go on with his education. He was subsequently drafted by the Montreal Expos in the 3rd round of the 1981 MLB June Amateur Draft from Miami-Dade College, Kendall Campus in Miami. And then he was later drafted by the Montreal Expos in the 1st round, the 19th, of the 1982 MLB June Draft-Secondary Phase from University of Miami in Coral Gables.

In 1982 he reported to the West Palm Beach Expos and Class A team in the Florida League where he played in 40 games and had a .246 batting average. This young catcher–he played first base during seventeen games in his career–went on to join the Major League Montreal Expos in 1987, appearing in two games. He returned the following year and had a .236 batting average in 92 games.

He played professional baseball from 1982 through 1994, ending his 19-season career with the Omaha Royals, the Triple A franchise of the Kansas City Royals. Santovenia played a total of 791 games in the minors with a .247 batting average and seven seasons in the major leagues, appearing in 297 games and hitting .233.

In the middle of his career, he became a U.S. Citizen, in 1985, in the Miami District Court.

Following his retirement as an active player, Santovenia became an assistant Coach at the High school level and a hitting coach in the Tigers minor league system.

Additional sources:
José (Chamby) Campos, personal interview with author,
January 26, 2018.
Danny Gallaher 2015 post Baseball Hot Corner "Former Expo Nelson Santovenia Teaching Tools of the Trade in Tigers System"

Year	Age	Tm	Lg	Lev
1982	20	West Palm Beach Expos	Florida State League	A
1983	21	Memphis Chicks	Southern League	AA
1984	22	Jacksonville Suns	Southern League	AA
1985	23	Indianapolis Indians	American Association	AAA
1985	23	Jacksonville Expos	Southern League	AA
1986	24	Jacksonville Expos	Southern League	AA
1986	24	Indianapolis Indians	American Association	AAA

Year	Age	Tm	Lg	Lev
1987	25	Jacksonville Expos	Southern League	AA
1987	25	Montreal Expos	National League	MLB
1988	26	Indianapolis Indians	American Association	AAA
1988	26	Montreal Expos	National League	MLB
1989	27	Montreal Expos	National League	MLB
1990	28	Indianapolis Indians	American Association	AAA
1990	28	Montreal Expos	National League	MLB
1991	29	Indianapolis Indians	American Association	AAA
1991	29	Montreal Expos	National League	MLB
1992	30	Vancouver Canadians	Pacific Coast League	AAA
1992	30	Chicago White Sox	American League	MLB
1993	31	Omaha Royals	American Association	AAA
1993	31	Kansas City Royals	American League	MLB
1994	32	Omaha Royals	American Association	AAA

Leonardo (Leo) Sutherland Cantino

Sutherland was born on April 6, 1958 in Santiago de Cuba but attended high school in California where he was drafted by the Cleveland Indians in 1975. However, he went on to Golden West

College in Huntington, California where he was drafted by the Chicago White Sox in the 1st round (3rd) of the 1976 MLB January Draft-Secondary Phase.

He began his playing career with the White Sox Rookie team in the Gulf League and went on to play a total of seven seasons in the minors including 767 games and batting .269. The young outfielder played two seasons in the majors with the White Sox in 45 games and a .248 batting average ending his playing career in 1982 at the age of 24.

Sutherland came to the U.S. via the Freedom Flights Program.

Additional source: José (Chamby) Campos, personal interview with author, January 26, 2018.

Year	Age	Tm	Lg	Lev
1976	18	GCL White Sox	Gulf Coast League	Rk
1977	19	Appleton Foxes	Midwest League	A
1978	20	Appleton Foxes	Midwest League	A
1979	21	Knoxville Sox	Southern League	AA
1980	22	Iowa Oaks	American Association	AAA
1980	22	Chicago White Sox	American League	MLB
1981	23	Edmonton Trappers	Pacific Coast League	AAA
1981	23	Chicago White Sox	American League	MLB
1982	24	Edmonton Trappers	Pacific Coast League	AAA

Oscar José Zamora Sosa

The Oscar Zamora story is a bit different than others. He came to Miami from La Habana on October 31, 1960 with his brother, Pablo Oscar, born on October 6, 1941. His name at the time was listed as Oscar José Pérez Zamora Sosa, but he changed his name from Oscar José Pérez to Oscar Zamora on his application for U.S. Citizenship in 1975, which had been transferred from the Miami District to Chicago, Illinois.

On that application, his date as a permanent resident on October 31, 1960 was crossed out and someone wrote in ink that he had been a permanent resident only since March 28, 1968. His immigration record clearly shows October 31, 1960 as the date of arrival, the date the last professional baseball season in Cuba was getting underway. A pitcher, he was born on September 23, 1944 in Camagüey, Cuba. He attended Miami Edison High School and Miami-Dade College, North Campus.

Zamora was signed as a free agent and started his career with the Salinas Indians of the California League in 1965. He then moved that same season to the Dubuque Packers in the Midwest League. Both teams were at the Single A Level. Playing a total of fifteen seasons in the minors, he had a 96 and 75 record with a 3.03 ERA.

During his career he was able to reach the majors on four different occasions. He secured a 13-14 record with a 4.53 ERA playing for the Chicago Cubs and the Houston Astros. The Cubs fans made up the following song, to the tune of Dean Martin's song hit "That's Amore":

When the pitch is so fat
That the ball meets the bat

That's Zamora
When the ball hits the wall
And the runners all score
That's Zamora

Zamora also pitched for the Miami Amigos of the Inter-American League in 1979. He completed his career in 1982 at the age of 37 playing for the Single A Miami Marlins. That same year he also played in the Inter-American League, which had been spearheaded by Bobby Maduro. However, Zamora, who was running a shoe business at the time, would only attend games when he was pitching.

Additional source: The Hardball Times-The Short and Wild Life of the Interamerican League July 8, 2014 by Bruce MacKinson

Year	Age	Tm	Lg	Lev
1965	20	Salinas Indians	California League	A
1965	20	Dubuque Packers	Midwest League	A
1966	21	Pawtucket Indians	Eastern League	AA
1966	21	Portland Beavers	Pacific Coast League	AAA
1967	22	Pawtucket Indians	Eastern League	AA
1968	23	Reno Silver Sox	California League	A
1968	23	Waterbury Indians	Eastern League	AA
1969	24	Peninsula Astros	Carolina League	A
1969	24	Cocoa Astros	Florida State League	A
1970	25	Columbus Astros	Southern League	AA
1971	26	Oklahoma City 89ers	American Association	AAA
1972	27	Oklahoma City 89ers	American Association	AAA
1973	28	Denver Bears	American Association	AAA
1974	29	Denver Bears	American Association	AAA
1974	29	Chicago Cubs	National League	MLB

Year	Age	Tm	Lg	Lev
1975	30	Chicago Cubs	National League	MLB
1976	31	Wichita Aeros	American Association	AAA
1976	31	Chicago Cubs	National League	MLB
1977	32	Wichita Aeros	American Association	AAA
1978	33	Charleston Charlies	International League	AAA
1978	33	Houston Astros	National League	MLB
1979	34	Miami Amigos	Inter-American League	AAA
1979	34	Did Not Play		
1982	37	Miami Marlins	Florida State League	A

During this "Transition" period two Cuban-born players were selected to the All Star games.

José Canseco was selected six times and Rafael Palmeiro four. It is ironic and with much regret that these players performed at the highest level on the field of play but their reputation and possible consideration for further awards including their selection to Baseball's Hall of Fame was marred by their off-field reported behavior during the *so-called steroids era.*

#1 Rusney Castillo with author. Author's Collection.

2 Left to Right: Paulino Casanova, Jacinto Jackie Hernández, Gonzalo Cholly Naranjo and José Tartabull at Casanova's Baseball Academy. Author's Collection.

#3 Palatka Redlegs 1960 Championship team. Players identified by Iván Davis:

Top Row standing left to right: John Flavin, Pedro (Jay) Martínez, Miles McWilliams, player not identified, Daniel Bartko, player not identified, Mel Queen.

Middle Row left to right: Ted Davidson, Mike (Mickey) Mattiace, Bill Reeves, Sammy Thompson, next three players not identified.

Bottom Row seated left to right: player not identified, Iván Davis, Dave Bristol, Tommy Helms, next two players not identified.

Photo Courtesy of Iván Davis.

#4 Left to Right: Jackie Hernández, Leo Posada, Miguelito de la Hoz, Cholly Naranjo and José (Chamby) Campos. SABR Convention Miami 2016. Author's Collection.

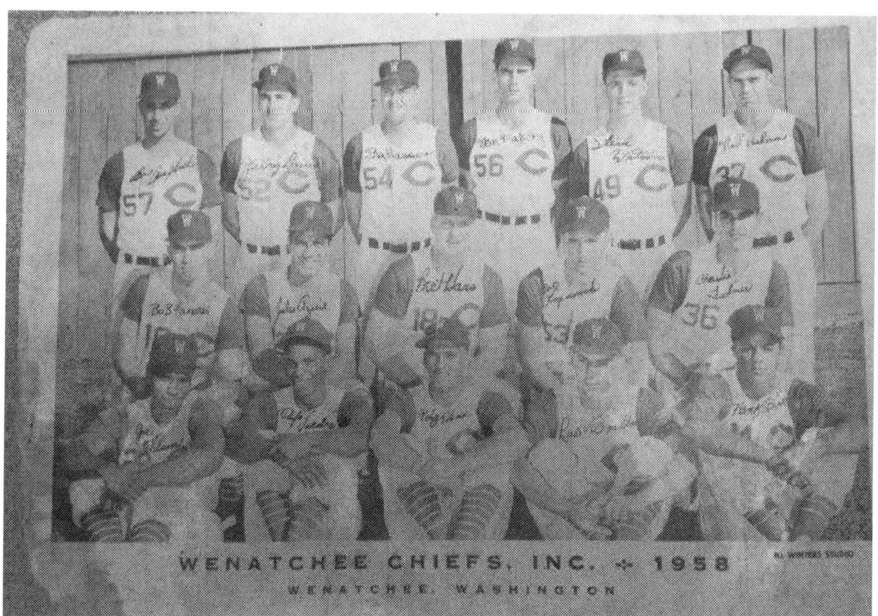

#5 Bottom Row Middle: Elio (Toby) Toboso as a member of the Wenatchee Chiefs in 1958. Courtesy of Efraín Rosales and Leonel Morales.

#6 Dagoberto Campaneris 2015. Author's Collection.

#7 Luis Tiant Jr. and Rusney Castillo. Author's Collection.

#8 Jacinto Jackie Hernández. Author's Collection.

#9 Left to Right: Miguel de la Hoz, Leo Posada, José (Chamby) Campos (Sports Radio personality in Miami), Jacinto (Jackie) Hernandez, Jorge Maduro (son of Bobby Maduro President and owner of the former Cuban Sugar Kings), author, and Gonzalo (Cholly) Naranjo. Author's Collection.

#10 Rogelio (Limonar) Martínez. Courtesy of Olga (Martínez) Fernández.

#11 Almendares team 1960-61. Courtesy of Miguelito de la Hoz.

Back row, left to right: Andrés Ayón, Marcelino López, Vicente Amor, René (Latigo) Gutiérrez, Orlando McFarlane, Carlos Paula, Lázaro Gonzalo (Cholly) Naranjo, Humberto Fernández and Orlando Peña.

Middle row, left to right: Julio (trainer), Leopoldo Posada, Miguel de la Hoz, Gabriel Antonio Martínez, José Ramón López, Enrique Izquierdo, Miguel Cuellar, Guillermo Jorge (clubhouse attendant) and General Manager Monchy de Arcos.

Front row seated, left to right: Julio Guerra, Angel Scull, Carlos (Patato) Pascual, Coach Juan Ealo, Manager Regino Otero, Coach Reinaldo Cordeiro, Antonio (Tony) Taylor, José Ramón Villar and Edmundo Amorós.

Front on ground, left to right: Radio Alvarez (known as Yayo) and young man not identified.

#12 José Iglesias with author. Author's Collection.

#13 Rodolfo Arias surrounded by his personal baseball memorabilia with author. Author's Collection.

#14 Luis Tiant Jr with author. Author's Collection.

#15 Pedro Sierra with author. Author's Collection.

#16 Juan Carlos Díaz with author. Author's Collection.

#17 Hector Maestri, first player standing, middle row left to right. Photo available through eltubeyero 22 March 4, 2014 by Andrés Pascual.

PART IV

"The Defectors" 1990–2017

Chapter 1

DEFINING THE DECISION

The period of baseball migration from Cuba known by the exodus of the *defectors* has been the subject of much writing, speculation and opinions, not all based on the reality of what living in Cuba is for those residing there on a permanent basis.

While avoiding repeating much of what been published already, I will focus my writing on establishing the context for why this exodus may have taken place, citing a few examples of those that have taken that step to *defect*.

However, before going any further, the term *defector* merits some consideration.

Language and terms used to refer to these players as *Defectors* suggest an action that does not always resonate with those people and players I have spoken to, some of whom left under these circumstances.

The word as defined reflects, "To desert one's country, cause, allegiance etc., especially, in order to join the opposing forces. To desert a cause, country etc., especially, in order to adopt another. Furthermore, to join the 'enemy', a term which is seen as a person who feels hatred for, fosters harmful designs against, or engages in antagonistic activities against another; an adversary or opponent, an armed foe, an opposing military force, a hostile nation or state, something harmful or prejudicial, the Devil; Satan.[55]

While it is easy enough or tempting to let one's political inclination to accept such terminology when referring to these baseball players leaving the island, it does not begin to acknowledge the genesis of the decision to leave by so many talented young men which I will elaborate on later.

To further suggest that these players *abandoned* their country is a way of parroting the Cuban government's position. It is offensive to these players and many others in the hundreds of thousands, in and out of baseball who have fled the island and continue to do so.

It has been noted correctly that the U.S. is a country of immigrants, given all that has happened over the years as people have come from all parts of the world.

Have they/we abandoned their country? Of course not. History is filled with the stories of people, not just from Cuba, who have returned to their homeland when they could be or continue to be of help from a distance or may have died to change what was abhorrent in their home land.

Are we not proud of the heritage and background? Of course, we are. One has to merely look around and see the expressions of pride by people everywhere as we celebrate our heritage and background at homes, neighborhoods and cities.

The basic premise for leaving Cuba permanently by baseball players began in earnest following the start of the Castro revolution taking power. Prior to that time, since the late 1800s, as we have seen, ball players simply travelled to and from both countries in order to engage in their chosen career as a professional baseball player year around which enabled them to better support themselves and their families while testing their talent against the best the sport offered.

The so-called *defections* since 1990 were driven by the same politically driven dynamics that led non-baseball players and baseball players alike to flee the island. Namely, the lack of basic freedoms and the inability to pursue your dreams without government controls or interference. This is a historical context that need not be forgotten or revised. There are those who have attempted to revise history and speak from a theoretical perspective and their own political ideology which is not always grounded in reality.

Leaving one's country voluntarily is a wrenching decision that few can relate to if they have not experienced it themselves, or else are close to those that actually have taken that step. There are those who have felt close to these players and yet were surprised when learning that these same players who professed support or acceptance to their way of life in Cuba would leave at a later date. This suggests another simple reality, which when in Cuba, people, including ball players do not have the freedom to express what they think for fear of reprisal. If they do, they must deal with the one entity that controls all forms of life on the island, the Cuban government led, by the only one political party allowed to exist legally, the Communist Party. And so, acting with discretion and secrecy is preferred in order to avoid being accused of fostering thoughts that are deemed contrary to the *revolution*, the Cuban Government. People in Cuba have been detained by the authorities or stripped of their jobs for simply being accused of harboring thoughts not consistent with government policies and views. The idea that those that left have done so as a result of the financial rewards that awaits them is to ignore the fact that living in Cuba is not a paradise-like experience unless you are connected to he high levels of the Party. Speaking of conditions in Cuba, Bill Lee the former lefty for the Boston Red Sox, and well known for his liberal political ideas, said, "I preach socialism fluently until the time comes when I actually have to participate in it."[56]

The reaction by the Cuban government as players left has been sadly predictable. In some cases, it has chosen to say where players have gone and simply say they live in the *exterior-out* of the country.[57] At other times, the government has devalued the memories of these players, as reflected in the official baseball guide of the 2002 season which describes players with an asterisk, *, as having *abandoned* the country. Some of the names classified as such are Ivan Alvarez Echevarría, Rubelman Acosta Díaz, René Arocha, Luis Rolando Arrojo, Danis Baez, Francisco Casanueva, Juan Chavez, José A Contreras, Ricardo Díaz, Osvaldo Fernández Guerra, Osvaldo Fernández Rodriguez, Manuel Hernández, Eisler Livan Hernández, Orlando

Hernández, Luis Hernández, Manuel Hurtado, José Mesa, Vladimir Nuñez, Edilberto Oropeza, Rolando Pastor, Omar Pérez, José Prado, Pablo Pozo, Ariel Prieto, Eduardo Rodríguez, Euclides Rojas, Rafael Rodríguez, Larry Rodríguez, and Julio Rojo.[58]

A critical and hard-to-envision mindset is the one expressed by Carlos Rodríguez, Baseball Commissioner, who said when asked, "We have a right to protect our athletes. You train an athlete since he was a child, since he was young, and then he gets to the point where he's producing important results.... And you're going to come and take him away? Nobody has that right. It's not morally correct or ethically correct, and we're right to take the necessary measures to protect ourselves from such piracy."[59] It is as if he is talking about a physical property to be controlled by the government not human beings.

And so, in the midst of this controlling environment, what were the options for these men? Many chose to stay and others have chosen to leave. The reasons stated by some who chose to leave do not differ in some instances than those before them who left in order to seek their own destiny despite the personal sacrifice they knew would need to be endured. "Coming here means leaving behind your friends, your childhood, to struggle by yourself against a world of different things to try to reach a point where you can be successful and help your family" Larry Rodríguez's grandfather who raised him died and he was unable to see him. "Can't forget the sadness to have left my family[60], and sought freedom where they had none. I didn't have all the liberty and freedom I wanted, talked to family and left such as Yuniesky Betancourt reflected on during his interview.[61]

The case of René Arocha who is touted as the first *defector* by many, reflects the thinking of an older ball player who saw things in Cuba in a similar way. He spoke at length, explaining that others will come to the U.S. when Fidel Castro changes his mind and begins to understand the damage he does to the Cuban people. Not only to let the players come, but to have a democracy where each person has the liberty to speak and say what he feels. "This is a very difficult decision. It is not at all easy. It's incredible the strength you have to have to leave behind not only your family, but to leave your roots, and to understand that you don't know when you will be able to return. That is what is hard.[62] This message was further reinforced by Euclides Rojas who stated that Arocha left in search of freedom whether he was able to play baseball or not.[63]

They also knew the price they would pay, like many before them, for being away from their parents. For these players it was the most difficult experience they endured, but they wanted to play baseball and help their family.[64] Just as many of the young ball players had experienced following the end of the last professional baseball season, their parents lent their support. Euclides Rojas' mother said to him, "I don't want to harm you anymore, there's no future for you here."[65]

They chose to test their skills against Major League Baseball players just as they tested the same skills against amateurs in other countries with lesser baseball traditions. "They just want to play the best baseball in the world, and they were willing to risk their lives to do it. Forget politics or family."[66] Baseball Commissioner Carlos Rodríguez reflecting on El Duque, took the opportunity to, in effect, devalue his former star by saying, "Duque pitched for the national team, but he always pitched against a team like the Italians. He never pitched against high quality players."[67] It may or it may not be always accurate to make that suggestion for ball players but they understandably want to test themselves against the best.

While some saw the opportunity to help their families financially, others felt poorly treated and restricted by Cuban government officials and institutions. They expected these players to give it all for the System and offered limited and sometimes no rewards. Many of them suffered through sanctions preventing them from playing baseball fully, or at all, such as Rusney Castillo, Adrian Hernández, and Kendry Morales, among others. Repudiation-related techniques or harassment were also experienced by some just because the government thought they wished to leave. Many players noted how treatment was delivered to those where accused or thought to wish to leave

Cuba. Juan Carlos Bruzón indicated that the *repudio* against Alberto Hernandez backfired. "…the same thing could happen to us" we realize that if we were to going to realize our dreams wc had to get out of Cuba." Many saw this as an act of hypocrisy. All players in all provinces were talking about it.[68]

In some cases they knew of people who left, people both in and out of baseball, and the more exposure they had to a different way of life, the more they became interested in seeing it for themselves. It is not surprising to note that at this time, Cuba continues to see young people leave the island while the general population is getting older. There are too many sources to mention here of the upcoming crisis facing the country as the demographical shift is taking place.

Chapter 2

MEANS USED TO EXIT CUBA

Arriving in the U.S. these players did not follow the basic travel avenues we saw used in the 1920s, 30s, 40s…. in ferries or airplanes as they traveled between the two countries or the more challenging efforts in 1960-61, seeking a visa to a third country (Mexico) in route to the U.S. These players have had to also endure sacrifices and dangers, but different than those before them. And yet, they have continued to come, to the best of their ability despite the risks.

Some, like Euclides Rojas, left in 1994 with his family during the *balseros* crisis. This was an exodus that saw thousands of Cubans–over 37 thousand–take to the strait of Florida in makeshift rafts and take their chances on the ocean with its dangerous currents, and sharks. I personally witnessed the exodus (with my oldest son) since I had arrived back in Cuba during that summer after an absence of 33 years from my home land.[69]

Others arrived with their parents like the case of Yonder Alonso. He was born in La Habana, Cuba on April 8, 1987 with parents Luis and Damarys, who left in 1996. His father played and coached for the Industriales team of the Cuban National Series, and taught his son Yonder to play as well. Alonso attended Coral Gables High School in Coral Gables, Florida, and was selected by the Minnesota Twins in the 16th round of the 2005 Major League Baseball draft. Alonso was selected to the All Star game in 2017.

More prominently published by the media are those who left through the use of boats and rafts, such as Kendry Morales, José

Fernández, Osvaldo Fernández and Yunel Escobar, among many others. Remaining behind during tournaments outside of Cuba became another method used by some, such as Noel Argüelles, Rolando Arrojo, Danis Baez and Aroldis Chapman. Travelling to a third country such as Haiti, like in the case of José Abreu and Rusney Castillo, or to Mexico like Roenis Elias and Yuniesky Betancourt became another form of escape. Another means of leaving Cuba has been to seek the opportunity of having family or other relationships that enable them to leave, such as Juan Carlos Díaz and Alexei Ramírez. Ariel Prieto arrived in April 1985 after his wife whose father had come to the U.S in 1981. He became a U.S. citizen and was given an exit visa with her spouse.

The cases of Rey Ordoñez and Edilberto Oropesa, who climbed up a fence in the field of play was a daring piece of escape widely published in the media.

Sadly, other cases like the experience of Geikel Coneydo a prospect in 2007, did not make the headlines or did not fit the image of those leaving by boat or staying behind in tournaments. Those are the stories of another real human drama, and this particular case reflects the true sacrifice of families. Coneydo who had been placed in a baseball academy by the Cuban government who considered him a prospect, experienced the separation of his parents. His father was in the Cuban military and was supportive of the Castro regime while his mother and ten of her relatives left the island under the auspices of a refugee program. Ultimately, Coneydo was allowed to leave. His mother and family continued to ask for him, and his father finally signed the necessary papers that would grant the young man's ability to enter the U.S.[70]

Secrecy was of the utmost importance. The reality of living in a political environment where one could be banned, if not worse, by communicating with players who had left, or were thought to harbor ideas about leaving. For many, their families would not learn of their leaving until the players felt safe enough following their arrival in a particular, and safer, destination.

Their baseball accomplishments have varied, as many before them in previous migrations had experienced. Some only reached the low minors but others made it to the majors and became stars.

A Note to readers: I have opted not to include individual records or accomplishments of the players on Part IV, the "Defectors." They have benefited for being the most recent arrivals and therefore, their baseball accomplishments and stories are available more readily to the fans and the general public and many have not completed their careers. It is not the same as those who arrived previously, especially, in the early days discussed in Part I "The Pioneers." They performed long ago and are no longer in the public eye or not as well known.

I did include the individual statistics and stories of those in Part II, "To Stay or Not to Stay" and III, "The Transition Period." They were, in fact, the primary reason and the attention of this effort, and I found it appropriate and necessary to ensure full attention was paid to this particular set of players.

A final word about the talent of these players. It has been of interest by some to do a comparison of the talent and accomplishments between this latter group of players and those who played prior to the Castro Revolution years. I have not found that to be a useful and fair assessment effort. The reality that I choose to convey is that players in all eras have excelled to the best of their ability, depending on many factors, some of their own doing, others due to external conditions. The personal challenges experienced, both at home in Cuba and in the U.S., may have prevented or helped players excel. And the competition that they faced in the field of play could have contributed to their ability to perform, among other factors. Therefore, I instead choose to celebrate the accomplishments in and the contributions of everyone who has participated in the game of baseball without devaluing any one particular group. And most clearly, I want to pay tribute to those who experienced the sacrifice that only came about because they simply wished to pursue a professional baseball career.

Cuban-born players during this period selected to the All Star Game through 2018 were:

Player	# of Selections
Abreu, José	2
Alonso, Yonder	1
Arrojo, Rolando	1
Baez, Danys	1
Céspedes, Yoenis	2
Chapman, Aroldis	5
Contreras, José	1
Díaz, Aledmis	1
Fernández, José	2
Hernández, Livan	2
Iglesias, José	1
Puig, Yasiel	1

Additional sources:

Kendry Morales Enrique Rojas 9/21/09 Hitting on all cylinders all shores espndeportes.cpm

José Fenández, Juan Rodríguez 4/2/13 Sun Sentinel Miami Marlins Top Prospect José

Fernández credits personal pitcher coach Orlando Chinea for speedy ascent to the majors

Yunel Escobar mopupduty.com 5/30/11

Noel Argüelles Dick Keagel MLB.com 12/6/09

Royals nearing deal for Argüelles, Rolando Arrojo Reading Eagle 7/11/96,

Danys Baez Making a Pitch for Freedom Morning call Manny Husenick articles mcall.com

A. Chapman Life just begginning Cuban Phenom espn.com Nov 1, 09

José Abreu Ebro Jorge 8/12/13 El Pelotero Cubano José Daniel Abreu abandona la isla El Nuevo Herald
Yuniesky Betancourt The Seattle Times Bishop Greg 3/15/07 Mariners Betancourt can't leave journey from Cuba behind
Juan Carlos Díaz Prest Ashley 8/7/09 and that one is…Juan gone winninpeg free press
Alexis Ramírez Manuel Jimenez 9/21/07 Top Cuban ball player defects
Rey Ordoñez Jennifer Frey 10/27/07 Deceptive Practices Prieto played his way out of Cuba and into the major leagues
Edilberto Oropeza A winning team Latimes.com 7/16/96
Euclides Rojas Jennifer Frey 10/27/07 Deceptive Practices Prieto played his way out of Cuba and into the major leagues
A. Hernández Baseball news Adrian Hernández defects from Cuba Cuba Culture News Havana Journal 3/10/04
Osvaldo Herández charlotte.com 7/31/95
Other sources in the form of books and personal interviews with this author are cited in the Resources Consulted and Acknowledgement sections.

PART V

"Uncertainty and Change" 2014–18

Dealing with uncertainty and change is not a new experience for Cubans. This includes Cuban players who are experiencing yet another adjustment period. This adjustment is one that affects Cubans, both in the island and in the U.S. as the presidency of Barack Obama brought about a series of proclamations and changes in regulations, some of which had been implemented. And then another potential set of changes occurred during the new presidency, by Donald Trump.

Meanwhile, the Cuban government under Raúl Castro has maintained the same political position as it has since 1959 with no signs of real change. Raúl Castro has made one point perfectly clear, the current system of government will not change and so, to those that would hope for a more open and free society, it continues to be an elusive expectation regarding any real change. There are those who have applauded some of the changes brought about in Cuba whereby individuals have been allowed to have their businesses and even maintain others on their payroll. While there are significant limitations regarding the type of businesses that are allowed, or the number of people who are employed, it is considered a step forward in a government-controlled society.

And so, I raise the following open question: why can the Cuban government allow another business, like a baseball team, be privately owned by an entity other than the Cuban government? One can only guess the response to this open question, but the principle of private ownership would be essentially the same. Or would it?

The planned *step-down* from a leadership capacity by Raúl Castro provided fodder for much discussion. However, as widely expected Cuba's National Assembly on a vote of 603 to 1 elected Miguel Diaz-Canel as the Country's new President. Confirming the concern by many, Díaz-Canel pronounced that he believed in continuing the current system, thus assuring everyone that current policies will remain, and no real change will occur. Meanwhile, Raúl Castro will remain as the First Secretary of the Communist Party, the true head of government. The most recent proposal by Raúl Castro published in July of 2018 to once again amend the Cuban Constitution has raised a great deal of speculation. Among the many proposed changes include, the abolition of the word "Communist" while maintaining "Socialist" as the de facto system. The Communist Party will remain as the vanguard of the system and will oversee the government in Cuba.[71] The translation of this *proposal* for many, is that no changes are forthcoming as they relate to government controls, human rights and civil liberties. Whether any of the proposed changes will have an impact on baseball players in Cuba and its citizens will have to wait as the "formal review" process is completed and the articles of the new Constitution are implemented.

While all of this is taking place, it seems that travelling to Cuba by former and current baseball players who wish to visit their homeland and family members still living there have continued. However it is a visit, and not designed to move back to live permanently. For many that had been against such travel, they have become more open to the idea of returning as time has gone by. And perhaps, in some cases, given their own advancing age leaves them more open to make these visitation trips.[72] Some players are being allowed to return on low key personal trips. One such player that I interviewed under the condition of anonymity, expressed how welcomed he felt during his return trip and how much he enjoyed his ability to visit with family in his hometown at a time of an important family event.

Another player, José Tartabull, started to return regularly after a 43-year absence, but is clear that, in the future, even if things were to change for the better politically, he would go to visit but not to stay.[73] This is not in an of itself surprising. For many players, their families have grown in the U.S. including their children and grandchildren and other meaningful connections making a permanent return another challenging effort of a different kind. A more recent short-term returnee, former pitcher Pedro Ramos, went back after 55 years to his native Pinar del Río in the western part of the island in August of 2016.

Former Pitcher and Red Sox Hall of Famer Luis Tiant thought quite a lot about his fellow Cubans over the years. For many years he was unable to return to his home country since a previous request had been denied. There was a time when he did not wish to return but, as years went by, the pull to return home was too strong to resist. He ultimately did so in 2005, which was the subject of a movie entitled The Lost Son of Havana, a film by Jonathan Hock from Hockfilms New York, 2009. Like many before him, he had suffered leaving at such an early age, but was happy to return and see his country and family before he died in order to "complete my life." Thinking about the family, "It hurts," he said, and had wondered whether, when meeting his family, he would break down and cry. Hugging and crying did take place. He, like others, felt welcomed, including welcome from old acquaintances, former fellow ballplayers, and families of ballplayers who had left Cuba. I had the honor and privilege to meet Luis Tiant's family in Cuba on two separate instances prior toTiant's trip, while I travelled there to visit my own family. I witnessed first-hand the love and affection they had for this man who had left at such a young age.

Memories rushed back to Tiant during that trip. "You feel like you are born again,"he told me. His family simply said "You arrived in time to see us alive,"also expressing how proud they were of him, and making it clear he was not and should not be blamed for having left when he did. Saying goodbye at the end of his trip, Tiant felt, "This is my country. My heart is better, my head is better. When I die, I will die happy-I am free-I am free inside". He would reaffirm that sensation "When I die, I die happy. I am a free man now."[74] For many of us who have returned this is a sensation that we share.[75]

Tiant returned to Cuba in 2016 and threw the ceremonial first ball of the game between the Cuba and Tampa's major league team. During that trip he was able to again meet with his family members but under rules established by the Cuban government, unlike the previous trip.

He could only see them at a designated hotel, like othe players who had travelled to the island had been required to do.

Nevertheless, there are those that for their own personal and appropriate reasons have made it clear they will not return to Cuba until the Castro regime goes completely away. This is a view held by many fellow Cubans here in exile and whose views need to be, in my opinion, respected and understood in their proper light. It is not possible to forget what families and friends, some of whom are no longer with us, suffered through the years since 1959. René Arocha the first so-called *defector* said he doubted that much had really changed. "Players are going to keep coming because there is still no freedom there," he said. "If I go, I want to go wherever I want, whenever I want. That is freedom."[76] Orestes Destrade has said that negotiations between the two countries must reflect a "quid pro quo" to include Freedom Rights.[77] This is a sentiment many of us share, and it is only one example of the kind of conditions that many want to see before they would even consider a possible return, albeit temporarily.

In the midst of possible changes, will baseball fans be able to recognize and acknowledge the contributions by those that gave so much to the sport of baseball? The notion that we are all Cubans, regardless of when we came, makes it hardly possible for many in the U.S. to cheer for the Cuban National Team as they represent a regime that has caused so much suffering since 1959, almost 60 years.[78]

Could a baseball Hall of Fame in Cooperstown, Miami or Cuba serve as the impetus for such recognition? To express such recognition would likely require a separation of baseball from politics. To set some context on what seems to be a simple step-one can simply look at history. The Cuban Baseball Hall of Fame, *Salón de la Fama del Beisbol Cubano*, was created in 1936 by the National Director of Sports. The first ten players were elected on July 26, 1939 and elections were held annually until 1961 when professional baseball was forbidden. The *Federación de Peloteros Profesionales Cubanos en el Exilio* (Federation of Cuban Professional Players in Exile) was organized in Florida and continued to elect players from 1962 to 1986.

Back in 1985, the *Casa del Baseball Cubano*-the Cuban Baseball House-was founded by Lorenzo Fernández and Antonio Pacheco at a modest site but containing a very impressive set of baseball related memorabilia. I was fortunate to get a tour of the premises by Lorenzo Fernández with my father who he knew for many years due to their connection to the Sports Complex of the Rosario Sugar Mill-*Deportivo Rosario*-in our hometown of Aguacate. As we walked through each of the small rooms decorated with photographs of former players, I could not help but admire Fernández's passion and knowledge.[79] Although the house is no longer in existence, its history stands as a proper tribute to the game and the players–and their families–who endured much sacrifice over the years.

Elections to the Hall of Fame in Miami resumed in 1997 but were again suspended in the following year. In 2003, the Cuban Sports Hall of Fame in Florida decided to continue the Hall of Fame, absorbing all members who had been elected from 1939 to 1998. Cuba had not recognized members of the Hall after 1961 although, more recently, they have begun to do so as the Government opened a Hall of Fame in 2016 in the site of the Palmar del Junco Park in Matanzas. A recent inductee in Cuba's Hall of Fame, in February of 2018, was Rogelio (Limonar) Martínez bringing a continuing source of pride to our family.

In the spirit of transparency, while this set of actions can bring a certain measure of hope to some, there are those who are of the opinion that this set of recent elections represent nothing more than the means to incite some of the former players to return to Cuba, and by their presence give credibility to Cuba's policies.

And so my basic question will remain unanswered for now. Is it possible that those who love and pay tribute by their contributions to the sport of baseball and its players put aside political differences and government-imposed restrictions? At the present time, this does not appear to be possible.

A CONCLUDING MESSAGE

It is hardly possible to finish a book such as this due to that continuing dynamic of baseball players who may wish to play professionally but are not allowed to pursue that career in their home country. The reality facing us is that, in the absence of any kind of a resolution or real change, people in Cuba have and will continue to leave the island, which will bring as a consequence an impact in many sectors of society, including baseball. The significance of the movement and migration of Cuban born baseball players to the U.S. and its impact in Major League Baseball has been nothing but great. A relatively small country has produced, over the years athletes that continue to contribute to the quality of the sport of baseball.

It is also worthy of note that, whether you read about the Pioneers and the players who travelled to and from Cuba through 1960 to play professional baseball, or about those players who were confronted with the decision "To Stay or Not to stay" in Cuba during 1960-62, some of which left and others didn't, as we have seen; or whether the story of the so-called *Defectors* is considered, all of these groups of players have had one thing in common: Cuban-born players who wish to play the game have and will go to any length to pursue their chosen professional careers regardless of the sacrifice they must endure. This sacrifice is difficult for people in an open society to fully comprehend given the many freedoms that we so enjoy.

There are many stories within the Cuban baseball history that have been written and many that remain to be written. I am particularly honored to have taken *pencil to paper* to capture the story in part of the period of time prior to, during, and following the last professional baseball season and its consequences. It has been largely forgotten over the years, and the men and their families who endured the pain of that period I believed deserve the proper level of recognition.

As previously mentioned, Paulino Casanova who passed away on August 12, 2017 related to me on several of my visits with him at his Baseball Academy, the idea that the players of this era (to meaning those involved just prior to and those during the last professional baseball season in Cuba, were *Los Olvidados*-the forgotten ones). I hope this modest effort has in some way brought about the recognition and the respect he and so many others so richly deserve.

SUMMARY DATA INTRODUCTION

The following spreadsheet is intended to provide a glance at the players featured in this book in some greater detail.

At the risk of including previously written information, I want to ensure that to those who focus on this data base are as clear as possible for the inclusion or exclusion of players.You will note the use of the label "Part" reflecting the periods identified in this book.

Purposely, players included in Part I, "The Pioneers" and Part IV, "The *Defectors*" are not included for the following basic reasons.

The first reflects on the fact that both of these "Parts" are written to serve as a context for the primary focus of the research. They also serve as a context for the issues associated with the players that participated in the last professional season in Cuba, 1960-61, and of those who found themselves playing in Cuba and the U.S. prior to, during, and following that same period through 1962 and thus were faced with the *question* of what to do with their lives given the suspension of the professional baseball league in Cuba. The second, in the case of those in Part IV "The *Defectors*", those players as indicated earlier are the most recent arrivals, and in some cases, players who remain active and who have been the subject of much publicity and writing efforts. Many are better known than those who struggled with the *question* back in 1960-61.

Players who are found in Part III, "The Transition Period" are included on the basis that dealing with the *question* as to whether to "stay or not" became the challenge for them or their parents. Some left via specific programs in place at the time such as the Freedom Flights-*Vuelos de la Libertad*, the Mariel boatlift or the Pedro Pan Program, like this author did. At least one other came on a raft when his parents sought to escape and leave behind their life in Cuba. Where available, these stories are included in the text under each player.

Part II players, "To Stay or Not to Stay", reflect a more complicated set of stories. One group represents players who were in the active roster and participated in the last professional season in Cuba. Their team in Cuba is noted in the order that they finished, Cienfuegos as Champions followed by Almendares, Habana and Marianao. Other players were not in the active roster but played in the practice squad and never participated in a game. A perfect example is that of Paulino Casanova who was on the on-deck circle when the last out to finish the season was recorded and so he was denied the opportunity to fulfill his dream to play professional baseball in Cuba. Others, because of their age, or unable to break into the club, never participated but were able to secure a U.S. baseball contract and had to decide what to do about their chosen profession. There are also those who were playing in the U.S. minors and remained or went back to Cuba only to return later on.

In several cases, research has not always unveiled the actual date when players arrived in the U.S. but their baseball career makes it possible to presume they did or did not return to Cuba. Thanks to a number of sources, it has been possible to come to a reasonable conclusion what happened to each player in question. However, some of my conclusions were subject to interpretation and I welcome any comments that will help to ensure that an accurate record is ensured and preserved.

Of the total of players or managers that are featured in this book, it should be noted that some of these players played for more than one team during the 1960-61 season and therefore, the number of players will fluctuate when attempting to determine certain statistics. In addition, some players or managers as expressed in the individual write ups, came to the U.S. and then returned to Cuba while others, stayed in Cuba and later on came to the U.S.

What is clear, is that the vast majority of the players chose to pursue their professional baseball career, and thus came or stayed in the U.S. despite the sacrifices that such a decision brought about. The one exception (noted with an asterisk) as to whether he stayed or left was the one player who passed away during the baseball season in the U.S. and therefore did not have the option to make a choice due to his tragic and premature death.

	A	B	C	D	E	F	G
1	**Players featured in Parts II and III**						
2	**Legend** X= Left or Stayed in Cuba (year undetermined), * Died during U.S. Season						
3	**Last Name**	**First Name**	**Team/League**	**Position**	**Left Cuba**	**Stayed in Cuba**	**Part**
4	Arcia	Jose	U.S. Minors	IF	1961		III
5	Canseco Capas	Jose	U.S. Minors	OF	1965		III
6	Canseco Capas	Ozzie Osvaldo	U.S. Minors	OF	1965		III
7	Destrade Cuevas	Orestes	U.S. Minors	IF	1968		III
8	Fossas Morejon	Antonio "Tony"	U.S. Minors	Pitcher	X		III
9	Garbey	Barbaro	U.S. Minors	1B/OF	1980		III
10	Gonzalez	Orlando	U.S. Minors	1B	1961		III
11	Lauzerique	George	U.S. Minors	Pitcher	1956		III
12	Menendez	Antonio Gustavo	U.S. Minors	Pitcher	1965		III
13	Nieto	Adrian	U.S. Minors	Catcher	1994		III
14	Palmeiro Corrales	Rafael	U.S. Minors	1B	1971		III
15	Ramos	Roberto	U.S. Minors	Catcher	X		III
16	Sanchez Matos	Israel	U.S. Minors	Pitcher	1967-68		III
17	Santovenia Mayol	Nelson	U.S. Minors	Catcher	X		III
18	Sutherland Cantin	Leonardo	U.S. Minors	OF	X		III
19	Zamora	Oscar	U.S. Minors	Pitcher	1960		III
20	Ala	Aurelio "Joe"	U.S. Minors	3B	1961		II
21	Alarcon	Inael	U.S. Minors	OF	1961		II
22	Campaneris	Dagoberto	U.S. Minors	SS	1962		II
23	Cardenal	Jose	U.S. Minors	OF	1960		II
24	Casanova Ortiz	Paulino	U.S. Minors	Catcher	1961		II
25	Chinique	Oscar	U.S. Minors	Pitcher	1961		II
26	Consuegra	Sandalio	U.S. Minors	Pitcher	1961		II
27	Diaz	Mario	U.S. Minors	2B	1962		II
28	Dieguez Padilla	Jose	U.S. Minors	IF	1962		II
29	Dihigo	Martin	U.S. Minors	OF	1961	X	II
30	Fernandez Arba	Pedro	U.S. Minors	OF	1962		II
31	Fuentes Peat	Rigoberto	U.S. Minors	IF	1962		II
32	Garcia	Reinold	U.S. Minors	2B	1962		II
33	Gomez	Preston	U.S. Minors	Manager	X		II
34	Hernandez Zulueta	Jacinto "Jackie"	U.S. Minors	SS	1961		II
35	Iglesias	Juan Antonio	U.S. Minors	IF	1961		II
36	Izquierdo	Ricardo "Lefty"	U.S. Minors	Catcher	1962		II
37	Jimenez	David	U.S. Minors	Pitcher	1960		II
38	Martinez Oliva	Orlando	U.S. Minors	IF	1961		II
39	Martinez	Pedro	U.S. Minors	Catcher	X		II
40	Martinez Santos	Rodolfo	U.S. Minors	IF/OF	1960		II
41	Mirabal	Vladimir	U.S. Minors	2B		X	II
42	Miranda	Guillermo "Willy"	U.S. Minors	SS	X		II
43	Monteagudo	Aurelio	U.S. Minors	Pitcher	1962		II
44	Moret	Pedro	U.S. Minors	NA		X	II
45	Oliva	Edilio	U.S. Minors	Pitcher	1961		II
46	Oliva Lopez	Pedro Tony	U.S. Minors	RF	1961		II

	A	B	C	D	E	F	G
47	**Last Name**	**First Name**	**Team/League**	**Position**	**Left Cuba**	**Stayed in Cuba**	**Part**
48	Paz	Carlos	U.S. Minors	2B/Pitcher	X		II
49	Pedroso	Gerardo	U.S. Minors	OF	X		II
50	Perez	Atanasio "Tony" "Tany"	U.S. Minors	1B	1960		II
51	Ribet Jr.	Elio	U.S. Minors	Pitcher	*	*	II
52	Rojas	Hilario	U.S. Minors	IF	1962		II
53	Sanchez	Roberto	U.S. Minors	IF	1961		II
54	Sierra	Pedro	U.S. Minors	Pitcher	X		II
55	Telleria	Emiliano	U.S. Minors	OF	1960		II
56	Toboso	Elio	U.S. Minors	OF		X	II
57	Torres	Jesus	U.S. Minors	IF	1960		II
58	Velazquez	Nestor	U.S. Minors	IF	1961		II
59	Ramos	Pedro	Cienfuegos	Pitcher	1961, 1962		II
60	Maestri	Hector	Cienfuegos	Pitcher	1961,62,65		II
61	Diaz	Antonio	Cienfuegos	Pitcher	X		II
62	Sanchez	Raul Guadalupe	Cienfuegos	Pitcher	X		II
63	Maroto	Enrique	Cienfuegos	Pitcher	1966		II
64	Pascual	Camilo	Cienfuegos	Pitcher	1961		II
65	Garcia	Maximo	Cienfuegos	Pitcher	1961, 1962		II
66	Concepcion	Dagoberto	Cienfuegos	Pitcher	1961		II
67	Tano	Roberto	Cienfuegos	Pitcher	1961		II
68	Azcue	Jose J.	Cienfuegos	Catcher	1962		II
69	Suarez Tejerina	Arturo Adolfo	Cienfuegos	Catcher	1962		II
70	Alvarez	Rogelio	Cienfuegos	1B	1961, 1962		II
71	Cesar	Jose Angel	Cienfuegos	2B	1962		II
72	Alvarez	Oswaldo	Cienfuegos	2B	1961, 1962		II
73	Sablon	Hiraldo	Cienfuegos	3B	1961		II
74	Cardenas	Leonardo "Leo"	Cienfuegos	SS	X		II
75	Valdes-Vila	Hernan	Cienfuegos	IF		X	II
76	Martinez Azcuiz	Jose	Cienfuegos	IF	1961		II
77	Mejias Gomez	Roman	Cienfuegos	OF	1961		II
78	Gonzalez	Andres Antonio "Tony"	Cienfuegos	OF	1961		II
79	Zambrano	Mario	Cienfuegos	OF	1962		II
80	Vistuer	Juan	Cienfuegos	OF	1961		II
81	Alvarez	Ultus	Cienfuegos	OF	X		II
82	Castano	Antonio	Cienfuegos	Manager	1961, 66	X	II
83	Ayon	Andres	Almendares	Pitcher	1962	X	II
84	Pena Guebara	Orlando Gregorio	Almendares	Pitcher	1961		II
85	Cuellar Santana	Miguel Angel	Almendares	Pitcher	1961,62		II
86	Lopez y Pons	Marcelino	Almendares	Pitcher	1962		II
87	Naranjo	Gonzalo "Cholly"	Almendares	Pitcher	1961 1995	X	II
88	Amor	Vicente	Almendares	Pitcher	X		II
89	Guerra	Julio	Almendares	Pitcher	X		II
90	Lopez Hevia	Jose Ramon	Almendares	Pitcher	1961		II
91	Gutierrez	Rene A "Latigo"	Almendares	Pitcher	X		II
92	Pascual	Carlos	Almendares	Pitcher	1962		II

	A	B	C	D	E	F	G
93	**Last Name**	**First Name**	**Team/League**	**Position**	**Left Cuba**	**Stayed in Cuba**	**Part**
94	Davis	Ivan	Almendares	Pitcher	1993	X	II
95	Izquierdo Valdez	Enrique "Hank" Roberto	Almendares	Catcher	1961		II
96	McFarlane	Orlando Jesus	Almendares	Catcher	1961		II
97	Amoros	Edmundo	Almendares	1B	1967	X	II
98	Taylor Sanchez	Antonio Nemesio "Tony"	Almendares	2B	1961		II
99	De la Hoz Piloto	Miguel Angel	Almendares	3B	1961		II
100	Fernandez	Humberto	Almendares	SS	X		II
101	Martinez Diaz	Gabriel Antonio	Almendares	IF	1962		II
102	Rivero	Jose Mario	Almendares	IF	1962		II
103	Scull	Angel	Almendares	OF	X		II
104	Posada Hernandez	Leopoldo Jesus "Leo"	Almendares	OF	1961		II
105	Paula	Carlos	Almendares	OF	X		II
106	Villar	Jose R.	Almendares	OF	1961, 1962		II
107	Almenares	Pedro	Almendares	OF		X	II
108	Otero	Regino	Almendares	Manager	1961		II
109	Tiant	Luis	Habana	Pitcher	1961		II
110	Gutierrez	Rene A "Latigo"	Habana	Pitcher	X		II
111	Rodriguez Borrego	Fernando Pedro	Habana	Pitcher	X		II
112	Bauta	Eduardo	Habana	Pitcher	X		II
113	Castellanos	Silvio	Habana	Pitcher	X		II
114	Moreno Gonzalez	Julio	Habana	Pitcher	1962		II
115	Naranjo	Gonzalo "Cholly"	Habana	Pitcher	1961 1995	X	II
116	Segui	Diego	Habana	Pitcher	1962		II
117	Muniz	Gustavo	Habana	Pitcher	X		II
118	Rojas	Minervino	Habana	Pitcher	1962		II
119	Gutierrez Herrera	Roberto A	Habana	Catcher	1961		II
120	Noble	Rafael Sam	Habana	Catcher	1961		II
121	Herrera	Francisco "Panchon"	Habana	1B	1961		II
122	Rojas	Octavio "Cookie" "Cuqui"	Habana	2B	1961		II
123	Quintana	Patricio	Habana	3B	X		II
124	Rodriguez Ordenana	Hector A	Habana	SS	1961		II
125	Mendoza	Rigoberto	Habana	IF	1961		II
126	Terry	Lazaro	Habana	IF		X	II
127	Morejon Torres	Daniel	Habana	OF	1961, 1962		II
128	Valdespino Borroto	Hilario "Sandy"	Habana	OF	X		II
129	Cardenal	Pedro	Habana	OF	1961		II
130	Zayas	Luis	Habana	OF		X	II
131	Baro	Asdrubal Alberto	Habana	OF		X	II
132	Guerra	Fermin "Mike"	Habana	Manager	X	X	II
133	Arias Martinez	Rodolfo "Rudy"	Marianao	Pitcher	1962		II
134	Fornieles Torres	Jose Miguel "Mike"	Marianao	Pitcher	1961		II
135	Montejo Bofill	Manuel	Marianao	Pitcher	1962		II
136	Oliva Acosta	Antoliano Angel	Marianao	Pitcher	1961		II
137	Alvarez	Fidel	Marianao	Pitcher	1961 Mex		II
138	Piedra Torrens	Juan Andres	Marianao	Pitcher		X	II

	A	B	C	D	E	F	G
139	**Last Name**	**First Name**	**Team/League**	**Position**	**Left Cuba**	**Stayed in Cuba**	**Part**
140	Carrillo Alfonso	Pedro	Marianao	Pitcher		X	II
141	Gomez	Lazaro	Marianao	Pitcher	X		II
142	Alvarez Cortes	Alberto	Marianao	Catcher	1962		II
143	Friol	Rene	Marianao	Catcher	1962		II
144	Becquer	Julio	Marianao	1B	1961		II
145	Fernandez	Lorenzo	Marianao	2B	1961		II
146	Flores Apodaca	Oscar	Marianao	3B	X		II
147	Versalles	Zoilo	Marianao	SS	X		II
148	Valdivielso	Jose	Marianao	IF	X		II
149	Laza Rosell	Martin	Marianao	IF	1962		II
150	Seara	Ramon Luis	Marianao	IF	X		II
151	Tartabull Guzman	Jose Milages	Marianao	OF	1962		II
152	Delis	Juan Francisco Cachano	Marianao	OF		X	II
153	Sardinas	Oscar	Marianao	OF	1962		II
154	Minoso	Orestes "Minnie"	Marianao	OF	1961		II
155	Leroux	Orlando	Marianao	OF		X	II
156	Fernandez	Jose Maria	Marianao	Manager		X	II

ACKNOWLEDGEMENTS

Where does one begin to say thank you? While it is true that writing is a solitary endeavor, the reality when working on a book such as this one required a great deal of support by many others. The information provided thorough the sources cited throughout the text and in the "Resources Consulted" section reflect the wealth of information I was able to secure in putting this project together.

There are no enough words to express my thanks and appreciation to former and present baseball players who willingly sat through interviews at different times and addressed questions that would bring in some cases personal and painful memories;

Rodolfo Arias

Paulino Casanova

Rusney Castillo

Iván Davis

Miguel De la Hoz

Roelis Elias

Antonio (Tony) González

Jacinto (Jackie) Hernández

Yoán Moncada

Lázaro Gonzalo (Cholly) Naranjo

Leopoldo Posada

Octavio (Cuqui) Rojas

Israel Sánchez

José Tartabull

Antonio (Tony) Taylor and

Luis Tiant Jr.

Some of the above players also enable the opportunity to meet other players and or secure information not readily available. Their contribution cited throughtout the text was most appreciated and proved to be invaluable.

I am indebted to my cousin Olga (Martínez) Fernández daughter of Rogelio (Limonar) Martínez, and the families of Francisco (Panchón) Herrera and Luis Tiant Senior for their contributions.

Clemente Amezaga opened the door for me to be able to find critical official documentation about the players' entry into the U.S. during the initial period of my research, and provided valuable fact-checking.

César Brioso who without reservation shared his research approach and interests in Cuban baseball while researching his own book on the subject.

David Brody a *Boston Globe* bestselling fiction writer and author provided the necessary access to resources required to make this publication possible.

José (Chamby) Campos a radio personality in Miami Florida where he has hosted his own program for over 15 years and as of this writing is the voice of the University of Miami baseball, basketball and football programs (since 1999). "Chamby" facilitated my ability to be able to speak or secure information that brought light to areas (that would have been difficult for me to obtain) given his knowledge and rich connections to those in the Cuban baseball scene in the Miami Florida area.

Cuba's Efraín Rosales and Leonel Morales both of whom live there today contributed valuable information about Elio Toboso not previously known.

Eloisa Echazabal a fellow Pedro Pan and well-known lecturer and an expert of the Pedro Pan experience.

Omelis Hongamen former scorekeeper at the "Pedro Betancourt" and "Popular" baseball leagues.

Library services at the J. V. Fletcher Library in Westford Massachusetts by Kristina Leedberg Head of Information Services and staff who "walked me" through the process to seek critical information related to immigration, marriages, and burials and were always available to answer my many questions and assist with my research and to the Collier County Library in Naples Florida who made their research equipment available.

Jorge Maduro (the son of "Bobby" Maduro) brought to bear a thoughtful understanding of the 1959-61 period given his direct line to that critical time of the Cuban Baseball history.

Peter Olivieri Professor Emeritus Information Systems and Computer Science at Boston College who provided sage advice as the material related to the U.S. Minor Leagues became almost overwhelming and provided much needed technical support.

Andrés Pascual lent his extensive knowledge of baseball in Cuba not just professional baseball but its rich amateur history through a lengthy interview and "eltubeyero22".

SABR members Rory Costello and Bill Knowlin who always responded to my requests for information and guidance at different times through this long process.

The book would not have been completed without the effort by my editor Richard Meibers who made it possible for my second language be worthy of my readers' attention and the technical advice provided by Nina Mangan. Soumi Goswami provided the formatting support while Dan Van Oss of Covermint Design delivered the final creation of the front and back covers.

The Topps Company allowed me to include many of the players' baseball cards and so am appreciative of the "Topps[R] trading cards used courtesy of The Topps Company, Inc."

The trading card featuring Pedro Sierra was included due to the courtesy and support of Jim Burgess President of Baseball in Living

Color. "Trading Faces trading card courtesy of Trading Faces/base-ballinliving color"

Ximena Valdivia Director of the Archives and Special Collections at Barry University in Miami Florida who supported my research about the Pedro Pan Program.

My wife Judy who patiently listened to my continuing struggle and "updates" as this effort evolved over time and provided editing support at a crucial time when it was most needed.

As usual there are those who preferred their names not be made public or cited in every instance and provided a great deal of support at a time when I was questioning the direction to take on this project.

Finally I wish to thank those who unknowingly inspired me to write what I consider a topic that needed to reflect a more accurate account and context for what really transpired during that time in light of what had been written previously. I suspect they know who they are and we will remain as people with different opinions on some of the topics addressed here.

END NOTES

1. Major League Cuban" a film by Joe Cardona and Ralf Gonzalez 2017 South Florida PBS Inc. and Royal Palms Films (MLC).
2. Jamail, Milton H. *"Full Count Inside Cuban baseball"*. Carbondale and Edwardsville: Southern Illinois University Press. 2000.
3. González, Echevarría, Roberto. *"The Pride of Havana A History of Cuban Baseball"*. New York Oxford: Oxford University, 1999.
4. Santana Alonso Alfredo l. *"Un Astro del Montículo El Diamante Negro"*. Imprenta Alejo Carpenter 2009.
5. Fordham Summer 2002 by Mari-Claudia Jimenez and Christopher Schmidt-Nowara page 32.
6. Carteles Magazine February 20, 1955.
7. Jamail, Milton H. *"Full Count Inside Cuban baseball"*. Carbondale and Edwardsville: Southern Illinois University Press. 2000
8. Thomas, Hugh 1971. *Cuba, or the pursuit of freedom*. Eyre & Spottiswoode, London. Revised and abridged edition 2001, Picador, London. Chapters 16 & 17.
9. Bjarkman Peter C. "Adolfo Luque the Original Pride of Havana". Elysian Field Quarterly Winter 2003 page 21-39.
10. García, Gilberto *"Beisboleros: Latin Americans and Baseball in the Northwest, 1914-1937"*. Columbia, The Magazine of Northwest History, Fall 2002.
11. Santana Alonso Alfredo I. *"Un Astro del Montículo El Diamante Negro"*. Imprenta Alejo Carpenter 2009.
12. Memories and Dreams May-June 2006.
13. Skinner, David. *"José Méndez: Havana and Key West."* The National Pastime. The Society for American Baseball Research, Cleveland Ohio: 2004. 17-23.
14. Santana Alonso Alfred l. *"El Inmortal del beisbol Martín Dihigo"* Editorial Científico-Técnica 2007.
15. Steven Goldman *"TheTwice Missing Cubans"* August 4, 2016.
16. Adrian Burgos "Making Cuban Stars: Alejandro Pompez and Latinos in Black Baseball, "Playing America's Game: Baseball, Latinos, and the Color line (Bekerley: University of California Press 2007), 112-37.

17. Lowry, Philip *J. Green Cathedrals.* New York: Walker & Company, 2006. 96.
18. Nowlin, Bill and Krieger, Kit. *La Tropical Park, Then and Now.* The National Pastime. The Society for American Baseball Research. Cleveland Ohio: 2005. 3-5.
19. Cardona, Joe and González Ralf "Major League Cuban" a co-production of South Florida PBS and Royal Palms Films 2017.
20. GM Branch Rickey Note New York Times February 15, 2015, page 6.
21. Brioso, César Cuba Béisbol Ramon Roger Article
22. "Defining Moments A Cuban Exile's Story about Discovery and the Search for a Better Future" Create Space José I. Ramírez 2013.
23. baseball-reference.com
24. paxety.com/site1940Constitution.
25. cedema.org Manifiesto de la Sierra Maestra.
26. Figueredo Jorge S. Cuban Baseball A Statistical History 1878-1961 McFarland and Company inc., Jefferson North Carolina and London Pages 463-4.
27. Daniel James Cuba The first Soviet Satellite in the Americas Avon Book 1961.
28. Jorge Maduro interview and Ancestry.com.
29. Costello Rory SABR.org BioProject Bobby Maduro
30. Stars and Stripes July 10, 1960 edition page 18 and 22.
31. Octavio Cuqui Rojas interview with author on November 2016.
32. Daniel James Cuba The first Soviet Satellite in the Americas Avon Book 1961.
33. Figueredo Jorge S. Cuban Baseball A Statistical History 1878-1961 McFarland and Company inc., Jefferson North Carolina and London Page 473
34. Barry University Archives and Special Collections Department Ximena Valdivia
35. Ramirez, Jose I Defining Moments Create Space 2013.
36. Theodore Draper, Castro's Revolution: Myths and Realities.
37. Cardona, Joe and González Ralf "Major League Cuban" a co-production of South Florida PBS and Royal Palms Films 2017.
38. Interview Omelis Hongamen
39. Fainure, Steve and Sánchez Ray. *The Duke of Havana.* New York: Villard, 2001 page 23.
40. Luis Tiant interview with author.
41. Cardona, Joe and González Ralf "Major League Cuban" a co-production of South Florida PBS and Royal Palms Films 2017
42. Miguel de la Hoz Interview.
43. Bjarkman Peter C. Cuba's Baseball Defectors The Inside Story 2016 page 69
44. Bjarkman Peter C. Cuba's Baseball Defectors The Inside Story 2016 page 51

45. Jamail, Milton H. *Full Count Inside Cuban baseball.* Carbondale and Edwardsville: Southern Illinois University Press. 2000.

46. amnesty.org

47. Ramírez, José I. *Defining Moments A Cuban Exile's Story about Discovery and the Search for a Better Future.* North Charleston, South Carolina: CreateSpace, 2013.

48. Courtesy of baseball-reference.com.

49. "Rogério Manzano site – Tigres de Marianao entry (Spanish)"

50. The Pride of Havana: A History of Cuban Baseball – Roberto González Echevarría. Publisher: Oxford University Press, 1999.

51. uscg.mil

52. Ramírez, José I. *Defining Moments A Cuban Exile's Story about Discovery and the Search for a Better Future.* North Charleston, South Carolina: CreateSpace, 2013.

53. Miami Herald October 15, 2006.

54. Cardona, Joe and González Ralf "Major League Cuban" a co-production of South Florida PBS and Royal Palms Films 2017.

55. Dictionary.com.

56. Lee, Bill and Lally, Richard. *Have Glove Will Travel.* New York: Crown Publishers, 2005. 182.

57. Martínez de Osaba y Goenaba, Juan A. *El Niño Linares.* La Habana, Cuba: Abril 2002.

58. Pérez Dominguez, *Guía oficial Beisbol Temporada* 2002. Alejo Carpenter Printing, La Habana, Cuba 9.

59. Price, S. L. *Pitching Around Fidel A Journey into the Heart of Cuban Sports.* New York, New York: Ecco Press. 2000 109.

60. Miami Herald June 28, 2004 but seeing no future they left. Source: Interview Roelis Elias

61. seattlepi.com Mariners/MLB February 24, 2005

62. US Baseball Weekly July 28-August 3 1993.

63. Cardona, Joe and González Ralf "Major League Cuban" a co-production of South Florida PBS and Royal Palms Films 2017.

64. Interview Yoán Moncada

65. Fainure, Steve and Sánchez Ray. *The Duke of Havana.* New York: Villard, 2001. 53.

66. Price, S. L. *Pitching Around Fidel A Journey into the Heart of Cuban Sports.* New York, New York: Ecco Press. 2000. 127.

67. Price, S. L. *Pitching Around Fidel A Journey into the Heart of Cuban Sports.* New York, New York: Ecco Press. 2000. 107.

68. Fainure, Steve and Sánchez Ray. *The Duke of Havana.* New York: Villard, 2001. 166-67.

69. Ramírez, José I. *Defining Moments A Cuban Exile's Story about Discovery and the Search for a Better Future.* North Charleston, South Carolina: CreateSpace, 2013.

70. The New York Times June 22, 2007 From Cuba, With a Dream of the Majors by David Picker.

71. granma.cu 23 July, 2018

72. Omelis Hongamen telephone interview with author.

73. José Tartabull, personal interview with author

74. Boston Globe interview published April 4, 2009.

75. Ramírez José I. *"Defining Moments A Cuban Exile's Story about Discovery and the Search for a Better Future"* Part I. Create Space. 2013.

76. Archbold Randal C. "This Cuban Defector Changed Baseball. Nobody Remembers." March 18, 2016.

77. Cardona, Joe and González Ralf "Major League Cuban" a co-production of South Florida PBS and Royal Palms Films 2017.

78. Cardona, Joe and González Ralf "Major League Cuban" a co-production of South Florida PBS and Royal Palms Films 2017

79. The House That Beisbol Built June 24, 1991 by John Hughes Staff Writer.

RESOURCES CONSULTED

Books

Betancourt Hernández, Aldo. *Historia de Mi Pueblo,* Self-published, 2008

Bjarkman, Peter C. *A History of Cuban Baseball 1864-2006*. Jefferson, NC, and London: McFarland, 2007.

Bjarkman, Peter C., Nowlin, Bill eds. Baseball's Alternative Universe Cuban Baseball Legends Phoenix, AZ: SABR, 2016.

Bjarkman Peter C. "Adolfo Luque the Original Pride of Havana". Elysian Field Quarterly Winter 2003, 21-39.

Bjarkman, Peter C. and Rucker, Mark. *Smoke The Romance And Lore Of Cuban Baseball.* Kingston and New York New York: Sports Illustrated, 1999.

Bjarkman Peter C. *Cuba's Baseball Defectors The Inside Story* 2016, 51 and 69.

Kelley, Brent *The Negro League Revisited*, McFarland & Co. 2000, 324-327.

Burgos Adrian. *Making Cuban Stars: Alejandro Pompez and Latinos in Black Baseball, Playing America's Game: Baseball, Latinos, and the Color line* (Bekerley: University of California Press 2007), 112-37.

Draper Theodore, *Castro's Revolution: Myths and Realities*. Praeger Publications, 1962.

Fainure, Steve and Sánchez Ray. *The Duke of Havana.* New York: Villard, 2001.

Figueredo, Jorge S. *Cuban Baseball A Statisitical History 1878-1961.* Jefferson, North Carolina and London: McFarland and Company, 2003.

Figueredo, Jorge S. *Who's Who in Cuban Baseball 1878-1961*. Jefferson, North Carolina and London: McFarland and Company, 2003.

Freedman, Lew. *Latino Baseball Legends: An Encyclopedia* Greenwood Publications, 2010.

González, Echevarría, Roberto. *The Pride of Havana A History of Cuban Baseball.* New York

Oxford: Oxford University Press, 1999.

Henninger Thom *Tony Oliva* University of Minnesota Press Minneapolis London 2015.

Jamail, Milton H. *Full Count Inside Cuban baseball.* Carbondale and Edwardsville: Southern Illinois University Press. 2000.

James, Daniel. *Cuba The First Soviet Satellite in the Americas.* New York: Avon Books Division, 1961.

Lee, Bill and Lally, Richard. *Have Glove Will Travel.* New York: Crown Publishers, 2005, 182.

Lowry, Philip *J. Green Cathedrals.* New York: Walker & Company, 2006, 96

Martínez de Osaba y Goenaga, Juan A. *El Niño Linares.* Habana: Casa Editorial Abril 2002.

Martinó, Henry, Fernández, Edwin and Valero, Eduardo. *Jonrón.* San Juan, Puerto Rico: Gabiota, 2006.

Nowlin Bill, Tan Cecilia eds. *The Red Sox team that saved baseball.* Rounder Books 2005, 63.

Price, S. L. *Pitching Around Fidel A Journey into the Heart of Cuban Sports.* New York, New York: Ecco Press. 2000.

Ramírez, José I. *Defining Moments A Cuban Exile's Story about Discovery and the Search for a Better Future.* North Charleston, South Carolina: CreateSpace, 2013.

Rodríguez, Carlos. *Guía Oficial Beisbol.* La Habana, Cuba: Alejo Carpenter, La Habana, 2002, 9.

Santana Alonso Alfredo l. *"Un Astro del Montículo El Diamante Negro".* Imprenta Alejo Carpenter 2009.

Santovenia Emérito and Shelton Raul M. *"Cuba y Su Historia".* Tomo Primero Miami Florida: Rema Press 1966, 98.

Simon, Tom Ed. *Deadball Stars of the National League.* Washington D.C. Brassey's Inc.: 2004.

Thomas, Hugh *Cuba, or the pursuit of freedom.* Eyre & Spottiswoode, London. 1971, Picador, London, 2001, Chapters 16 and 17.

Torres, Angel. *La Leyenda del Beisbol Cubano.* Miami, Florida: Review Printers, 1996.

Van Hyning, T.E. (2004). *Puerto Rico's Winter League: A History of Major League Baseball's Launching Pad.* McFarland & Company, 2004, 19.

Zminda, Don Editor *GO-GO to Glory The 1959 Chicago White Sox* SABR 2009.

Films

Cardona, Joe and González Ralf, *Major League Cuban* South Florida PBS and Royal Palms Film 2017.

Hock Jonathan, *The Lost Son of Havana* Hockfilms New York. 2009.

Internet Resources

Araton, Harvey 2009-03-17 *Tony Pérez on Cuba and Its Team* NYTimes.com.

Archibald Randal C. *This Cuban Defector Changed Béisbol. Nobody Remembers.* March 18, 2016. nytimes.com.

baseballinlivingcolor.com

Brunt, Larry. *Carlos Paula The Man that Integrated the Washington Senators* baseballhall.org/discover.

Briley, Ron, Costello, Rory and Nowlin, Bill *"Román Mejías"* SABR Bio Project (http://sabr.org/bioproj/person).

Brioso César Cuba Béisbol-Cuban Baseball Hall of Fame *Ramon Roger* article. cubanbeisbol.com.

cnlbr.org

Costello, Rory and Ramírez, José *"Tony Gonzalez"* SABR Bio Project (http://sabr.org/bioproj/person).

Costello, Rory and Ramírez, José *"Tony Taylor"* SABR Bio Project (http://sabr.org/bioproj/person).

Costello, Rory and Ramírez, José *"Jackie Hernández"* SABR Bio Project (http://sabr.org/bioproj/person).

Costello, Rory and Ramírez, José *"Paul Casanova"* SABR Bio Project (http://sabr.org/bioproj/person)

Costello, Rory. *"Sandy Consuegra"* SABR Bio Project (http://sabr.org/bioproj/person).

Costello, Rory. *"Willy Miranda"* SABR Bio Project (http://sabr.org/bioproj/person).

Costello, Rory. *"Ray Noble"* SABR Bio Project (http://sabr.org/bioproj/person).

Costello, Rory. *"Julio Moreno"* SABR Bio Project (http://sabr.org/bioproj/person).

Costello, Rory. *"Rogelio Martínez"* SABR Bio Project (http://sabr.org/bioproj/person).

Costello, Rory. *"Bobby Maduro"* SABR Bio Project (http://sabr.org/bioproj/person).

CubaCollectibles.com Oscar Sardinas Baseball card #50

ebooksread.com/authors-eng/mass-northeastern-university-boston/cauldron-volume-1956-tro/page-4-cauldron-volume-1956-tro.shtm

Ecured.cu/Orlando_Leroux

Ecured.cu/ Antonio_Guerra_Silva

Ecured.cu/Pedro Almenares

elfinanciaro.com.mx

Elsoldemexicocom December 4, 2006.

.http://grfx.cstv.com/photos/schools/mifl/sports/m-basebl/auto_pdf/1011-basebl-mg3.

Gallagher Danny. *Former Expo Nelson Santovenia Teaching Tools of the Trade in Tigers System*. May 14, 2015 baseballhotcorner.com

Goldman, Steven *TheTwice Missing Cubans* August 4, 2016. TheNationalpastimemuseum.com

Gutiérrez, Daniel; González, Javier (2006); *Records de la Liga Venezolana de Béisbol Profesional* LVBP.com

Hughes, John *The House That Beisbol Built* June 24, 1991. sunsentinel.com.

Hulbert Joanne. *"José Tartabull"* SABR Bio Project (http://sabr.org/bioproj/person)

Justonebadcentury.com/chicago_cubs_tales9_27_asp

Ladson Bill 14 September 2005 Cardenal wants to help MLB .com.

Ladson Bill October 8 2009 Nationals cut ties with Cardenal. MLB.com.

Markusen, Bruce. The Short, Wild Life of the Interamerican League *The Hardball Times* July 8, 2014. fangraphs.com.

Merkin, Scott Feb 21, 2014. MLB.com.

Miami News Google News 2014.

mlb "The San Francisco Giants partner with Lazer Broadcasting on a three-year deal" (Press release). San Francisco Giants. March 24, 2017. MLB.com.

Negro League Baseball Museum e-museum.

NLBM Legacy 2000 Players' Reunion Alumni Book, Kansas City Missouri: Negro Leagues Baseball Museum, Inc., 2000.

Nowlin Bill SABR Bio Project "Fermín Guerra" (http://sabr.org/bioproj/person)

Pascual Andrés, eltubeyero22.files.wordpress.com/2015/08.

Pascual Andrés, eltubeyero22, November 21, 2011.

Pascual Andrés El Ultimo Campenato de Beisbol professional Cubano eltubeyero22 November 20, 2011.

Ramírez, José *"Cholly Naranjo"* SABR Bio Project (http://sabr.org/bioproj/person)

Ramírez, José *"Pancho Herrera"* SABR Bio Project (http://sabr.org/bioproj/person).

Ramírez, José *"Rudy Arias"* SABR Bio Project (http://sabr.org/bioproj/person).

Reds.enquirer.com "Perez: From Cuba to Hall" January 13, 2000.

Rogério Manzano site – Tigres de Marianao entry (Spanish)

Romero Esteban, *Un grande de la receptoría* by Esteban Romero Swingcompleto. com.

Schworm Peter *In Cuba, diamond diplomacy Senior softballers from Bay State find the bases for understanding in Havana* November 24, 2009. Boston.com.

seattlepi.com Mariners/MLB February 24, 2005.

Sherwin, Bob. *Palmeiro Born In Cuba, Raised in Miami and Third Hispanic to Hit 3000* July 17, 2005. nytimes.com.

thekingdomofbaseball.proboards.com/thread/1861/tendremos-reescribir-historia-baseball-cubano#ixzz4JbAVg7iP

Welch, Matt *The Cuban Senators* March 3, 2002 espn.com.

Magazines/Journals

Ahern, Maurice L. Fordham University's library Archivist letter to Warren F. Broderick. Courtesy of Hall of Fame Library.

Armour, Mark. El Tiante, *The Baseball Research Journal.* Cleveland Ohio: SABR, 2001.

Baseball Guides from 1956, 1958, 1960, 1964 and 1967.

Bjarkman Peter C. *The Cuban Comet* Elysian Fields 2002, 22-37.

Dawidoff Nicholas. "The Struggles Of Sandy A," *Sports Illustrated*, July 10, 1989.

Enders, Eric. The Society for American Baseball Research. *Deadball Stars of the National League.* Washington D.C.: Brassey, 2004.

García, Gilberto Beisboleros: Latin Americans and Baseball in the Northwest, 1914-1937. Columbia, *The Magazine of Northwest History*, Fall 2002.

Harris John R. and Burbridge Jr. John J. The Short but Exciting Life of the Havana Sugar Kings. *The National Pastime* SABR 2016.

Hnos. Nuñez Liga Cubana Base Ball Profesional Temporada 1957-1958 Score Cards.

Jimenez Mari-Claudia and Schmidt Christopher Nowara Correspondence Courtesy of Hall of Fame Library Fordham Summer 2002, 32.

Nowlin, Bill and Krieger, Kit. *La Tropical Park, Then and Now The National Pastime.* Cleveland Ohio: SABR, 2005.

Rivas Jorge Asdrúbal Baró: Un pelotero admirado y querido *Trabajadores*

20 November 2014.

Skinner, David. José Méndez: Havana and Key West *The National Pastime*. Cleveland Ohio: SABR, 2004.

Price, S. L. The Best little sports machine in the World *Sports Illustrated* May 15, 1995, 60.

Newspapers

Boston Globe Peter Gammons Feb 21, 1992, 47.

Boston Globe interview published April 4, 2009.

Boston Globe published February 14, 1998.

Carteles Magazine February 20, 1955.

Daytona Beach Morning Journal August 19, 1969.

Harrison, Bill. High school softball spotlight's on Niles North's Brittany Sanchez: Like major league father, like daughter. Chicago *Tribune* May 01, 2010.

Kepron Tyler. Baseball Mazzilli is back in New York and wearing Stripes. *New York Times*. January 1, 2000.

Lapointe, Joe. A Cuban with Clout *New York Times* May 7, 1984.

The *Lethbridge Herald* June 24, 1977, 6

Madden Bill To José Cardenal First things First *Daily News* New York. February 23, 2000.

Miami Herald October 15, 2006.

Miami Herald June 28, 2004.

New York Times GM Branch Rickey Note *New York Times* February 15, 2015, 6.

Nuevo Herald Angel Torres

Picker, David. From Cuba, With a Dream of the Majors. *The New York Times* June 22, 2007

Sarasota Herald Tribune July 17, 2003

Stars and Stripes July 10, 1960 edition, 18 and 22.

Starts and Stripes April 14, 1954 Volume 12 Number 359.

Starts and Stripes September 30, 1960 199.

Stars and Stripes November 29, 1959, 19.

Strauss Ben In Havana, Remembering a Minor League Championship Correspondence with Cuban baseball researcher Rogelio Manzano *New York Times* March 23, 2013.

US Baseball Weekly July 28-August 3 1993.

AUTHOR'S NOTE:

I have also consulted several websites to gather, and confirm information. The following sites proved to be very valuable to that end and in directing me to other sources:

amnesty.org

ancestry.com

Baseball-reference.com

baseballhappenings.net/2014/02

cedema.org *Manifiesto de la Sierra Maestra*

chicagotribune.com 2011

CNN ireport.com August 1, 2015

cubanbaseball.com

cubanosfamosos.com

Ecured.cu/Federacion_Cubana_de_Beisbol

ElUniversal.com

findagrave.com

Herald.com

paxety.com/site 1940Constitution

uscg.mil

Made in the USA
San Bernardino, CA
19 December 2018